The
DREAMS of REASON

The Computer and the Rise of
the Sciences of Complexity

Heinz R. Pagels

Simon and Schuster

New York / London / Toronto / Sydney / Tokyo

Copyright © 1988 by Heinz R. Pagels
All rights reserved
including the right of reproduction
in whole or in part in any form.
Published by Simon and Schuster
A Division of Simon & Schuster Inc.
Simon & Schuster Building
Rockefeller Center
1230 Avenue of the Americas
New York, NY 10020

Designed by M. B. Kilkelly/Levavi & Levavi
Manufactured in the United States of America

1 2 3 4 5 6 7 8 9 10

Library of Congress Cataloging in Publication Data

Pagels, Heinz R., date.
The dreams of reason.

Bibliography: p.
Includes index.
1. Computers and civilization.   2. Science—
Philosophy.   3. Complexity (Philosophy)   I. Title.
QA76.9.C66P34   1988   303.4'834   88-6559
ISBN 0-671-62708-2

Acknowledgments

Texts are like living beings, adaptive and vulnerable, brought into the light of existence by the labors of their authors. In such a birth process it is extremely helpful to have many midwives—friends and colleagues who can be confident critics of the text. I have benefited by comments from John Brockman, David Campbell, Peter Carruthers, Dan Dennett, Hubert Dreyfus, Mitchell Feigenbaum, Joseph H. Hazen, Nick Herbert, Peter Lax, Seth Lloyd, Richard Ogust, David Olds, Elaine Pagels, Eugene M. Schwartz, David Shaw, Joseph Traub, Hao Wang, and Katherine Watterson. My editor, Alice Mayhew, helped at every stage. The Board of Governors of the New York Academy of Sciences is to be thanked for its sympathetic interest in my writing about science and the Aspen Center for Physics for its hospitality during the summer of 1987. I would like to thank Barbara Munsell for her volunteer and dedicated assistance. Dotty Hollinger faithfully typed the manuscript with its numerous changes.

In memory of our son

Mark

His home
Is the Universe

Contents

10   Contents

Preface

It seems that we live in two different worlds—the world of our mind and the natural world of things. This dualism, a rift in the perceived order of reality, stands as a persistent challenge to Western thought. Can we accommodate it?

Most natural scientists hold a view that maintains that the entire vast universe, from its beginning in time to its ultimate end, from its smallest quantum particles to the largest galaxies, is subject to rules—the natural laws—comprehensible by a human mind. Everything in the universe orders itself in accord with such rules and nothing else. Life on earth is viewed as a complex chemical reaction that promoted evolution, speciation, and the eventual emergence of humanity, replete with our institutions of law, religion, and culture. I believe that this reductionalist-materialist view of nature is basically correct.

Other people, with equal intellectual commitment, maintain the view that the very idea of nature is but an idea held in our minds and that all of our thinking about material reality is necessarily transcendent to that reality. Further, according to this view, the cultural matrix of art, law, religion, philosophy, and science form an invisible universe of meanings, and the true ground of being is to be found in this order of mind. I also believe that this transcendental view, which affirms the epistemic priority of mind over nature, is correct.

These two views of reality—the natural and the transcendental —are in evident and deep conflict. The mind, it seems, is transcendent to nature. Yet according to the natural sciences that transcendent realm must be materially supported and as such is subject to natural law. Resolving this conflict is, and will remain, a primary intellectual challenge to our civilization for the next several centuries. The great temptation will be to resolve the conflict by collapsing the differences between these views into one viewpoint or the other and then claiming a solution. The Buddha, it is said, when confronted with a similar temptation, held aloft a flower and smiled, indicating that neither dualism nor nondualism provide a resolution. That insight, however, provides us with the beginning of an inquiry, and not its end.

The emergent new sciences of complexity and the order of being that they study are a first step toward a resolution of this problem. What are the sciences of complexity?

Science has explored the microcosmos and the macrocosmos; we have a good sense of the lay of the land. The great unexplored frontier is complexity. Complex systems include the body and its organs, especially the brain, the economy, population and evolutionary systems, animal behavior, large molecules—all complicated things. Some of these systems are simulatable on computers and can be easily modeled rather precisely; others cannot be simulated by anything simpler than the system itself. Scientists, in a new interdisciplinary effort, have begun to meet the challenge of complex systems and, remarkably, are understanding how complexity can emerge from simplicity. For example, cellular automata, an artificial set of video dots that rearrange themselves according to definite, simple rules on a screen are an example of complex behavior emerging from simplicity. The evolution of life and culture may be another example, in this instance, of a threedimensional cellular automata made of atoms instead of video dots and which fills the entire universe. All of existence may be viewed as a complex system built out of simple components.

Some of the themes of the new sciences of complexity—the importance of biological organizing principles, the computational view of mathematics and physical processes, the emphasis on parallel networks, the importance of nonlinear dynamics and selective systems, the new understanding of chaos, experimental mathematics, the connectionist's ideas, neural networks, and parallel distributive processing—are described in the first part of this book. Where these new developments are headed no one can tell. But they portend a new synthesis of science that will overturn our traditional way of organizing reality. Already institutes and centers for the study of complexity are springing up on campuses and within corporations around the world—a sign of what is to come.

In this book I will focus on three main themes: first, the rise of the sciences of complexity that stand at the newest frontier of knowledge; second, the role of the computer as a research instrument and the reordering of knowledge it implies; and finally, the philosophy of science.

The primary research instrument of the sciences of complexity is the computer. It is altering the architectonic of the sciences and the picture we have of material reality. Ever since the rise of modern science three centuries ago, the instruments of investigation such as telescopes and microscopes were analytic and promoted the reductionalist view of science. Physics, because it dealt with the smallest and most reduced entities, was the most fundamental science. From the laws of physics one could deduce the laws of chemistry, then of life, and so on up the ladder. This view of nature is not wrong; but it has been powerfully shaped by available instruments and technology.

The computer, with its ability to manage enormous amounts of data and to simulate reality, provides a new window on that view of nature. We may begin to see reality differently simply because the computer produces knowledge differently from the traditional analytic instruments. It provides a different angle on reality. I will be describing some uses of the computer—simulating intelligence, simulated annealing, modeling molecules, computer modeling of both real and artificial life, the discovery of deterministic chaos, nonlinear dynamics, modeling evolution, neural nets, Boltzmann machines, experimental mathematics, to name a few. The technology that emerges from these applications will have profound implications in the commercial and business world, the financial services industry, the legal profession, and the military. The world will be changed. As a new mode of production, the computer creates not only a new class of people struggling for intellectual and social acceptance, but a new way of thinking about knowledge. It will transform the scientific enterprise and bring forth a new worldview.

The second part of the book deals with the impact of the sciences of complexity on the philosophy of science. Philosophy of science has fallen on hard times, deserted by even the professional philosophers, some of whom think it has come to an end. Once the handmaiden of theology, in this century philosophy became the whore of science, and finally, today, it is all but abandoned. Practicing scientists like myself tend to be antiphilosophers, often rejecting the efforts of professional philosophers to clarify and interpret our enterprise. This was not always the case. A few decades ago many scientists, especially my tribe—the physicists—were intellectually interested in, debated, and wrote about the philosophy of science. Today the pendulum has swung from thinking to doing. The external activities of scientists are more ethically oriented and less philosophically inclined. They have become involved in issues—the environment, war and peace, and human rights. So writing about the philosophy of science today, especially by an "antiphilosopher," requires an explanation.

Thinking about and doing science have become two very distinct professional activities, one philosophical, the other empirically investigative. This schism between the philosophy of science and science itself was wrought by Kant more than two centuries ago and has persisted until the present day. I believe that these two activities will become less distinct in the future, an influence of the new sciences of complexity. I welcome that. Philosophers and scientists may begin to collaborate more directly, especially in the cognitive sciences. It may turn out that philosophy has not so much come to an end, rather it has reintegrated with the activity of science, to where it was prior to the Kantian schism.

I am not a philosopher, and what I am writing in this book does not qualify as professional philosophy because it is not sufficiently closely argued. But I am trying to expose the new outlook on science that is arising out of the study of complexity, and I am using the themes and problems of traditional philosophy to do this —the nature of physical reality, the problem of cognition, the mind-body problem, the character of scientific research, the nature of mathematics, and the role of instruments in research.

I am profoundly biased in my views by my training as a professional physicist. As a physicist I feel more at home writing about the natural sciences. But some of the most exciting new developments in the sciences of complexity deal with social, economic, and psychological behavior. Interestingly, the interdisciplinary nature of these new sciences will in some cases cut across the traditional distinction between the natural and the social sciences. This will be lauded by some people and abhorred by others.

A recurrent theme in my thinking about science is the notion of "a selective system," a generalization of the Darwin-Wallace idea of natural selection to a general pattern-recognizing system. Empirical science itself exemplifies such a selective system. Instead of selecting species, natural science selects the theories of nature, our repertoire of reality. Empirical science may be viewed as a selective system for finding the invariant rules that order the universe. While these ideas are familiar in biology, the impact of the selective systems way of thinking on the social and psychological sciences is just beginning. It has been a long time in coming, and it will change them profoundly, a change that will be resisted by more traditionally oriented scientists.

I believe that the problem of the dualism of mind and nature will not so much be solved as it will disappear. Fundamental problems have disappeared before. Centuries ago natural philosophers debated the distinction between "substance" and "appearance," a distinction that vanished as empirical science matured. Likewise the radical distinction between mind and nature will disappear with the development of the new sciences of complexity and the categories of thought that development entails. As we deepen our understanding of how the mental world of meaning is materially supported and represented, an understanding coming from the neurosciences, the cognitive sciences, computer science, biology, mathematics, and anthropology, to name but a few contributing sciences, there will result a new synthesis of science, and a new cosmopolitan civilization and cultural worldview will arise. I am convinced that the nations and people who master the new sciences of complexity will become the economic, cultural, and political superpowers of the next century. The purpose of this book is to articulate the beginnings of this new synthesis of knowledge and to catch a first glimpse of the civilization that will arise out of it.

INTRODUCTORY
MEMOIR

Chapter 1

Big Sur and
the Apples of Cézanne

When the penis goes up, reason goes out the window.
—ROBERT M. HUTCHINS,
from the satiric short film *Zuckerkandel*

Straddling two of our planet's great tectonic plates, California is a geologically violent place where the land has only temporary stability. Here the Pacific plate, slipping against the continental land mass along the San Andreas Fault, moves ever northward and finally, in the vicinity of the Aleutian Islands, subducts deep into the molten bowels of the earth. California's geologic activity produces one of the most dramatic meetings of land and sea that I have ever seen, especially the coast near Big Sur south of the city of Carmel and north of Morro Bay. Here the Santa Lucia Mountains, which long ago moved north with the plate, rise a thousand feet right out of the Pacific, directly confronting the irresistible force of the sea.

Big Sur is an awesome and for the most part still primitive place that owes much of its magic to the quality of its light—diffuse in the winter and in early-morning fogs and lucid and intense during the summer afternoons. The mountains are covered with grasses, dry and golden in the hot summer sun. Cooler forested areas, shaded by cedars, pines, oaks, and redwoods, shelter wildlife. Just off the coast lie the giant feather boa, bull and bladder kelp beds undulating in a complex pattern with the waves. It is a rocky coast punctuated with occasional beaches harboring a rich and varied marine life, including tidepools filled with purple sea urchins, stars, hermit crabs, sea palms, and occasional black abalone. Pelicans, birds that seem to have forgotten evolution, patrol the surf, while cormorants rest on the cliffs, awaiting the fish that are attracted to the upwelling plankton carrying currents out of the depth.

The main evidence of human presence is the coast highway (Route 1), which was built in the 1930s with convict labor as part of the coastal defense system and which is the only rapid access to the region. With the highway came people, mostly artists and Bohemians, to join the ranchers who were already there; a few inns, restaurants, and houses were built, but the lonely damp winters, inaccessibility, and absence of jobs kept the extensive development that California has seen elsewhere, and most people, out.

As an easterner I never heard of Big Sur until 1960, my first year in physics graduate school at Stanford University. I was twenty-one. Grad students like myself used to hang out around the old student union fountain hoping to make friends. There I met Hal, who after serving in an army intelligence unit became a perennial Stanford student. Hal was a second-generation native Californian of Irish extraction, with a deep tan, jet-black hair, and blue eyes and, in the tradition of Irish poets, an adventuresome rebel.

Hal knew the Big Sur area, and one day he invited me to take a long weekend trip down there with him; in effect he was going to play Virgil to my Dante. He owned a number of VWs modified according to his specifications—the tops were cut off to the windowsills, for example—and outfitted with powerful Porsche engines. Around the bare edges of the cut-off cars Hal put polished white wood moldings so that the vehicles looked like bathtubs on wheels—very fast bathtubs. One such bathtub was to be our mode of transportation.

On the way to Big Sur from Stanford we took the back roads (Hal seemed to know them all) through the artichoke fields surrounding Monterey Bay. The salt smell of the sea filled the air. In Monterey we spent the better part of the morning exploring the old canneries that once packed the fish that fed England during

World War II. They were salty ruins now, becoming reclaimed by the sea they bordered, their work done. This was John Steinbeck's country, a rough place with human exploitation just below the social surface, a gathering place for life's losers and a few winners. (Today some of the canneries are restored, a gentrified tourist draw; the Monterey Bay Aquarium, opened in 1985, brings the local sea life to public view.) Hal knew some of the Italian fishermen who supplied the restaurants and could recount the days when the bay was still filled with fish.

After Monterey we headed south on Route 1, past Carmel and the Carmelite church, past Point Lobos and its tenacious cypresses, past the Lighthouse at Point Sur, and into the Santa Lucia Mountains that plummeted down to the sea, the waves resounding on the rocks hundreds of feet below. Everything became strangely silent, as if we had entered a primordial space and time, all thought of returning gone. A threshold was passed. But where had I been?

Kierkegaard, the Danish philosopher, once remarked that the irony of life is that it is lived forward but understood backward. In retrospect it was important for me to get to know Big Sur at that point in my life; the power of nature opened me to my own feelings and reflections about existence. I was young, an intellectual idealist and full of words, more so than now, committed to a great adventure of the human mind. In graduate school I pursued the subjects that challenged me most—high-energy physics and its mathematical language of quantum field theory; I could not imagine doing anything except physics research. Making money seemed unnecessary and uninteresting to me, as to many of my contemporaries who had grown up in the years of great affluence in postwar America. There were intellectually exciting ideas in the air, problems to be solved, reputations to be made.

The West Coast universities were successfully raiding the East Coast universities for some of the best faculty talent. At Stanford physicists were planning "the monster," a giant linear accelerator that propelled electrons down a two-mile pipe to their target. Here it was that quarks, the constituents of nuclear matter, were to be discovered. Biologists had cracked the genetic code; molecular biology made great strides, and a fundamental approach to the problem of life was in the making. Psychologists were breaking new ground with the theory of cognitive dissonance. Econometrics was born. Electrical engineers were deep into developing new theories of electronic control and information systems. Fred Terman, the energetic university provost, had gotten federal legislation changed in the late 1950s so that the university could lease property in a new industrial park, the seed for the growth of Silicon Valley. He developed the intimate liaison between the technical and financial community, lacking in other parts of the United States, which assured the future of high-technology development in the vicinity of Stanford. In Santa Clara County the apricot orchards were being felled to make room for homes and offices. A new technological revolution based on the electronic computer that would move the populations of cities and shift the center of economic power, create and destroy jobs, and transform the means of war was about to be unleashed.

Besides theoretical physics, I was attracted to intellectual recreations, mostly art and philosophy. I began to study paintings, trying to figure out what artists were doing and to break out of the province of my visual conventions. More than any other painter it was Cézanne who first taught me that there were different ways to see the ordinary world and that the form of my experience was the product of my culture.

A friend, Jon Ketchum, held seminars at his house in Palo Alto, and there I read Immanuel Kant and Edmund Husserl, the transcendental philosophers. From my housemates, fellow grad students, I picked up bits and pieces of dynamic programming, econometrics, molecular biology, and biochemistry. I audited courses at the university (not for credit, but for fun), and I remember that at one of these courses Donald Davidson, the analytic philosopher, was explaining Tarski's semantic concept of truth to a class of undergraduates: this involves the analysis of the sentence " 'Snow is white' if and only if snow is white." I never understood the semantic concept of truth, nor most of language philosophy with its hierarchy of truth levels. This, however, was not the fault of my philosophy teachers.

I suppose my mind had been ruined for philosophy by studying too much physics, with its simple (some would say naive) pragmatism. Physicists are quick to distinguish physics from mathematics, the formal language they use to express physical laws. Theoretical physicists who get completely absorbed in the beauty of mathematics, as they often do, and lose sight of the physics remind me of language philosophers who have lost sight of the world that the language is about in the first place. The answers I got whenever I questioned what the language philosophers actually did convinced me that it was the same thing the linguists had been doing all along —understanding how words are properly used.

It seemed obvious to me that if you want to understand a spoken language, you ought to study the people who speak it and speak it well. The simultaneous translators often employed by various state departments are masters of spoken language. One of these, a Soviet citizen, is truly remarkable in that he knows dozens of languages, Oriental as well as Western. If you want to understand how languages work, this is the sort of person you ought to meet and study. After he listens to someone speak, he translates the remarks into whatever language is desired—any one of dozens. How does he do it? According to him, he "hears" the remarks not in any language at all, but rather as "a matrix of meanings"—a conceptual format of some kind that he creates. When asked to translate into a specific language, he consults the matrix and expresses that meaning into a language. It would appear that spoken language is subordinate to a nonverbal format, a deeper logical structure that is independent of any specific language. This seemed rather clear to only a few people in the early 1960s, although it has become better accepted today, most notably through the work of Noam Chomsky.

Ironically, Wittgenstein, the father of modern language philosophy—the view that there is a formal correspondence between objects, thought, and language—ended his *Tractatus* with the sentence "Whereof one cannot speak, thereof one must be silent." This was profoundly misunderstood by many philosophers, who took his aphorism as a rallying cry for the elimination of metaphysics and theology. However, Wittgenstein himself came to believe in his later years that the key to knowledge and understanding lay in the world of silence beyond language. After all, we invent language, including formal languages like mathematics, to express our experience. It can be seen as a playful game. But anyone who has attempted to express something clearly and has struggled with language to make sure it is adequate to the silent thought to be expressed knows that language is the instrument of thought, sometimes even an obstacle to expression and not an easy game. Thought is simply not identical to language.

One reason Hal and I were traveling to Big Sur was that Hal

wanted to introduce me to a language philosopher who, whenever he could leave his university position, took up residence alone in a trailer on the coast. It was a perfect place for meditation.

I was suspicious of philosophers. They seemed to play an infinite game of "target and target shooters"—one philosopher sets up the target position, and others shoot at it. Then they reverse roles. Furthermore, their enterprise seemed to me too much dependent on their personal intellectual styles to have anything to do with what I conceived of as deep truth, which I felt ought to be universal and not particular (here my bias as a physicist comes out again). Philosophers had no tool—like experiment, the physicists' appeal to nature, or the mathematicians' appeal to axioms—to keep them honest. How could they tell if they made mistakes? I had read a few of this philosopher's articles and was ready for battle.

Hal knew where he lived and had met him before. By the time we arrived it was already the dead heat of the afternoon. We pulled off the highway and down a dusty dirt road leading to the rocky shore. There was the trailer all right, at the edge of a cliff forty feet above the sea, sitting in the partial shadow of a madrona tree, but there was no sign of life. Spinning dust devils in the dirt, our bathtub halted in front of the trailer. The heat was immense. We got out of the car and knocked on the door, which slowly swung open. And there before us was the philosopher. He lay asleep on his back, stretched out on the top of a table in the center of the trailer, completely naked, his penis erect, perpendicular like a demonstration in geometry. Nothing interrupted this tableau except for a chair, some scattered books including the *Tractatus*, and a single fly struggling to find its way out of the chamber. "I don't think," said my friend, "that we should disturb his dream," and we left. I never met him.

Back on the highway, Hal and I speculated on what grammatical fantasies could produce such a sight. Perhaps the discovery of a new, more intimate verb form joining subject and object? The answer came several years later from experiments done on sleeping men at Stanford which definitively proved that male erections coincided with REM (rapid eye movement) cycles, also coincident with dreaming, which occur periodically many times during normal sleep. When friends from Stanford Hospital reported this to me, my reaction was amazement—how could such a fact have been missed by wives and mistresses, who for countless millennia had the opportunity to observe it? But that's one of the points of science—it begins with *indifferent*, careful observation.

Later that day we set up camp under an oak high in the mountains south of Lucia where the phone lines end. Here we would have sun all day long—even the morning fog would not reach our elevation. As the sun sank in the Pacific, the hills were turning a brilliant yellow, then orange, casting long shadows. Nothing was nearby except the presence of the church, a Camaldolese hermitage, and the army, the Hunter-Liggett military reservation on the other side of the mountains (sometimes we could hear the big guns go off). Hal opened a bag filled with handguns and gave me a .45, keeping a .38 for himself. I thought his military craziness had got the better of him, but he insisted that this was lawless land and weapons were a matter of personal security. No telling whom one might meet in these mountains—escaped criminals or possibly a couple of guys like us. The next morning we blasted away at targets, the mountains resounding in gunshot echos. Like dogs, we were marking our territory.

Later in the day we drove down to Slate's Hot Springs, a resort directly on the coast that featured hot natural baths. The water, smelling of sulfur, was heated by volcanic rocks in the earth below. The property was originally the 1882 homestead of Tom Slate, who sold it in 1910 to Henry Murphy, a physician from Salinas. He and his wife shared the ambition of making it into a European-style spa. The Murphys had three daughters and a son, John. John Murphy's sons, Dennis and Michael, "the sinner and the saint," who, legend has it, were models for the characters Cal and Aaron (symbolizing Cain and Abel) in John Steinbeck's novel *East of Eden*, were to play an important role in the future of the Hot Springs.

As we rolled down the drive in our bathtub to the main building, Hal said that the Hot Springs was not the place for guns, and we left our weapons in the car. The resort had a gun freak for a guard, and it was better not to upset him (the guard, it turned out, was the writer Hunter Thompson). I recall that the place was managed by an old lady who belonged to a religious community and wanted to use it as a meeting place for her co-religionists from Fresno. There was a "sweetness and light" portrait of Jesus on the wall. The resort was too remote for the religious community to come to with any regularity, but the San Francisco gay community, attracted by the hot baths, came in numbers instead. Besides the gay presence, the clientele included some local Bohemians and artists and faculty from Stanford University humanities departments who brought undergraduates down for special weekend seminars. Among the undergraduates that weekend was a girlfriend of Hal's (I realized now his trip had a hidden agenda), who was, however, quite indifferent to his courtship. She later ran off with one of the gays, leaving my friend quite chagrined.

A year or so later I returned to Big Sur, looking for Hal, who, no longer a student, was camped out somewhere south of Lucia. His camp had grown—several army tents, a generator, trucks and jeeps, rocket launchers (no rockets in evidence)—it looked like the invasion headquarters of a banana republic. Sheltered under one of the tents was an extensive set of filing cabinets. Looking under "C," I found the drawer contained three used carburetors. Hal had a couple of friends, a mulatto with a ring in his ear and a one-armed sailor with pornographic tattoos. They were all armed. It was not clear to me what they were up to, and I didn't ask. Hal told me there was someone I ought to meet, "a philosopher, a shrink of sorts," and we went to the Hot Springs for dinner. The picture of Jesus was gone.

The scene at Slate's had changed dramatically. Michael Murphy had returned from a visit to Aurobino's ashram in India and after spending some time in San Francisco decided with Richard Price to manage the property given to him by his grandmother and set up an educational center, the Esalen Institute (named for the indigenous people who lived in the area before the Spanish Conquest). Dennis Murphy subsequently joined them.

The center was based on the views of Aldous Huxley, Carl Rodgers, Abraham Maslow, and others who emphasized the importance of nonverbal learning and the positive rather than the pathological aspects of mental life. Esalen eventually became the pioneer institution in humanistic psychology, and many of the people who went there went on to start up similar institutes. Books were never much in presence there, although more recently some have made their appearance in a small shop. Simple consistency is not the Esalen way.

I sat across the dinner table from "the philosopher," whom I took to be a German-Jewish psychoanalyst, a victim of the recent European exodus who had somehow managed to find his way to the continental edge of the Western world. I asked this chain-smoking Santa Claus how he came to be here, and he spoke of the analytic movement in the 1930s and his break from it. We went on to discuss psychoanalytic theory, which I thought resembled the work of a literary or cultural movement; it certainly did not qualify as a science, which I felt always has to contain a recipe for its own destruction. Psychoanalysis had no such recipe. An "elephant-shit" conversation was Santa Claus's term for this kind of talk. I liked him.

Just as I felt we were warming up, a beautiful woman came to him and after a few soft words began weeping on his shoulder; he wept, too, tissues much in evidence. A family problem, I thought; too bad. Soon we resumed our previous conversation. Then another beautiful woman came to him weeping, and the whole business started over again. I turned to Hal and said, "Let's get the hell out of this funny farm!" The Santa Claus, who was Fritz Perls, the gestalt analyst, must have overheard me; in any case he explained that he was running a gestalt workshop that weekend and invited me to join.

I did, and rejoined him on other weekends. The workshops "turned my head around." I liked the experiential approach, the absence of theory, the fulfillment of practice, and the discovery, usually but not always traumatic, of parts of myself that I didn't know existed. I learned a lot from working with and watching other people in the group, a kind of collective learning experience.

But I learned most from my body, listening carefully to its signals rather than simply, usually unconsciously, reacting to them. I discovered my "silent partners" within me—my personifications of unconscious processes—whose wisdom, fear, or attraction for people is expressed in my body and intuitive feeling, and who, in their own silent language, react to the world and people around me. Better get on good terms with my partners, I thought, since I have to go through life with them. I saw these parts of myself, learned to talk to them, and sometimes had to struggle to keep all the actors on the stage working to hold the drama of my being together. Such experiences would push me to the threshold of confusion and madness, or so it seemed. But those thresholds, I found out, are the gates of learning, and one always feels confused and unbalanced crossing them as with any real learning. Reason alone will not get you across. In the end you have to trust the organism. If you don't trust the organism, you risk falling into the trap of a religious, political, or intellectual fundamentalism—a form of certainty that terminates creative growth. That I really didn't go mad instilled me with an enormous confidence in my effective wholeness. I realized that "reality," like time and other deep concepts, is simply understood and felt, but almost impossible to express in language. Ask anyone if they know what reality and time are, and they will think that the answer is obvious. Yet they will struggle, grasping at metaphors, to express it in the limiting form of language.

In my twenties I came to some conclusions about who I was, not the personality and other behavioral decorations, but who I was within that still, quiet place where mentally healthy people go when they want a respite from themselves and the world of sensation. What I found there (once I removed the mental clutter) was somewhat disappointing. What "I" am is a grammatical form—the first person singular—the logical structure in language that reports that my mental and physical acts are done by me. This "I"—the irreducible ego—has the same remarkable quality of certain existence that the existence of truth has. For you cannot deny the possibility of truth without contradiction: to say "There is no truth" means (if it means anything at all) that the statement in quotes is false, which means there *is* truth. Likewise I cannot deny the existence of my ego, for that would be denying the existence of the denier—a subjective contradiction. One can elaborate on this elementary but profound insight of Descartes (the philosopher who had it first three hundred years ago) about the nature of the ego, but it seems to me that if one is to think at all, then one cannot ignore it. There is, I'm afraid, not much comfort in this bare-bones ego because as a logical form it is impersonal and universal, like the number one.

Fortunately I found this is not all that there is to my being. There are all those silent partners, the personality, the decorations, the animal within, the ocean of the self, and God. Nothing dramatizes the existence of those silent partners so well as one of Rodger Sperry's, Michael Gazzaniga's, and their collaborators' split-brain experiments. They examined patients with their brains cut in half for medical reasons so the language faculty located in the left hemisphere was effectively separated from the right—the home of some of those silent partners. The people in this radical condition superficially behaved rather normally until they were studied closely. The investigators showed that the right brain could be trained to carry out a task while the left side (the side with the language faculty) was unaware of the training, by being blindfolded. When the blindfold was removed so the person could see the task performed, the person—the side of the brain that has language—responded, "Whoever did that, it wasn't me." The bare-bones ego was responding to an act of an isolated silent partner.

Most of these reflections from my twenties are from that "first person perspective," the view of my self from inside. People have an intense desire to know themselves and the world, a desire that matures (if it ever does) in their twenties. My favorite Jesuit sage, Gracian, who was the abbot of a monastery in the seventeenth century and recorded his reflections in his *Manual*, remarked that in his twenties man is dominated by desire, in his thirties by expediency, and in the forties by judgment. I'm into judgment now— right on Gracian's schedule—and now my judgment indicates that introspection is actually a very poor way to understand cognition and emotion, even in oneself. Consciousness is capable of other perspectives—"the third person perspective"—the view from outside, the view of science. It is, in some ways, the most difficult consciousness to achieve because everything in one's being cries out against it. It is a hard threshold for most people to cross—to see themselves as a fair witness would. But I am convinced that to deeply understand the nature of cognition and emotions, even one's own, you have got to ultimately understand how the brain and body work—a story for another chapter.

After leaving graduate school I went to the Institute for Field Physics at the University of North Carolina in Chapel Hill to pursue physics research. The next summer I traveled around the world, spending a lot of time in Asia, giving lectures at the universities, and exploring foreign cultures. When I returned I joined the theoretical physics group at Rockefeller University in New York City. On a visit to Chapel Hill at the beginning of the next summer to see some friends, I met Barry, a young Native American. When I mentioned that I was driving west to work in California for the summer, he decided to join me for the trip. I gave lectures at a few universities and labs along the way, and Barry told me the ancient stories that his Indian grandmother told him.

We arrived in San Francisco during the "summer of love" in 1967, and I dropped Barry off in the Haight-Ashbury district, then crowded with hippies and weirdness. It turned out that Barry was a craftsman, he made Indian artifacts and knew the import system, and I suggested that the two of us set up a small gift shop right on Haight Street. I would stake him out, and he would manage the business. After renting a shop for him, I began my summer research at the Lawrence Radiation Lab across the bay in Berkeley.

Two weeks passed, and I went back to the Haight to check on business. No Barry. I went to the commune where he was staying —a boardinghouse filled with Oriental religious icons, reeking of incense and vegetarian cooking and filled with a sample of America's youth in various states of ecstasy. A relatively coherent girl informed me that Barry had "freaked out on acid" and was now living the natural life in Golden Gate Park. She led me to him. Parts of Golden Gate Park are thickets of trees and bushes, transversed by a maze of narrow paths. It was night when we finally found my business partner squatting in a clearing next to a fire strewn about with bottles, cans, and chicken bones. He had on shorts, was covered with a blanket, and on his otherwise naked body and face were painted the symbols of his people. Without looking up, he said, only slightly apologetically, "Heinz, I'm an Indian, not a businessman."

I sympathized with what he had just gone through. I had been exposed to LSD some four years earlier. Around 1963 Leo Hollister, a psychopharmacologist at the Veterans Administration Hospital in Palo Alto, was asking for volunteers to be injected with this substance. Leo was interested in studying the effect of LSD on fatty acids in the blood. The volunteers got fifty dollars, an opportunity not to be missed by poor grad students like me. I had read R. C. Zaehner's *Mysticism Sacred and Profane*, Aldous Huxley's *The Doors of Perception*, accounts of their drug experiences, and a few articles from the pharmacology literature and was ready to have a go at it. I got my fifty dollars and a mystical experience in the bargain. A few days later I told my friends about *my* experience (as if the experience belonged to me) and said to just wait until this drug hits the streets. It didn't take long. Ben Weininger, a psychotherapist from Santa Barbara, once remarked to me that when people have mystical experiences it is a signal from the organism that it needs more socialization. People start interacting in new ways. That happened for millions of Americans in the late sixties.

Later in the summer Barry and I traveled south to Big Sur. Young people were migrating north out of Los Angeles and south from San Francisco, drawn to Big Sur by its natural power and isolation from society. The highway was littered with dropouts into the drug culture and young men avoiding the draft into the Vietnam War. We met up with Hal at his new encampment at Lime Kiln Creek, a beautiful stream that emptied into a Pacific beach not far from the moss-covered waterfall. Hal told me of strange events in the mountains—stories about communes and savagery. He insisted that we visit a commune deep in the mountains, a two-hour jeep ride away. We got there in the afternoon. The communards thought they were the wave of the future, an experimental community, but in fact they had reverted to the authoritarian tribalism of the human past. The place was run by a heavyset headman or shaman (I called him "Rasputin") dripping in beads and hair. Several underlings carried out his orders—he ruled using fear and magic. The women were shared or parceled out by the headman. There was lots of garbage about, large bones, pieces of animals, and, of course, drugs. I later visited some more positively oriented communities in the neighborhood of Taos, New Mexico, small groups with spiritually committed individuals sharing their labor and striving to lead a new and better life; but this place was definitely not one of them.

Hal and I spent the night some distance away sleeping on our revolvers (this time he didn't need to convince me we needed them). At the encampment far below us a fire blazed, drums played, dancers danced. We heard screams and groans (pain or pleasure?) until all fell silent. I fell asleep as the moon, rising over the mountains, reclaimed dominion over the night.

The next morning one of the young men wanted a ride back to the highway, and we took him with us. With my usual insistence on knowing the economic underpinnings of personal and social existence, I questioned him about how the commune managed to feed itself. He told me they trapped animals and preyed on tourist cars down on the highway during the weekends. He went on to explain in an indifferent sort of way that they had begun to eat people. He then said he had found a friend's head in a tree and, thinking he might be next, wanted out. I had no way of knowing if he had been lying, hallucinating, or if it was for real. It was certainly believable.

Years later when I recounted this tale to a French physics colleague, he responded, "That is silly! There's been no cannibalism in Africa for years." When I replied that he had misheard me and the story was about California, not Africa, he said, "Oh, California! Anything is possible in California."

I remember seeing the kids along the coast highway in the late 1960s. Sometimes they emerged from the brush after weeks in the mountains with no contact with human society. They had lived with the alternate ancient reality, with the primal gods that created the planet and moved in the wind and waters, without a guide, lost in mind and body. When they emerged mostly, but not entirely, mad, they often embraced the telephone poles along the highway or touched the road—the first human artifacts they had seen for weeks. They were reconnecting with the network, the road spanning a continent, connecting to that tenuous collective dream of history, the world of language, buildings, law, art, and science, the world dream that is spinning itself out on the edge of the abyss. They were coming home.

As it turned out, the future in California belonged not to rural communes and the counterculture, but to the electronic engineers and entrepreneurs. In a few years the high-technology computer revolution was under way in Santa Clara County. Fortunes were being made (and lost); the dialectic between ego and id was taking another turn. The war was over. Young Americans returned to an earlier set of values emphasizing individual and economic fulfillment; once again it was important to find a good job. But the price for adopting a set of values or a way of life remained unchanged. The price was, and always will be, one's life.

I lost track of Hal. An acquaintance, a self-styled leftist revolutionary in his Stanford days but now a well-heeled pornographer in San Francisco, told me Hal was now teaching at Sonoma State College. Barry wrote me several years later. He had gotten a job as a bellhop in the St. Francis Hotel in San Francisco and was now living with his wife. Enclosed with the letter was the money he borrowed. The last line of his letter summarized his reflections on the life he had been living: "There are things in this Universe that man was never meant to know." Meanwhile I was back east working on the symmetries of the quantum particles, pushing the edge of darkness, in the only way I knew how, farther away.

Part I
THE SCIENCES
OF COMPLEXITY

Chapter 2

A New Synthesis
of Science

*A science of computing is beginning to emerge, like Hercules,
from its cradle.*
                                                    —PETER D. LAX, 1985

Thirty years ago, a typical college student was offered a choice of
courses in the natural sciences—biology, physics, and chemistry
—as well as courses in the behavioral sciences—psychology, anthropology, sociology, and economics. The various courses were
neatly packaged, and there was only modest overlap between
them; each science had its own intellectual turf. The division of
the science departments and indeed the division of knowledge
itself reflected, or so it seemed, the actual order of nature, mind,
and society.

Even today those divisions between the sciences have not altered very much, a testament to the endurance of institutional
structure in the face of an almost complete change in personnel.
Yet something is stirring in the way the sciences are ordered and
divided. Murray Gell-Mann, the physicist, caught the spirit of this
change in his 1984 remarks to participants at the Santa Fe Institute, a newly proposed center for the study of complexity: "It is
usually said that ours is an age of specialization, and that is true.

But there's a striking phenomenon of convergence in science and scholarship that has been taking place, especially in the forty years since the Second World War, and at an accelerated pace during the last decade. New subjects, highly interdisciplinary in traditional terms, are emerging and represent in many cases the frontier of research. These interdisciplinary subjects do not link together the whole of one traditional discipline with another; particular subfields are joined together to make a new subject. The pattern is a varied one and constantly changing."

The movement described by Gell-Mann has less to do with the rise of some new outlook on science than with the realization on the part of many specialized researchers that the problems they are struggling with are shared by other researchers in disparate fields. For example, problems in neuroscience, anthropology, population biology, learning theory, cognitive science, nonlinear dynamics, physics, and cosmology (to name but a few fields) have overlapping components. It is too soon to see where this new horizontal integration among disparate sciences is headed, but it has taken root and is growing rapidly. It could herald a new synthesis of knowledge based in some general way on the notion of complexity.

The material force behind this change is the computer, the instrument of the sciences of complexity. In an impressive vindication of the thesis that new modes of production create new social classes, the computer has indeed created a new class of people who understand and have mastered it. This class is struggling for its recognition within the traditional society. Not only has a new social class been brought into existence by the computer, but the very structure of knowledge is being altered as well. The computer as a research instrument provides us with a new way of seeing reality, and the architectonic of the sciences must change accordingly.

In this chapter I will be exploring this new movement and the dramatic reordering of knowledge it portends. Knowledge exists both within itself in an abstract, philosophical sense, and without, externally represented in social institutions and human activities. I will start by examining the latter.

The first, and most obvious, place to look for the institutionalization of knowledge is, of course, in the universities. Universities are intellectually conservative institutions and adapt to change only gradually. This conservatism exists to protect a university's primary asset—intellectual excellence. Universities are fragile social structures embodying in their faculties a network of skills and knowledge centuries in the making, a network that is more easily destroyed than preserved. One has but to see the heroic start-up struggles of universities in the developing world to see what an immense accomplishment a modern university represents.

The challenge to universities in democratic societies is to promote the highest and best in intellectual work, preserve a tradition of values and freedom, protect dissent, and educate the young. All of this is to be done within the context of the wider society that is governed by the opinion of a numerical majority, a majority that may not share the values a university seeks to promote. While the dialectical tension between the university and society is a dynamic force for change, it can also be the undoing of the fragile university. Some think the university has already been undone.

I've asked a number of university presidents what they see as the most dramatic change in institutions of higher learning since the Second World War. I was surprised how many responded by saying the greatest change was the rise and influence of the large professional schools—law, medicine, and business, as well as graduate schools. Universities, rather than transmitting a tradition of human values to a new generation, have become "knowledge factories" producing the skilled and educated individuals a society needs to survive in the modern world. University presidents for their part have mostly become fund-raisers and ceased to exercise educational leadership. Which leaves one wondering who is minding the shop.

Over this same postwar period there has been a continuous decline in the status of university personnel, especially on the junior faculty level. In the last decade this decline had become dramatic, comparable to that of high school teachers in the 1960s. Such a decline in social status is what might be expected if faculty are viewed as employees of a "knowledge factory" rather than the transmitters and teachers of a high culture and the values that create civilization. When Dwight Eisenhower as the new president of Columbia University in the 1950s was introduced to the senior faculty, he remarked how pleased he was to meet with the employees of the university. The physicist I. I. Rabi interrupted him: "Mr. President," he said, "we are *not* the employees of the university.

We *are* the university!" Perceptions were different then. In spite of the fact that many of the major U.S. universities have handsomely increased their endowments, universities in kind and character are not the institutions they once were. Universities are supported today by those who see them as an adjunct to the society they serve, not as institutions that exist for their own sake. Some intellectuals see these changes in the university as a decline of the higher culture. Others see evolution and progress. Which change you see depends, ironically, on how you were educated.

While a lot of scientific activity, especially research, takes place in universities, not all of it goes on in universities. Corporations have both large and small research facilities. Major industrial laboratories, exemplified by the AT&T Bell Labs in Murray Hill, New Jersey, or the IBM research facilities near Yorktown Heights, New York, have made major contributions to both pure and applied knowledge. Such corporate labs exist in Japan and Europe as well. Working in such facilities is almost indistinguishable from working in a university, except that one is paid more and doesn't have to teach. Small industrial organizations have smaller labs that are more specialized and dedicated to solving particular problems appropriate to that industry. A vast body of our knowledge about physical processes and properties of materials comes from such industrial research.

The government also plays a major role in scientific research. The U.S. government has huge laboratories at Los Alamos, Livermore, Argonne, plus the Brookhaven National Lab, the Stanford Linear Accelerator Center, the Fermi National Laboratory, the National Institutes of Health, VA Hospitals, and different facilities especially dedicated to military research. Today the federal research budget in the United States is roughly 75 percent military and 25 percent civilian, up from a fifty-fifty split some years ago; this change has drawn some criticism, especially from the university community.

Sometimes people suppose that all of the fundamental research is done in universities while the applied, presumably more commercially or militarily useful, research is done in corporate or military labs. But that distinction is breaking down. The National Science Foundation under the leadership of Erich Bloch (formerly a research scientist with IBM) is setting up a number of research centers near universities that involve university-corporate collaborative research. The reason for this initiative is that many science policy leaders think that the United States has not been sufficiently effective in translating its superiority in fundamental research into applied, commercially viable products so that it can enhance its international competitiveness. Whether these centers will help solve that problem remains to be seen. But I am reminded by the fact that the collaboration between German universities and the nascent German-Swiss pharmacology industry before the First World War not only created a major new industry, but also provided the basis of most of our start-up knowledge of organic chemistry.

Corporations have also entered the field of private education. Since the early 1980s corporate spending on educating employees (about $100 billion) has annually exceeded the total budget of all higher education in the U.S.A., according to David Harman, an educator at Columbia University. The corporations are not, of course, teaching the university curriculum. Their curriculum consists of job training courses, personnel management, administration, executive training, and so forth. The extent of this emergent new educational enterprise is bound to have an impact, but few people have considered what it may portend for the future.

The visible order of knowledge is changing, compelled by forces both internal and external to science. We have examined aspects of the external representation of science. But how is it that we come to order the sciences internally and the relations among them? It is one thing to find theories in the sciences, like the theories of physics and biology, and quite another thing to find how they relate to one another and, when taken all together, how they form a picture of reality. The problem of ordering knowledge is itself a problem in knowledge. It is deeply informed by our culture and our idea of reality.

Until the rise of empirical science, some three hundred years ago the architectonic of the natural sciences (natural philosophy), in accord with Aristotelian canons, was established by the *logical* relation of one science or another. Once a discipline was defined, its relation to other disciplines simply became a problem in logic. In the absence of scientific instruments all that reflective people could do in order to see reality was to use their minds and the logical order of thought that they found there. It should be no surprise that the medieval hierarchy of knowledge was established in accord with logical rather than empirical principles.

With the rise of empirical science and the materialist outlook

promoted by new instruments such as the telescope and microscope, the various sciences became ordered by *reductionalism* or
essentially by *size*. The properties of the small things determined
the behavior of larger things. Physics, which dealt with the smallest entities, was thus the most fundamental science according to
this scheme, then chemistry, biology, and so on up (or down) the
ladder to psychology and sociology. This reductionalist hierarchy,
prevalent when I was a student, is still the dominant view held by
most natural scientists today.

What the various sciences *do* has not altered its intent. What
has changed is that we, in forming a picture of all the sciences in
our mind, have appealed to new categories in organizing that picture, categories that are informed by new instrumentation.

Now that the computer has arrived—the instrument of complexity—we may begin to see the relation between various sciences
in entirely new dimensions; for example, one such dimension
might be the simplicity or complexity of a system, or whether or
not the system is simulatable or unsimulatable.

Part of the reason for the great success of the natural sciences
over the last few centuries is that they restrict their attention to
simple natural systems with only a few conceptual components
that can be held in the mind and be mentally managed. In view of
the complexity of the world around us, it is utterly remarkable that
the natural world admits a simple description in terms of simple
physical laws. How is this possible?

The genius of Isaac Newton first gave us the reason for this.
According to Newton's mechanics, the world can be conceptually
divided up into the "initial conditions," which specify the physical
state of the world at some beginning time, and "physical laws,"
which specify how that state changes. The initial conditions are
usually very complicated, a complication reflecting the complexity
of the world in which we live. The natural laws, on the other hand,
could be and are rather simple. This division—simple laws and
complicated initial conditions—has been retained to the present
day. In practice, one could only solve the equations that represent
the simple physical laws for systems with simple initial conditions
—the firing of a projectile, the motions of the moon and planets.

For physical laws the equations had only a few variables that
described qualitatively distinct features of the system—the position of a planet, its velocity and acceleration. Some complex sys-

tems are distinguished from simple systems by the fact that many qualitatively distinct variables are needed to describe their behavior. For some complex systems like the brain or the world economy, the number of qualitatively distinct variables needed to describe their behavior may be in the hundreds of millions (we really don't know how many variables are needed—that is part of the problem).

Unlike the simple system of Newtonian physics, it is hard for the human mind to intuitively grasp what is going on in such a complex system with all its variables. According to the cognitive psychologist George Miller's famous estimate, the mind can hold at most 7 ± 2 distinct items before its attention. A mind with such a low capacity for attention will never stand a chance grasping the behavior of a complex system with its hundreds of variables. With the aid of computers, however, we can begin to distill that complexity down to a humanly manageable amount of information so that we can apply our intuition to it and see what is going on. That distillation, however, is more an art than a science.

Scientists studying such complex systems have found an exciting alternative to all those thousands of variables. It turns out that for some complex systems there is an underlying simplicity—only a few variables are really important. The interaction of a few components according to a set of rules can be shown to produce complex phenomena. Perhaps all those thousands of variables are only superficial, and at bottom things are very simple. But until that simplicity, if it exists, is uncovered we will have to manage complexity directly. Fortunately, because of the computer, that is now possible.

We see that the first impact of the computer as a research instrument is a "vertical" one—a deepening of our grasp on existing problems within a scientific discipline. Using computers, physicists, chemists, and economists can tackle problems that they could not touch before simply because the computational power was not there. The new methods of analysis of complex systems apply not only to the natural sciences—astronomy, physics, chemistry, biology, and the new medicine—but to the social sciences as well—economics, political science, psychological dynamics. Computers, because of their capacity to manage enormous amounts of information, are showing us new aspects of social reality.

Vertical deepening, however, does not especially alter the way we view the whole of the sciences; it deepens what lies within an existing scientific territory. The exciting new development comes with "horizontal" integration, connections between the sciences, because that can restructure our picture of reality.

Such horizontal integration often goes by the name "interdisciplinary," and to many scientific intellectuals this is synonymous with flaky, unserious work. It is difficult to tell if a new interdisciplinary field is to be taken seriously purely on its intellectual merits, especially if one is unfamiliar with the disciplines. However, if the best and the brightest people in different disciplines are drawn to a new area, it is a good sign that something significant is happening. New highly interdisciplinary fields are emerging among the sciences, and in many instances these fields are at the scientific frontier.

This horizontal integration is an important aspect of the new synthesis of science. It is already altering the architectonic of the sciences. It has been going on for more than forty years, since the end of World War II, but only in the last decade, after the microchip technology made computers both powerful and inexpensive, has its impact been growing rapidly. Using computers, scientists can build mathematical models of complex phenomena—human learning, unconscious processes, animal and cultural evolution, the cell, violent behavior, the brain—to name but a few applications. In spite of the diversity of these phenomena, the mathematics used to model all of them has elements in common, and that feature is becoming the basis of a new way of integrating the sciences. For example, computer modeling of evolutionary phenomena suggests how evolution functions as a pattern-recognition system, promoting some species, extinguishing others, and this has implications for learning behavior and economic behavior. While the general lines of this new synthesis that cuts across traditional diciplines are not yet clear, there is a major movement. The old way of organizing the sciences is no longer adequate. What will come out of this current period of intellectual ferment no one can yet tell, but I have some guesses, not about the final structure, but about some of the themes of the emergent architectonic of the sciences of complexity.

The first theme is *the importance of the computer*—the primary research instrument of the sciences of complexity. The power of the computer in research lies in its capacity to computationally model and simulate complex systems. So impressive is the computer's capacity in this regard that Peter Lax, a mathematician at the Courant Institute at New York University, sees it as a new branch of science. "The traditional branches of science, the experimental and the theoretical, correspond to the traditional sources of knowledge. In the last two decades a third branch, the computational, has joined the other two, and is rapidly approaching its older sisters in importance and intellectual respectability. . . . This rapid rise of computing was made possible by striking improvements in computer hardware and software, and by equally striking improvements in the discretizations of the equations that model the physical phenomena, as well as by clever algorithms to solve the discretized equations." This newfound capability to simulate physical processes has exciting implications for the traditional relation between theory and experiment.

I began to see just how exciting while attending a seminar by a colleague of mine, a theoretical physicist. He described his theory of quantum particles and then went on to describe an "experiment" that supported his theory. The trouble was I couldn't imagine anyone doing that experiment—it was far beyond our experimental capability. Then I realized that my colleague was talking about a computer "experiment" (he was intentionally misleading us as a kind of joke) in which he modeled his equations for a quantum particle collision. Later, when I met another colleague, an experimental physicist who actually did real experiments colliding quantum particles together, I told him about the seminar. He responded, "But computer modeling isn't real experiment." When I suggested that perhaps his real experiments were nothing but analogue computations for the underlying theory, he got annoyed. But in fact nature can be viewed as an analogue computer.

One of the ways that future science will progress is by a combination of precise observations of actual systems followed by computer modeling of those systems. This differs from the traditional notion of experimentation in which one actively alters the conditions of the actual system to try and determine what is going on. For many actual natural systems, such as the interior of stars, one cannot even do experiments, and computer modeling is the only route one can take. Likewise, in the social and psychological sciences, one cannot in many instances do experiments, for practical or ethical considerations, and once again computer modeling offers a powerful new method to see what is going on. Computer modeling is a new way to do "experiments."

Another important development is the emergence of *the computational viewpoint in mathematics*—the notion that to know a mathematical truth you must be able to compute it. This is yet another theme of the new scientific synthesis, a theme that got its start with the invention of the Turing machine. A Turing machine can be thought of as a mechanical device, a printer, through which passes an infinitely long tape with a sequence of spaces containing either nothing or a dot. The machine can carry out four operations as it reads a space—move to the right, move to the left, erase a dot, print a dot. (The logician Hao Wang has shown that the erasure operation is superfluous, so only three operations are really needed.) This machine can carry out any program that can be expressed in a binary code. The most complex digital computer is formally equivalent to a Turing machine, it just does its work much faster.

But it is possible to go quite a bit beyond Turing's initial idea and to ask what is the cost or time it takes to prove something or solve a problem on a real computer. Maybe there are provable results in mathematics, but the cost of proving them is too high. In some cases one can estimate how long a proof would take. A practical, material factor, it seems, has entered the world of pure mathematics. However, the computers invoked by these computational considerations in pure mathematics are "gedanken computers," imaginary Turing machines, not real ones. But real computers may also have an important role to play in mathematics.

The role of the computer in pure mathematics is often debated. As Jacob Schwartz of the Courant Institute, and a leader in the use of computers, puts it, "The mathematician is always interested in general principles and less in individual facts, which is why, of all the sciences, math has been least influenced by computers." The movement in twentieth-century math has certainly been toward ever-greater abstraction and generalization. Yet the advent of the computer has stimulated a partial return to the constructive attitude of nineteenth-century mathematics and has led to *the rise of experimental mathematics*—another theme of the new synthesis. Who are "experimental mathematicians"? These are mathematicians who try out their ideas on computers; in essence the computer is used by them as a grand blackboard. The purpose of this new "blackboard" is often to get a feeling for whether or not their ideas are right, if a conjecture is really true. Because of the computer, abstraction and construction in mathematics, sometimes viewed as opposite poles, are becoming close partners in investigations.

Closely related to these ideas in mathematics is the rise of *the computational viewpoint of physical processes.* The basic notion here is that the material world and the dynamic systems in it are computers. The brain, the weather, the solar system, even quantum particles are all computers. They don't *look* like computers, of course, but what they are computing are the consequences of the laws of nature. According to computational viewpoint, the laws of nature are algorithms that control the development of the system in time, just like real programs do for computers. For example, the planets, in moving around the sun, are doing analogue computations of the laws of Newton.

From the traditional orientation of the natural sciences this computational viewpoint is completely empty of content. After all, everything is its own simulation. What more do we learn about nature by adopting this viewpoint? What is the reason for saying everything is a computational process?

Such criticism, however, misses the point. The computational viewpoint doesn't explain anything that cannot be explained in traditional terms. Yet it does create a new perspective (like the perspective created by the Copernican conversion) that unifies science in a different way. It creates a different framework for thinking about material reality that seems worthy of exploration. No one knows yet where it will lead.

Another important theme in sciences of complexity is *the notion of a selective system.* The Darwin-Wallace ideas of natural selection if generalized and abstracted to the notion of a selective system can be applied to a variety of other phenomena. Whenever one sees a pattern, an order, like that of life on earth, animal behavior, or the structure of society, one can ask: How did that pattern arise; how was that specific pattern selected? Selective systems provide us with a new way of answering those questions, a way that is having ever-greater impact on the social and psychological sciences. It may, in fact, now be possible to develop a science of society that is minimally distorted by the political and social values of the investigating scientist much as is the case in the natural sciences. (Even *that* ambition, I realize, reflects a value.)

I am especially struck by the rise of the evolutionary-biological paradigm in the social sciences as set forth in "Prospects for a Synthesis in the Human Behavioral Sciences," an essay by Irven DeVore, a self-described "behavioral biologist" at Harvard. DeVore is forthright about his own outlook when he says, "Much the most important intellectual advance during my professional life has been the development of [an] exciting new theory in vertebrate behavioral ecology, or 'sociobiology.' This family of theoretical advances is truly a revolution in our understanding of how evolution has shaped animal behavior. At the heart of this revolution has been the demonstration that natural selection is most accurately viewed from the 'point of view' of the individual and the gene, rather than a process that is operating on the group or species. We can now, with some rigor, analyze such complex behaviors as aggression, altruism, parental care, mate choice, and foraging patterns. . . . Many of us felt, almost from the beginning, that this powerful new body of theory would also revolutionize the study of human behavior." DeVore goes on to say that "there is at present no deep, elegant or even intellectually satisfying theory in social science." But he feels that the new biological ideas may be a step in the right direction.

The ideas of one of the founders of social science, Emil Durkheim, likened a society of individual humans to a whole organism in which social institutions are akin to organs and the individuals to cells within the organs. But this image, which has influenced many social scientists since Durkheim, is inadequate if not wrong —cells in an organism are genetically identical and cooperate, unlike individual humans who are all genetically distinct and do not always cooperate. As DeVore's remarks indicate, the important new element in modern evolutionary thinking is the notion of "the selfish gene"—it is genes that are trying to survive, and genes will do this without concern for the group or species unless it serves their purpose of survival as well. Many social scientists (in spite of the fact that they feel they have gone well beyond Durkheim's views) resist the idea that the survival of an individual's genes, along with those shared with kin, provide a foundation for thinking about human interactions, including the formation of social groups. Often they accept the importance of the biological viewpoint but still think that it is the group or species that is being selected rather than a set of genes. For example, sociologists often attribute significance to the social group or institution and study it as a social object. But if there is no material basis for such objects, they are not subject to a scientific theory (see the subsequent chapter "Waiting for the Messiah"). Put in Kantian terms, the commonplace error in seeking deep theories in the social sciences is applying the methods of theoretical reason, which applies to the natural world, to the domain of practical reason, which applies to moral and ethical judgments.

Anthropologist Richard W. Wrangham frames the debate when he warns that "a synthesis will not come easily . . . On the one hand biologists tend to trivialize the complexities introduced by features such as language, culture, symbolism, ideology and intricate social networks. On the other hand most social scientists have a strong aversion to reductionism even within their own fields, let alone when imported from the alien culture of biology. A shotgun marriage of biologists and social scientists is more likely to engender mutual hostility and deformed offspring than hybrid vigor." The differences alluded to here between the biological approach that sees a material, genetic basis for social behavior and the traditional social science approach that sees "types" and social forms as the real determinates has its correlates with the debate about the character of cognitive science.

The biological perspective on the social sciences is here to stay and will become part of the new sciences of complexity. Human social interactions, the formation of culture, can be studied as a selective system.

A major step in this direction has been recently taken by Robert Boyd and Peter J. Richardson in their important book *Culture and the Evolutionary Process*, a mathematical study of cultural transmission. Unlike the sociobiologists, Boyd and Richardson think that "the details of cultural transmission are likely to be essential to an understanding of the evolution of human behavior."

While sociobiological ideas have been applied with great effect to animal behavior, do they really apply to human behavior? After all, humans, unlike animals, have culture—a set of values and techniques that can be transmitted from generation to generation by learning, which is not a genetic mechanism. Boyd and Richardson's view, developed in great detail, sees both genetic and cultural transmission as important in determining human behavior—a dual inheritance theory. They argue, "If acquiring information by individual effort [genetic transmission] is costly compared to acquisition by social learning [cultural transmission], an explicit theory of the mechanisms of culture evolution may be necessary." This represents a compromise between the hard-core sociobiological outlook and the more traditional view that sees cultural and social factors as objective determinates of human behavior. In a sense they are quantitatively examining the boundary between the domains of the material and cognitive world. Irrespective of how one stands on this debate between genes and memes, it is a debate couched within the framework of the general idea of a selective system.

It is odd that evolutionary thinking has had little impact on psychology. As John Tooby, a colleague of DeVore's at Harvard, points out, "Humans, like all other organisms, were created through the process of evolution. Consequently, all innate human characteristics are the products of the evolutionary process. Although the implications of this were quickly grasped in investigating human physiology, until recently there has been a marked resistance to applying this knowledge to human behavior. But evolution and the innate algorithms that regulate human behavior are related as cause and consequence: lawful relations are being discovered between the evolutionary process and the innate psychology it has shaped. These lawful relations constitute the basis for a new discipline, evolutionary psychology, which involves the exploration of the naturally selected 'design' features of the mechanisms that control behavior. This synthesis between evolution and psychology has been slow in coming . . . the delay can be partly accounted for by two formidable barriers to the integration of these two fields: the initial imprecision of evolutionary theory and the continuing imprecision in the social sciences, including psychology." Tooby goes on to describe how this barrier is falling. The computer plays an important role in establishing the needed precision, for one can make computer models of the psychological algorithms that control behavior and show how they conform to adaptive paths. The application of these ideas to psychology, Tooby notes, "is clearly in its infancy. It will be a long time before we understand the boundaries between the 'biological' and 'cultural' psyche, but the task is under way."

The general notion of a selective system, fruitfully applied to many areas, is inspired by biological evolution. This pattern of inspiration will be a recurrent theme in the sciences of complexity —*the discovery of new general principles inspired by biological systems*. Evolution is one example of such a principle, but there are others. The immune response as understood by Niels Jerne can be used as a model of adaptive and learning behavior in computers. The various components of the brain, the visual and olfactory systems, have taught us new principles of network organization. Some of these biological principles of organization will be described in a subsequent chapter (Connectionism/Neural Nets).

I predict that the future will also see the rise of an interdisciplinary attack on fundamental biological systems—the cell, the brain, protein synthesis, evolution—representing a joining of physics, especially the physics of nonlinear systems, mathematics, and biology. We will also see *the rise of computational biology*—the study of biological systems and artificial life done on a computer. The import of the most precise natural sciences on biology is growing, and in the future this influence will be profound. Computer modeling will facilitate this influence. Biological systems will be viewed as extremely complex quantum mechanical entities (which is, after all, what they are) functioning according to well-defined rules. This development will also have its practical side. In his book *The Youngest Science*, Lewis Thomas describes the transformation of medicine from the art of the healing practitioner, who could do little, to the laboratory science of modern medicine with all the distress and hope that such a transformation entails.

Yet another theme in the new synthesis is *the study of nonlinear dynamics*. A subsequent chapter ("Life Can Be So Nonlinear") will focus exclusively on this mathematical development in the natural sciences. Suffice it to say here that most of the equations one encounters in the natural sciences are nonlinear equations. These equations are difficult, if not impossible, to solve analytically, but they cannot be ignored if we are to understand complex phenomena. With the arrival of the computer they can now be solved numerically to great effect. As a consequence scientists have uncovered chaotic solutions hidden in nonlinear, deterministic equations, chaos that describes phenomena like the weather or the behavior of neural nets. Many of these chaotic solutions and their properties are described in James Gleick's excellent book

Chaos. Other examples of nonlinear systems are the heart-lung system, evolution, the immune response, the global economy—just about anything that can be quantitatively described. The study of nonlinear systems, using computers, opens a vast vista on reality, a world never before seen.

Another theme under the aegis of complexity is *the emphasis on parallel (network) rather than serial (hierarchical) systems.* I remember hooking up light bulbs in a series circuit in electrical shop at my junior high school. In the series circuit, one wire ran from the power source to the first light bulb and then to the second and third and finally back to the power source. In the parallel circuit, two wires ran to the first light bulb, each connecting in effect to the filament in the bulb, and then the two wires continued to the next bulb and so on. The series curcuit had the advantage of fewer connections (one wire). But it was vulnerable—if one light bulb was removed or if it blew out, the circuit was broken and all of the lights went out. By contrast, the parallel circuit had more wire, more connections, but because of this redundancy it was much less vulnerable. If one light was removed, the others could continue to function.

This distinction between serial and parallel systems is quite general. The serial system can be generalized to a hierarchical system like the pyramidical organization chart for a corporation, the church, or the military. Hierarchical systems are such that there are a "top" and a "bottom" at every level. If you remove a "top," everything below it is cut off from the rest of the system—just like the series of light bulbs.

Parallel systems generalize to what I will call a "network." A network has no "top" or "bottom." Rather it has a plurality of connections that increase the possible interactions between components of the network. There is no central executive authority that oversees the system. A network has lots of redundancy, so that if a part of a network is destroyed, the whole network continues to function.

Most real systems are mixtures of hierarchies and networks. An example is the international banking system. Each bank or financial institution is internally a hierarchy, yet the global financial system consisting of all these financial institutions forms a network —no one is in charge. The brain is also a network, but it has hierarchical organization as well. (As yet, no master control system in the brain has been found.) The study of such mixed networks is part of the sciences of complexity.

It is interesting to apply these ideas contrasting hierarchies and networks to the architectonic of the sciences itself. The reductionalist architectonic of the sciences corresponds to a hierarchical system. Quantum field theory, since it deals with the fundamental laws governing the smallest things, is the "most reduced." Then come other sciences—nuclear physics, atomic physics, and chemistry—followed by the life sciences. The picture that emerges of the relation of the sciences to each other is like a corporate organization chart.

However, we might also view the architectonic of the sciences as a network—no "top" or "bottom," no master science. The various sciences are simply related to one another according to what aspect of reality is examined. We might divide the sciences into sciences of simplicity and complexity or into sciences of extension and intension and so on. A network could represent all these divisions. Some people don't like this network image because it isn't tidy, rigorous, and definite. But then again, this lack of tidiness also characterizes the logical relations between the various sciences, once one breaks out of the reductionist viewpoint.

Finally, and most important, the new synthesis will focus on *the study of complex systems*. I haven't yet given a definition of complexity (the next chapter will go into that), except to say that complex systems, at least at the phenomenal level, have many qualitatively distinct components. Their underlying mechanisms may be, however, rather simple. In the last few decades there has been rising interest in the brain, neural networks both biological and artificial, adaptive systems, behavior of social insects, games, and many other examples of complex systems. As our understanding of complexity develops, laws of complex systems may be found that apply to a variety of systems irrespective of what discipline they are found in. For example, laws of natural and artificial selection may turn out to have very general applicability to a variety of complex systems whether they be social, economic, or biological systems. We may thus see the unity of science in a new way.

The picture of the potential new synthesis of science I have given the reader in terms of these themes is necessarily incomplete because the synthesis is only in its beginning stages. This synthesis, like all major developments in science, will build on what we already know. In particular it will presuppose that the reduction-alist view of natural science is correct and will endeavor to show how complex behavior can arise out of simple elements. The many components of a complex system that we see may be the conse-quence of a few simple elements that we do not see.

The emergence of the sciences of complexity is one of the most exciting developments on the scientific frontier. It is difficult, even in one book, to survey that expanding frontier. But in the next several chapters I will provide the reader with some snapshots of what is happening at different points along that frontier in detail —from the abstract, mathematical ideas about complexity to the more applied ideas. Most of my snapshots will be from the natural sciences rather than the social sciences because that is the area I am most familiar with. But I believe, as I have indicated in this chapter, that some of the most exciting implications for the sci-ences of complexity are going to be in the social sciences.

In the last few decades we have witnessed the emergence of the computer culture—a new class of people and a new means of creating knowledge. The older culture, whether it is in the aca-demic or business community, does not yet fully grasp the impli-cations of this change. No one knows where it is headed; there are many prophets but no messiah. There is a kind of rough-and-tumble aspect to the sciences these days, indicating an era of fer-ment and change. Intellectual leaders will arise to attempt to bring order to this emerging synthesis, creating new institutions as they do so. This is, in fact, already happening as new centers for the study of complexity are being established in universities or as in-dependent institutes. Eventually even the departmental structure of universities will reflect the new synthesis of science.

A new worldview is struggling to be born as scientists proceed to examine the vast realm of complex systems. I cannot see the final shape of this new architectonic of knowledge, only some of its characteristics, which I have roughly outlined above. It will take decades and centuries before the dust settles and a new consensual framework of knowledge emerges—a framework that will be in-formed by our understanding of the invariant order of nature— the cosmic code.

The new knowledge that we acquire will have a transforming influence on the way our society is organized, how it uses infor-mation and technology. If complex systems can be understood from "the bottom up," it may take a lot of the guesswork out of planning. This knowledge, however, does not come automatically. Both human and material resources have to be allocated to this end. Substantial investments in educational and commercial development are required.

Advanced societies must begin to accept the challenge of this new frontier in science. I would urge that the United States build a policy and institutional structure in the information sciences and sciences of complexity similar to that which gave rise to the National Science Foundation and the National Institutes of Health some decades ago. Initial support for these sciences must be a government initiative which is then followed by commercial development. Government leaders must understand that targeting projects piecemeal is not productive; what is required is the promotion of an entire new scientific culture.

I am convinced that the societies that master the new sciences of complexity and can convert that knowledge into new products and forms of social organization will become the cultural, economic, and military superpowers of the next century. While there is great hope in this development, there is also the terrible danger that this new salient in knowledge will aggravate the differences between those who possess it and those who do not.

And now, to begin, let us start at the most basic level and take a look at what the mathematicians have to say about complexity.

Chapter 3

Order, Complexity, and Chaos

Most numbers in the continuum cannot be defined by any finite set of words.

—MARK KAC

What is complexity? Up until now we have been using the term "complexity" rather loosely to convey what it means in ordinary language—it refers to a state of affairs that has many interacting, different components. Now it is time to move beyond that loose definition. Complexity, as we shall endeavor to understand it in this chapter, is a quantitative measure that can be assigned to a physical system or a computation that lies midway between the measure of simple order and complete chaos. A diamond crystal, for example, with its neatly arranged atoms, is "ordered"; a rose, which has both randomness and order in the arrangement of its parts, is "complex"; the movement of gas molecules is truly "chaotic." Complexity thus covers a vast territory that lies between order and chaos. Interestingly, we understand a lot about completely ordered systems like crystals, for which the atoms are completely arranged in a lattice, or even the dynamics of single simple atoms like the hydrogen atom. We also understand a lot about completely chaotic systems like gases because we can apply the laws of statistics to them with great effect. The chaos guarantees very stable average behavior so that we can find appropriate laws. It is the realm of complexity that lies between order and chaos that is the greatest challenge to science. While we can define order and define chaos, how can we define complexity more precisely?

Mathematicians and scientists have had a look at complexity and tried to define it so that it accords with these intuitive notions and yet is precise. Some people resist such precise mathematical definitions of things because it removes the flexibility in how we think about them. Yet I believe that the mathematical approach, because it is precise, considerably deepens our understanding and grasp of what was previously elusive. Clarity is the first step to a deeper understanding.

For the moment let us forget about any vague idea of complexity that we might already hold and see what mathematicians and others have found. In this chapter we will be examining various concepts of complexity—algorithmic complexity, computational complexity, information-based complexity, as well as physical complexity, and logical depth. The basic approach we will at first follow is that if we can define complexity for an abstract object like a number, then we may be able to understand how that definition applies to other real objects in the physical world.

So as a start let us first examine the infinite continuum of numbers between zero and one when they are written out in decimal expansion. The first number in this set is .00000 . . . and the last one is .99999 . . . , where the " . . . " means it goes on forever. Some of the numbers in this continuum, like

$$.101010101010$$

seem rather ordered and simple. But we can also imagine generating the digits of a number by rolling a ten-sided die with the integers from 0 to 9 on the faces. Then we might come up with a number that is rather disordered, like

$$.185320942116$$

How can we characterize the distinction between the two numbers more precisely? In order to answer this question, we ask another: How can we compute these and other numbers?

In his seminal work, Alan Turing distinguished between "computable" and "noncomputable" numbers. To make this distinction precise, Turing imagined writing a program, what is called an algorithm, for a computer that would compute various numbers. As an example, let's take the number

$$.42857142 \ldots$$

At first this number looks rather random and complicated, and we might think that it was generated by rolling the die. But suppose we recognize that this number is simply 3 divided by 7 expressed in decimal form. Then the algorithm that computes this number simply states, "Divide 3 by 7 and print the result"—a simple program. Another example is Champernowne's number $C = 0.1234567891011121314151617181920\,21 \ldots$, which also looks complicated but as we see by inspection is really constructed by writing out the integers in order. Its program, which is also simple, could read, "Print the integers in order." Likewise the algorithm for $.101010101010$ would state, "Print 10 six times."

These are all examples of "computable" numbers because there is a simple algorithm that gives us the number even if the number is infinitely long, like the decimal expression of 3/7 or Champernowne's number. However, for some numbers, the "noncomputable" numbers, the only algorithm we know is to explicitly specify the number itself within the program. For example, the only algorithm that I know of for the number above, which was generated by rolling a die, is "Print .185320942116". That, of course, is still not too long a program. Yet if we were to continue the number $.101010101010$ out to one million 01's, the program length for computing this number does not change much—"Print 01 one million times". By contrast, if we continued the random number of rolling the ten-sided die another million times, the only program that would compute this number is "Print .185320942116 . . .", where the ". . ." means another million specific digits. That's a considerable increase in the length of the program.

We learn from Turing's ideas that it is possible to characterize different numbers by the length of the program that is required to compute them. For "computable" numbers, even if they are infinitely long, it is possible to write a relatively short program that will calculate them. For the "noncomputable," random numbers, the only algorithm that will do the job already contains all the information in the number explicitly—the algorithm is at least as long as the number. This distinction provides a *definition* of a random number, put forth independently in 1965 by A. N. Kol-mogorov, a Soviet mathematician, and Gregory J. Chaitin, then an undergraduate at City College of the City University of New York—random numbers require computational programs that are at least as long as the number itself. Both these mathematicians were unaware of the related proposal set forth in 1960 by Ray J. Solomonoff, who was trying to find a definition of the simplicity of scientific theories (rather than the complexity of numbers).

Although we have imagined the programs that compute the numbers as written down in ordinary language, it is clear that by assigning numerical values to the letters of the alphabet the program can itself be encrypted as a string of integers. So the full informational context of the program can be represented as a number in the continuum between zero and one—just like the number the program is supposed to compute. Hence the length of the string of integers representing the program can be compared to the length of the number it is supposed to compute.

We are almost finished. But before we give the "algorithmic definition of complexity," we have to say what a "minimal program" is. Any particular number can be computed by an infinite number of different algorithms. For example, the number 2397 can be gotten from the programs "Subtract 3 from 2400" or "Add 17 to 2380" or "Multiply 51 by 47" or an infinite number of different programs. Of special interest is the *minimal program*—the shortest one once we have encrypted it as a string of integers. There may be one, or there may be many such minimal programs. One thing is for certain, however: the string of integers, the number representing the minimal program, must be random. For if it is not random, then according to the definition we previously gave for random, we could write a shorter program that would compute the number representing that program in contradiction to the assumption that it was a minimal program.

We can now give the algorithmic definition of the complexity of a number. It is simply the length of the minimal program required to compute it. In this way we can assign a quantitative measure to every number in the continuum, and this is the algorithmic definition of its complexity.

For random numbers generated by the roll of a die, as we have seen, the complexity according to this definition is approximately equal to the length of the number because the minimal algorithm must contain the number itself. By contrast, for numbers that are highly ordered, like .010101 . . . or 3/7 = .42857142 . . . , the minimal program length is short and hence the complexity is low. For numbers in between those for which the minimal program length is short or those for which the length is approximately the length of the number itself are numbers with a mixture of order and randomness—the true realm of "complicated numbers." They lie between order and chaos.

Some people's reaction to all these mathematical definitions is that they only have to do with the complexity of strings of numbers. What does that have to do with the world of real physical objects that we endeavor to understand? One example will show us how these ideas can apply to the real world. Think of the DNA molecule for a specific animal (it could be you). This molecule is a sequence of base pairs that tell us how to make a genetic replica of that animal. The sequence of base pairs can be mapped onto a single number. For example, the four letters in the genetic code could be designated 0, 1, 2, and 3 respectively. Then the molecule is perfectly represented by a sequence like 023011032221. . . . So we can construct a finite number that represents the informational content of the DNA molecule and can now ask: What is the length of the minimal algorithm that will produce that number?

One thing we know is the code of triplet sequences of base pairs for the twenty amino acids—the building blocks for all proteins. Hence we know that the number is not completely random because there is lots of order in the number already—we can look at the number of a sequence of triplets. We also know empirically there is a lot of redundancy—repetition—in the DNA molecule (a puzzling finding), and that also represents order. Finally we know that this molecule, in principle, contains the instructions for making the animal, all the organs, the hair color, and so forth, and that also represents further informational content of a very high order. All of this argues for the fact that the DNA molecule and the number representing it is not random and yet is not perfectly ordered, either—it is a "complicated number." If we could find the length of the minimal algorithm, it seems that it would certainly be much less than the length of the DNA number and could provide a quantitative measure of the complexity of the animal.

It was easy to see how a number got assigned to the DNA molecule because it is just a coded string of base pairs. But in fact this kind of construction can be applied to anything that is made of matter. For simplicity we will restrict our attention to things made of the six dozen atoms. These atoms can be viewed as letters of an alphabet, and the alphabet can be coded into numbers, as is done in cryptography. Not only can the atoms be coded, but the explicit arrangements of atoms, their coordinates within the object, their angular momentum, and even their motion can be coded. So the material state of an object, like a chair, or the entire universe, can in principle be represented as a single number, a very long number to be sure.

Back in the 1930s, Kurt Gödel showed how to represent strings of symbols, like those appearing in a logical proof, as a single number (the Gödel or G-number). For every logical proof there was a unique number. Given the number, one could decode it and get the proof back. Our construction of numbers for physical entities is similar in spirit. It ought to be possible (depending on the laws of physics and the precise way we decide to codify structure) to represent the state of physical entities by a unique single number. I will call this number the E-number, "E" for Entity. (I will overlook here the important question of how difficult it is to actually find this number.) Reducing everything to numbers is the ultimate Pythagorean fantasy, a fantasy that leads to the realization of a science-fiction dream. For once we know the E-number of an object, we can imagine transmitting it via an electromagnetic signal to the other side of the galaxy, where it could be decoded and used to replicate the entity—a matter transmitter. That way people and things could get around the universe at least at the speed of light.

Such science-fiction ideas aside, once we have an object's E-number we can ask what is the algorithmic complexity of that E-number and thereby assign a quantitative measure to the complexity of that object. In this way we can assign a quantitative measure of complexity to people, chickens, rocks, or bacteria. So what?

For one thing, we have succeeded in making our definition of complexity quite precise. Consequently we can unleash the formidable apparatus of mathematical complexity theory on our problem of defining complexity of material entities. These virtues are not to be overlooked. Yet from the practical side we still have a problem. Before we can find the complexity of a number, we need to find the length of the minimal algorithm required to compute it. And to find that length we have to *prove* that a specific algorithm is indeed minimal. How can one do that? This question gets us into some tricky but intriguing Gödelian reasoning.

As Gregory Chaitin has argued, in order to prove anything in mathematics one needs a set of axioms (the unproven, and taken as given, propositions of the system) and the rules of inference—in short, what is called a formal system in David Hilbert's sense (see my subsequent chapter "Warriors of the Infinite"). Such a formal system of axioms, since it consists of strings of symbols that express the axioms, can be assigned a G-number, and thus we can ask questions about the complexity of such a number. The G-number representing the axioms of a formal system better be a random number. If it isn't, that means we can find an algorithm that is simpler than the number representing the axioms, and hence the axioms can be reduced to simpler axioms—they are *not* irreducible axioms and are really theorems based on yet simpler axioms.

Chaitin has also maintained that in addition to the axioms, one needs a program that will use the axioms to prove that a specific algorithm is indeed minimal. The program that searches for proofs can also be codified as a number. With the axioms and program in hand we can begin to try and prove that certain numbers are random by showing that their minimal algorithm is at least as long as the number. But can this be done? In fact it cannot. The reason is that a large number whose randomness we wish to prove contains a certain amount of information. The formal system of axioms that we use and the program we use to search for the proof of the randomness of that number can be codified into another number that also contains a certain amount of information. One cannot use a system that is specified by a certain amount of information to prove something about a system with a relatively larger amount of information. In mathematics one never gets out more information than one puts in in the first place from the starting axioms and rules. It is like expecting a mouse to swallow an elephant. Since we can always find huge numbers that contain an arbitrarily large amount of information, there will always exist numbers whose informational content exceeds that of any axiom system, and therefore one cannot find a proof that they are random. This also means that there exist numbers for which we cannot establish the minimal algorithm and hence define their complexity. As Chaitin says, "In such a formal system one cannot prove that a particular series of digits is of a[n algorithmic] complexity greater than the number of bits in the program employed to specify the series. . . . Hence there will always be numbers whose randomness cannot be proved." A reasonable conclusion.

This is a strange state of affairs. While we can prove that almost all numbers in the continuum are random, we cannot prove that any specific number is indeed random. Mathematics is filled with such ironies.

I have gone through these rather abstract mathematical ideas about algorithmic complexity to show not only how conceptually beautiful they are, but also the fundamental limitations of this or any related attempt to define complexity. The algorithmic definition of complexity provides a mathematical framework for our thinking about complexity and randomness, yet it does not provide a practical definition that we can use for physical systems.

We discussed *algorithmic complexity*—the length of the shortest program to do a computation. Another, related definition is that of *computational complexity*—how long a time it will take a computer to solve a specific problem, a direct measure of the problem's difficulty. Algorithmic complexity is in a sense a measure of complexity in space (the length of the minimal algorithm); computational complexity is a measure of complexity in time (the time it takes to solve a problem) as well as in space. Problems in computational complexity are a rich and a rapidly expanding field of investigation, both in mathematics and computer science.

We had already briefly mentioned this new field of computational complexity in our discussion of the computational outlook in mathematics. The theorems of mathematics, according to this view, do not simply exist in some transcendent realm of the mind but have to be actually proven—we have to decide if the theorem is true or false within a specific formal system of axioms and rules of inference. Suppose we know that a specific theorem is decidable within a formal system of axioms. Then we can ask, how hard is it to decide if it is true or not? That is a problem in the field of computational complexity. Here is an example:

The ordinary arithmetic we use is a formal system, but as Gödel showed, in the proof of the famous theorem that bears his name, it is undecidable—there are propositions within the realm of arithmetic that we cannot prove are true. But there is a restricted form of arithmetic that has only one operation—addition of the positive numbers and zero—called Presburger arithmetic, which is decidable; all statements are provable. So this axiom system is not subject to Gödel's theorem. M. J. Fischer and Michael Rabin have shown that in Presburger arithmetic the decision problem— whether a theorem is true or not—takes a superexponential amount of time in the length of the theorem statement. This means that while *in principle* all theorems in Presburger arithmetic are provable, *in practice* proving some theorems will take much, much longer than the lifetime of the universe. This insight can tell us how much it costs in computing time to establish the true theorems of even decidable systems. As Joseph Traub, chairman of Columbia University's department of computer science, exclaimed, "What an enrichment of Hilbert's question!"—referring, of course, to David Hilbert's question about proving all the true theorems of mathematics. Hilbert envisioned a mathematical project in which one set out to systematically prove all the true theorems of mathematics; but he never asked how *long* it would take to find the true theorems. While the computational viewpoint deepens our insight into the realm of the solvable, it still is often very hard to establish the actual computational complexity of specific problems (just as it is hard to find the minimal algorithm). Yet there has been significant mathematical progress in this area.

If we examine the computational complexity of specific mathematical problems, we are led to a classification of such problems into two broad categories—those problems that require a geometrical (exponential) amount of computing time and those that require only an arithmetic (power law) amount of computer time. The problems that require an exponential amount of computing time typically need millions of lifetimes of the universe to be solved, even on supercomputers. Forget about ever arriving at an exact solution. The problems whose computational complexity is only arithmetic in computing time can typically be solved in a reasonable amount of time (meaning the amount of time before the mathematician loses interest in the problem).

It is important to be able to distinguish between the two categories of problems, but it isn't always so easy. Often we don't know if it takes an exponential or power law amount of time to solve a problem. The traveling salesman problem—how to find the shortest route for visiting half a dozen or more cities, calling at each city once and returning to the original city—is a problem that people suspect is of the exponential kind, but they have not proved it. One can never tell if some clever person won't someday find an algorithm for solving this problem using only a power law amount of computing time. For many problems, however, the mathematicians know the classification—part of a growing body of pure knowledge in the field of computational complexity. They can thus determine how long it takes to solve certain problems.

The field of computational complexity, which has attracted many of the best mathematicians, has given rise to the nascent field of *information-based complexity*, developed by Joseph Traub and his co-workers. I want to describe this idea also because it has practical implications.

The kinds of problems that are examined by workers in the field of computational complexity are usually completely specified problems, like the traveling salesman problem. All the cards are faceup on the table. In principle, if you work hard enough (*how long may not be known*), you can find the answer because all the information needed to solve the problem is right there with the statement of the problem.

But in the real world the situation is seldom so pure and precise. Only some of the cards are faceup on the table. As every decision maker knows, the problems we encounter in the real world are often not specified precisely—information is incomplete, or we may know only approximate data. "Thus," as Traub observes, "computational complexity comes in two flavors, depending on which set of assumptions are made about information. Is information complete, exact, and free, as with the traveling salesman problem? Or is information partial, contaminated, and priced, as with a host of other real-world problems?" The goal of people working on information-based complexity "is to create a general theory about problems with partial or contaminated information, and to apply the results to solving specific problems in varied disciplines." This is the kind of approach that will be needed if we are to come to grips with problems in the biological, behavioral, and social sciences. For example, we have only partial or contaminated information about the brain, animal behavior, and the global economy. What can we expect to know (compute) about such systems, and how reliable is that knowledge? Those are problems in information-based complexity theory that are at the forefront of the new sciences of complexity.

This completes my brief survey of some of the important ideas about how to mathematically define complexity. From an intuitive point of view, these mathematical ideas of complexity, although they are precise, leave one feeling dissatisfied. Complexity, as a measure of physical objects, is supposed to lie somewhere between order and chaos. Yet with the algorithmic definition of complexity, the more random a number is, the more complicated (chaotic) it is. That definition does not correspond to an idea of complexity between order and chaos. Actually, the algorithmic definition of *complexity* seems to be a misnomer. It really is a definition of *randomness*, not of complexity.

To make this point clear, go back to the example of the DNA molecule—clearly a highly complicated molecule. Yet the DNA molecule has order, important order that represents the instructions for making an animal. If we compare a DNA molecule to another molecule of equal length in which the four base pairs are ordered at random (by rolling a four-sided die), then according to the algorithmic definition of complexity this random molecule is *more* complex than the actual DNA molecule. But in fact, nothing can be constructed from the information in that random molecule —it's just random nonsense.

Another example is provided by language. Spoken or written language is clearly very complex compared with the production of a monkey at a typewriter—a random string of letters. Yet the "algorithmic definition of complexity" assigns a higher complexity to the monkey's production. Therefore, the algorithmic definition of complexity, while it illuminates the problem of defining complexity, does not come to grips with what we are after.

Some scientists, dissatisfied with the algorithmic and computational definitions of complexity for this reason as well as the fact that one cannot use it in any way to practically establish the complexity of an object, have proposed other definitions of complexity. In 1985 T. Hogg and Bernard Huberman of the Xerox Palo Alto Research Center proposed *a physical definition of complexity* of a system that is based on its *diversity*. Their measure has the virtue of vanishing for both completely ordered and completely random systems and is maximal for the realm in between, in conformity with our intuitive notion of complexity.

To define complexity, Hogg and Huberman use the notion of a hierarchy that "can correspond to the structural layout of a system or, more generally, to clustering the parts by the strength of interaction. In particular, if the most strongly interactive components are grouped together and this procedure is repeated with the resulting clusters, one produces a tree [like an organization chart] reflecting the hierarchy of the system. In physics one sees this type of organization as quarks form hadrons, which in turn form nuclei, then atoms, molecules, and so on. Similarly, in computations one assembles subroutines into programs which form higher lever structures such as operating systems and networks." Once one has defined and established such a hierarchy, it is possible to assign a measure to its complexity, taking into account diversity in interactions among the components. According to Hogg and Huberman, this "is the essential feature that makes for complex behavior in systems made up of simple elementary parts."

Using the mathematical properties of hierarchies, Hogg and Huberman give a precise definition of complexity that captures the sense that it is maximal between order and chaos. The complexity of a completely ordered and repetitive hierarchy is zero, and so is the complexity of a disordered and chaotic one. A rose is more complicated than a crystal or a gas. This seems like progress. However, in order to use this definition of complexity one has first to establish the appropriate hierarchy, and how to do that is not always so clear. Maybe the complexity comes in defining the hierarchy and is not intrinsic to the system. Their definition has been criticized by some scientists as rather artificial.

Another approach to defining complexity has been pursued by Charles Bennett of IBM Research. He, too, is seeking a definition of complexity for which a rose turns out to be more complex than a gas of molecules. Instead of talking about the complexity of a system, he talks about its "organization"; but he is after the same notion.

Bennett is especially struck by the behavior of self-organizing systems. These are systems that obey the letter of the second law of thermodynamics (which requires a closed physical system to deteriorate) but violate its spirit. A self-organizing system lowers its entropy (a measure of its degree of disorganization) by expelling entropy into its environment and hence avoiding deterioration. An example of the development of a self-organizing system is the growth of a plant or a crystal. The point to be made about self-organizing systems is that first they are indeed complex—highly organized—and second they got that way by starting from a much simpler system. Bennett's idea of the organization or complexity of a system is closely related to how difficult it is to go from the simple starting system to the fully developed complex system.

He couches his ideas in terms of information theory and gives the following illustration: "The problem of defining organization is akin to that of defining the value of a message, as opposed to its information content. A typical sequence of coin tosses has high information content but little message value; an ephemeris, giving the positions of the moon and planets every day for years, has no more information than the equations of motion and the initial conditions from which it was calculated, but saves its owner the effort of recalculating these positions. The value of a message thus appears to reside not in its information (its absolutely unpredictable parts), nor in its obvious redundancy (verbatim repetitions, unequal digit frequencies), but rather in what might be called its buried redundancy—parts predictable only with difficulty, things the receiver could in principle have figured out without being told, but only with a considerable cost in money, time, or computation. In other words, the value of a message is the amount of mathematical or other work plausibly done by its originator, which its receiver is saved from having to repeat. . . .

"These ideas may be formalized in terms of algorithmic information theory: a message's most plausible cause is identified with its minimal algorithmic description, and its 'logical depth,' or plausible content of mathematical work, is (roughly speaking) identified with time required to compute the message from this minimal description."

Bennett identifies "logical depth" with the complexity of a physical entity. He implicitly appeals to *the computational view of physical processes*, in which physical processes are viewed as computing equations specified by the laws of nature. The solar system can, in this view, be seen as an analogue computer solving Newton's equations. By the same token we can stimulate the behavior or growth of a physical system on a digital computer. We may begin with a very elementary set of rules or algorithms to do such a computation (the "minimal algorithmic description"), like Newton's laws for the solar system or the rules of molecular combina-

tion in the case of living systems. The "logical depth" of an object
—its complexity—is measured by how long it takes a computer to
simulate the full development of that object beginning with the
elementary algorithm and taking no short cuts. Complexity, in this
sense, is a measure of how hard it is to put something together
starting from elementary pieces. For example, different kinds of
picture puzzles can be classified in terms of their complexity by
how hard it is to put them together.

These attempts to define complexity in terms of diversity in a
hierarchy or "logical depth" are extremely intriguing. Yet suppose
one finds such a definition of complexity. What good is it? Unless
the complexity of an object enters as a quantity in physical laws
like the temperature or entropy of a physical object, it is not very
useful—at least not to physicists. None of the present proposals
for defining the complexity of physical things implies that it is a
quantity that enters into physical laws.

If we look at the attempt to find a physical definition of the
complexity of an object, we see that there is something very odd
about it. For imagine that someone succeeds in defining complexity for physical objects, a definition everyone agrees on. Then we
can measure the "complexity" of an object the way we can measure its temperature. Rocks, chickens, and stars would all have
some amount of "complexity" associated with them. But what an
odd notion this would be. Rocks, chickens, and stars are all complex, but they are complex in different ways. They are qualitatively
different. Rocks are made of different compounds and crystals,
chickens of cells and stars of electrically conducting gases. To
reduce all those essential differences—essential to any description
of their complexity—to a *single* number seems to oversimplify the
situation. What is interesting about the complexity of physical
systems lies in their details—how they are put together. It would
be desirable to advance these vague notions about the complexity
of physical objects to something more precise. Yet a more precise
definition would have to respect the complicated nature of some
material objects, and so far no such useful definition has been put
forward. My own guess is that a useful definition of the complexity
of objects as a physical property intrinsic to the object will continue to elude us.

Perhaps, then, it is asking too much for complexity to play such
a direct role in physical laws. If, instead, we adopt the idea that

nature is a giant computer whose operations we imitate in our own simulations, then a quantitative definition of complexity may be useful. The notion of complexity has its natural home in the world of computation. Providing we adopt the computational view, then complexity can indeed correspond to something physical—the running time of a computer simulation of a physical process.

One example, albeit an extreme one, of the computational view of nature is the new perspective it provides on the growth of an animal. The processes of growth of a physical organism can be seen as a computational proceess calculating the content of that organism's DNA. Now, the information content of DNA, we have noted, can be codified as a number. The algorithmic complexity of that number is specified by the length of its minimal algorithm. I conjecture that the computational process of the minimal algorithm for DNA is approximately represented by the actual growth process of the organism corresponding to that DNA sequence. This conjecture supposes that the algorithmic complexity of the DNA (genotype) and the organism (phenotype) are approximately equal. Biological development is thus an algorithm—computational processes translating the genotype into the phenotype.

The computational viewpoint of the physical world can lead to a weird perspective. But it is that kind of weirdness that opens us to new insights. Conceivably we may even find a useful definition of complexity within that perspective.

The search for a precise definition of complexity is closely related to the desire on the part of some scientists to quantify the intuitive notion that as things evolve they seem to become more complex. This happens in spite of the fact that entropy—a measure of disorder—always must increase for a closed physical system (the second law of thermodynamics). Somehow nature is able to create little islands of order and complexity within the great ocean of entropy. The evolution of life seems to violate the spirit of the second law even while it adheres to the letter.

A property of dynamical systems is that they seem to give rise to more and more complex systems. Why is this? A human being is more complex than a protozoa—not better, not more important, but certainly more complex. It seems that by "experimenting" with the creation of more complex organisms, nature has found a technique that enables evolution to take off in new environments. If all the simplest ecological niches are already occupied by simple organisms, then a more complex organism—one that need not compete for those simple niches—can evolve and survive. This is probably part of the answer to why evolution has produced complex organisms. Adopting complex strategies can promote survival. If we but had a mathematical definition of complexity, this idea could then be explored quantitatively, as could cultural evolution and the emergence of complex social and economic systems.

Before leaving complexity and randomness I want to mention yet another attempt to capture chaos. The algorithmic definition of randomness, while it provides new insights, cannot, we have learned, tell us if a specific number is random. If we cannot tell what *in principle* is random, perhaps we can determine what *in practice* is random. If mathematicians can't tell us what is random, then perhaps we ought to turn to the physical world. Back in the 1930s Richard von Mises thought that we could define randomness by its appearance in physical processes, like a ball jumping about in a gambling wheel or coin flipping, in which, if it is truly random, you could never win or lose a bet on the average. That approach puts the notion of randomness on a practical basis.

Recently a group of statisticians at Stanford University, Persi Diaconis (a former professional magician), Bradley Efron, and Eduardo Engle have been examining physical processes and have come up with a quantitative definition of chaos. They have also found out that many physical processes one might think are random in fact are not. For example, shuffling cards five or fewer times does not really randomly mix the deck. Only after seven or eight shuffles are they suddenly random. Diaconis and his colleague Joseph Keller have also analyzed the rolling of dice and roulette, and the story here is similar. "If you look hard," Diaconis says, "things aren't as random as everyone assumes." But because they aren't so random, it is possible to examine these physical processes in detail and see how randomness fails. Then one learns something.

Coin flipping is a good example. When we flip a coin it has a starting velocity and spin. We can imagine plotting the initial velocity and spin of the coin on a two-dimensional graph with the velocity on the horizontal axis and the spin on the vertical axis. With the coin always in the same position initially, let's say heads up, we can map out the regions on the two-dimensional graph that result in heads and those in tails when the coin is flipped. Near the origin of the graph corresponding to low initial velocity and spin (so the coin doesn't even flip), the region is heads. As one moves away from the origin there are regions of both heads and tails. Far from the origin, corresponding to high initial velocity and spin, the regions of heads and tails become very narrow—a slight change in the initial conditions will produce a different result. So for these regions of high initial velocity and spin, coin flipping is very random. It would take millions of flips to see that it wasn't.

Diaconis has developed a theory that enables him to quantify precisely how random some of these physical processes really are. His theory also enables him to say what the degree of chaos is— how far one is from true randomness. Through his work and that of others we are getting a peek behind the veil of physical chaos.

Chaos has been with us for a long time. But only recently are we beginning to tame it. While statisticians are pursuing their methods of studying chaos, a major new development has occurred in physics—scientists discovered chaos in deterministic equations. This new discovery ties in profoundly with the ideas of complexity and computability discussed in this chapter. Chaos and the approach to chaos, it turns out, has an interesting structure that is just beginning to be understood.

Joseph Ford, of Georgia Tech, hails this new science of chaos as the "beginning of the third revolution in physics in this century," the other two revolutions being the theory of relativity and the quantum theory. I am inspired by Ford's expositions on chaos but disagree with his assessment. The previous "revolutions" in physics postulated new physical laws. By contrast, all the theoretical work on chaos, while it profoundly illuminates actual physical processes and deepens our understanding, does not postulate any new physical laws. Rather it analyzes existing physical laws in an exciting new way. Chaos was "sitting there" in the existing equations of physics waiting to be understood. In the next chapter we shall have a look at it.

Chapter 4

Life Can Be
So Nonlinear

Earliest men perceived . . . their world as largely chaotic, and so now do we! There is a difference, however. The cavemen viewed nature as indifferently rolling unbiased dice; modern men recognize that nature's dice are only slightly but nonetheless purposefully loaded.

—JOSEPH FORD

We have all heard the remark, "Everybody talks about the weather, but no one does anything about it." Well, that's not quite true.

John von Neumann, the mathematician, thought hard about how to control the weather. He knew that the future development of the weather could be triggered by small fluctuations in temperature, pressure, and humidity and thought that if we could alter those fluctuations, effectively killing them while they were still small, we could control the future weather. Aircraft could seed the clouds on Friday, thus altering the fluctuations so that it wouldn't rain on Sunday's picnic. That was one of von Neumann's dreams.

Von Neumann, however, was quite wrong about the nature of these fluctuations because it is not possible to control them. The deterministic equations that describe the future of the weather have hidden within them solutions that exhibit complete chaos, and these solutions, in fact, are the ones that correctly describe the weather. Infinitesimally small fluctuations can grow rapidly, more rapidly than we can anticipate or control, thus generating chaos. A sea gull flapping its wings in Cape Cod can generate a fluctuation that in principle can turn into a Pacific typhoon. That such utter chaos can emerge from deterministic equations is one of the remarkable discoveries of modern mathematical physics.

This discovery of *deterministic chaos* was made in 1963 by the meteorologist Edward N. Lorenz at MIT. Convinced that the well-known unpredictability of the weather ought to have an explanation in terms of deterministic equations, he began the search for such equations. The equations that describe the weather are known; but they are an infinite set of equations and as such are unmanageable. Lorenz's first step was to simplify these equations by making approximations until he had just three differential equations for how three quantities changed in time. What these three quantities represent need not concern us—they describe aspects of the weather. There was nothing particularly unusual about the equations that Lorenz found except that they were non-linear equations, which simply means that the sum of any two solutions to them is *not* in itself a solution. This nonlinear feature turns out to be essential for deterministic chaos to occur.

A word about "linear" and "nonlinear" is appropriate at this point. These terms simply refer to the properties of solutions to equations—whether or not you can add them up to get new solutions. If the equations describe some natural or social phenomena, then we can refer to those phenomena as linear or nonlinear as the case may be. For example, the wave equation, describing the motion of a water wave, is a linear equation. It has many different solutions, each with a different amplitude and a different wave-length. But because it is a linear equation we can add these solutions together to get a new solution to the wave equation. These new solutions simply reflect the physical fact that real waves, like water waves, can superimpose on one another, and all these su-perimpositions are also solutions to the linear wave equation.

Most of the equations that describe phenomena in the natural world, human behavior, neurofunction, population dynamics, and many other areas, are nonlinear. In spite of the fact that these are extremely interesting phenomena that we would like to under-stand, the fact that nonlinear equations are usually mathemati-cally intractable makes them almost impossible to solve. Previous to the deployment of the computer only a few general features of these nonlinear equations and their solutions could be analyzed; in a few rare instances exact solutions were known. But remark-ably, the kind of numerical analysis of equations done on comput-ers is, for the most part, indifferent to whether the equations are linear or nonlinear—it just grinds out the solutions. The advent of the computer meant that scientists no longer had to be intimidated by nonlinear equations. When one came up with a nonlinear equation in one's work, it no longer meant "insoluble, stop here."

Nonlinear science is the study of phenomena that requires non-linear equations for its mathematical language. Life is nonlinear, and so is just about everything else of interest. The human mastery of the nonlinear regime will open a vast new realm of existence. In this chapter we will be examining a few examples of this realm. The first such example is Lorenz's discovery of deterministic chaos.

Lorenz put his nonlinear weather equations on a computer, and the computer was printing out lists of the three quantities as time advanced. He would stop the computer, examine the lists of the three numbers, pick an intermediate set of three values, and then start up the computer with those intermediate values as the initial data. Normally one might expect that the computer would print out the same subsequent lists as before. After all, these were deter-ministic equations, and if the initial data were the same, the time development of the system should be identical to what it was be-fore. But, instead, the values of the three quantities on the lists would quickly differ from the original run, a difference that in-creased as the run went on. What Lorenz had discovered was deterministic chaos.

What had happened was that the values of the three quantities were not printed out to full machine accuracy. Hence when Lor-enz started up a second run with those intermediate values as initial data, they were ever-so-slightly different from those the computer had used before. That slight difference quickly got am-plified as the program ran (this is how a sea gull flapping its wings may cause a typhoon). This behavior—extreme sensitivity to ini-tial data—is the signal for deterministic chaos.

The differential equations Lorenz studied, like the equations of Newton, were classical physics equations and completely deterministic. Given some set of starting values for a physical quantity, the equations completely specify the future values. Usually if one makes small changes in the specification of the starting values, the final values are only slightly altered. For example, in firing a gun a small change in the position of the barrel results in a proportionally small change in the bullet hitting the target. This is typical behavior for most classical equations. The characteristic of Lorenz's equations for the weather, and other nonlinear equations that exhibit deterministic chaos, is that a small change in the starting values produces an exponentially large change in the subsequent values. Unless one knows the starting values to *infinite* accuracy (which in practice is impossible), one quickly loses all ability to predict the future values—just like weather prediction.

These ideas about determinism, predictability, and chaos tie in profoundly with the ideas about algorithmic and computational complexity introduced in the previous chapter. In order to see that connection, we must understand a few things about determinism in classical physics.

The notion of determinism, which lies at the conceptual center of classical Newtonian physics, asserts that if we know the initial state of a particle—its position and velocity—we can predict, using the equations of motion, its subsequent orbit. This aspect of determinism is beautifully illustrated by the image of the French mathematician Pierre Simon de Laplace, who went so far as to imagine a demon who knew the positions and velocity of every particle in the universe. Using Newton's laws, the demon could then know the entire future of the universe, a mechanical universe that functioned like a great clockwork.

In predicting future behavior, a lot of emphasis is placed on knowing the laws of physics, like the equations of motion. After all, it was the discovery of the laws of motion that made Newton famous and started modern physics on the long road to the present day. The initial conditions, which we also need in order to plug into the equations of motion to make predictions, get second notice. They don't seem too important; in any case they represent something we cannot control with great precision. For many problems in classical physics that precision is not especially important. For example, for the motion of a pendulum swinging back and forth or the motion of a planet around the sun, the accuracy with which we specify the initial conditions determines, by roughly direct proportion, the accuracy with which we know the subsequent motion.

If we adopt the computational viewpoint of physical processes, then we can view the initial conditions of our moving particle, now represented as a string of numbers, as the input to an orbital computation. The output is the mathematical specification of the orbit given by the solution to the equations of motion. For some systems, like the pendulum and the planet going around the sun, a small amount of input information will result in a large quantity of output information—the entire future orbit of the system. It would be as if we put the initial conditions as input into our "computer" and then were rewarded with *all* the future positions as output. Such "analytically soluble" systems—those for which one can explicitly write down the solution to the equation—are deterministic, predictable, and nonchaotic. They are the image of Newtonian determinism. If we know the present in terms of the initial conditions, we know the future and the past, just like Laplace's demon.

An analytically soluble dynamical system can be examined from the standpoint of algorithmic complexity. The initial conditions and the explicit solution to the equations can be thought of as an algorithm for computing the orbit. The orbit itself can be viewed as a set of numbers to be computed. Because the entire orbit is calculable from a rather simple algorithm, the orbit is nonchaotic and the numbers representing it are nonrandom relative to the initial conditions.

The situation is dramatically different for nonlinear equations, like Lorenz's equations, which have chaotic solutions. A small error in the specification of the initial conditions produced vastly different orbits. These chaotic orbits, viewed as a computational process, are described by Joseph Ford as follows: "Our orbital computation is found to require just as much informational input as it provides informational output. This means that our computations have now ceased computing or predicting anything because the output orbital data are so chaotic, so unpredictably random that our input information must, of necessity, be equivalent to a copy of the output. . . . To summarize, a chaotic orbit is its own briefest description and its own fastest computer; it is both determinate and random." We learn from this description that the nonchaotic orbits are what we called "simulatable" (this is what a computation does), while the chaotic orbits are "unsimulatable" (the only thing that can simulate the weather is the weather).

The subtlety of nature is vindicated. We see that hidden within the deterministic equations of classical physics is a chaos so complete that even Laplace's demon could not predict the future. Only if the demon knew the initial conditions with *infinite* precision and could remember *infinite* random numbers (this presumably requires an *infinite* demon) could he predict the future. In this sense the demon would have to be identical with an infinite universe itself, which is not at all what Laplace had in mind.

When Lorenz discovered deterministic chaos, he discovered what physicists call the "strange attractor." What is an attractor? An attractor is what a solution to an equation is drawn into and such a concept helps classify dynamical systems whether they be the solar system, a dripping faucet, a neural network, or the weather. In order to say what an attractor is more precisely, we will first describe the abstract notion of a "state space." Attractors, it turns out, live in state space.

A dynamical system is said to have a physical "state," which is completely specified once one specifies the values of all the independent physical variables for the dynamical system. For example, a simple pendulum that swings back and forth in a plane is described by two variables—the position of the bob and its velocity. More complicated dynamical systems may require many, even an infinite number of, variables to specify their physical state. Once you know the physical state of a system, you know all you can know about that system.

Mathematical physicists often find it extremely useful to think about the world in geometrical terms, and that kind of thinking also can be applied to thinking about physical states. We can imagine an abstract space called a state space (also called phase space), which has nothing to do with real three-dimensional space, in which the different dimensions correspond to the variables that describe the physical systems. For example, for the simple pendulum the state space is two-dimensional; one dimension represents the position of the bob, the other its velocity. For a dynamical system with three variables, we can still visualize the state of the system as a point in a three-dimensional space. But for more complicated dynamical systems with lots of variables we need many, perhaps an infinite number of, dimensions in the state space and we can no longer visualize the space. Still, the advantage of thinking in terms of such an abstract state space is that the precise physical state of a system, no matter how complicated or how many variables are involved, is represented by a single point in that multidimensional state space. By reading off the coordinates of that point in the state space, you specify the values of all the physical variables, and that is equivalent to specifying the state of the system. As the dynamical system changes in time that point can move around in the multidimensional state space, showing exactly how the system changes in time. If the physical variables never become infinite (which is the case for all real systems), the point moves around in a bounded region of the state space.

The reason I have gone through all this trouble to describe the abstract state space is because attractors "live" in state space. An attractor does just what the name implies—it attracts the point that is moving about in state space. Surrounding an attractor is a region of state space called a "basin of attraction." The point may start off anywhere in state space, reflecting the start-up conditions of the physical system. But eventually, if it is in a basin of attraction, it gets drawn inexorably into the corresponding attractor. A dynamical system may have one or more attractors, and which one the system settles into depends on which basin of attraction it starts up in.

There are several kinds of known attractors. The simplest kind of attractor is called *a fixed point*—after moving about in a basin of attraction the point in state space eventually comes to a stop at the fixed point. What does this correspond to in the real world? If we go back to our simple pendulum and suppose that it has friction, we would find that it eventually comes to rest—the position of the bob is fixed, and the velocity is zero. In state space this corresponds to a fixed point attractor. If we watched the point representing the physical state of the pendulum move in state space as the pendulum slowed down, we would see it go around an ever-decreasing orbit until it stopped at the fixed point.

A second kind of attractor is called *a limit cycle*. As the name implies, the point in state space instead of coming to rest cycles around on a specific closed loop. This means that some of the physical variables undergo periodic motion. Again, let's take our pendulum: suppose it has friction, and we supply it with periodic kicks (as is done in a metronome); we now will find that it will not come to rest but will oscillate, reflecting the limit cycle.

The discovery of limit cycles in nonlinear dynamical systems goes back to Balthasar van der Pol's mathematical modeling of the action of the human heart back in the 1920s. The equations that describe the heart are nonlinear, and the normal periodic beating of the heart is reflected as a limit cycle of these nonlinear equations. Under shock or stress this limit cycle can be disrupted and the system thrown over to another attractor—a fixed point; the heart stops, and death ensues.

Limit cycles also occur for complex chemical reactions (also as described by nonlinear equations), in which the concentrations of two or more chemicals will oscillate back and forth. Metabolic chemical reactions occurring in living organisms can also oscillate, and these are suspected to be the origin of animal clocks. Each of us has at least one such internal clock, as anyone who has experienced jet lag will testify. These internal clocks may be the limit cycles of nonlinear chemical reactions in the body and brain.

While the limit cycle is a simple loop in state space, the next most complicated attractor, *the quasi-periodic attractor*, can be viewed as an endless line drawn on the surface of a torus (donut-shaped surface) in state space, circling the torus on a kind of helical path. The system exhibits a quasi-periodic motion in which it almost returns to the same state but not quite. Such an attractor applies to the joint behavior of two coupled pendula with incommensurate periods. This system never quite returns to the same state; hence the term "quasi-periodic."

Finally, in this classification of attractors, we come to *the strange attractor*. In this case the point in state space moves about along a continuous path in a bounded region that never returns to the same point. (The path is *not* jumping about in a chaotic fashion, it is continuous.) The crucial feature of these strange paths (and what distinguishes them from the quasi-periodic case for which the paths also do not return) is that if you examine two nearby paths in state space and follow them along, they rapidly diverge, moving far apart. This behavior reflects the sensitivity of the chaotic solution on the choice of initial data. A tiny difference in the initial data, corresponding to nearby paths in state space, is quickly amplified. The other attractors do not have this property. Hence if we know the initial state of a system (only approximately, which is all we can really achieve), this knowledge has no predictive value when there is a strange attractor present because the future orbit depends so sensitively on our choice of the initial state.

Strange attractors, an endless path in the abstract state space, are rather beautiful geometrical objects. They can be constructed using computers and viewed on a video screen. The path of the strange attractor in state space may, in its endless meandering, fill a subspace of the whole space, and this subspace can have a bizarre noninteger fractal dimension. There is no way we can exactly mathematically construct the geometrical path of such strange attractors; there are no equations that precisely describe them, as we can often find for the other attractors. The only realistic way we can construct strange attractors and see what they look like in state space is by generating them on computers—the way they were first discovered. Strange attractors are an offspring of the computer.

One way of imagining a strange attractor is described by James P. Crutchfield, J. Doyne Farmer, Normand H. Packard, and Robert Shaw in a *Scientific American* article:

> Chaos mixes the orbits [paths] in state space in precisely the same way as a baker mixes bread dough by kneading it. One can imagine what happens to nearby trajectories on a chaotic attractor by placing a drop of blue food coloring in the dough. The kneading is a combination of two actions: rolling out the dough, in which the food coloring is spread out, and folding the dough over. At first the blob of food coloring simply gets longer, but eventually it is folded, and after considerable time the blob is stretched and refolded many times. On close inspection the dough consists of many layers of alternating blue and white. After only 20 steps the initial blob has been stretched to more than a million times its original length, and its thickness has shrunk to the molecular level. The blue dye is thoroughly mixed with the dough. Chaos works the same way, except that instead of mixing dough it mixes state space.

In spite of the fact that strange attractors pop up in lots of equations today, the idea about these attractors was slow in coming. In 1944 Lev Landau, a Nobel Prize-winning Soviet physicist, proposed that the onset of turbulence in fluids like a gas or liquid was characterized by an infinite sequence of instabilities, each adding a new frequency to the motion until it is "complicated and confused." We can see this onset of turbulence when the laminar flow of the smoke rising from a cigarette begins to swirl and twist about or in the transition from smoothly flowing water to churning water. However, Landau's important work did not identify the turbulent state as true, utter chaos (which we believe it to be today), but rather as a complicated form of quasi-periodic behavior that mimicked chaos. Furthermore, in his view there was no well-defined onset of turbulence.

In 1963 Lorenz wrote his classical paper "Deterministic Nonperiodic Flow," in which he suggested that turbulence was truly nonperiodic (chaotic) rather than quasi-periodic motion. Unfortunately his important work, the discovery of deterministic chaos, escaped the notice of scientists for more than a decade. The distinction between quasi-periodic and nonperiodic chaos is subtle and important: two nearby paths in quasi-periodic motion always stay nearby, while for chaotic motion they diverge rapidly.

In 1971 David Ruelle and Floris Takens wrote a paper entitled "On the Nature of Turbulence," in which they showed that most fluid flows would produce chaotic solutions after a few instabilities. They also coined the term "strange attractor." Following this, in 1975 Tien Tien Li and James Yorke first used the term "chaos" to describe the new erratic solutions. The true nature of the approach to turbulence and chaotic solutions was now becoming understood. According to these investigations, as one approached turbulence the period of the dynamical system would first double, then double again and again, until as a definite point true chaos set in.

During the summer of 1975 a friend, Mitchell Feigenbaum, from Los Alamos Laboratory, was visiting the Aspen Center for Physics, a summer research institute. He was examining the period doubling of a certain equation as it approached chaos, calculating everything by hand. It was odd that he would undertake such a laborious hand calculation when at Los Alamos, his home base, they had giant computers where he could do his calculation in milliseconds instead of hours. Mitch said he did it the slow way because he liked playing with numbers.

A month or so later Mitch was back at Los Alamos doing a similar calculation with a different equation. What surprised him was that even with this different equation the *approach* to chaos was characterized by the same number that had cropped up in his calculation in Aspen. Then he knew he was onto something. In short order he realized that the approach to chaos was characterized by two universal numbers, numbers like π, the ratio of the circumference to the diameter of a circle, which are purely geometrical and have nothing to do with the detailed dynamics (that is why the dynamical equation he used did not matter). Had Mitch used a big Los Alamos computer that homed in on a solution quickly, he would have missed this important discovery. His impulse to play directly with numbers was not misplaced.

Many of the ideas about chaos flew in the face of accepted wisdom about the behavior of dynamical systems coming from mathematics and physics, and some of the early chaos workers found it hard to get their ideas accepted by their colleagues. This was especially true of the "Dynamical Systems Collective" at the University of California at Santa Cruz, led by Crutchfield, Farmer, Packard, and Shaw. I recall visiting their "lab" back in 1981 and thinking that most of their equipment came out of the local hardware store. They had a difficult time convincing their colleagues that they were doing something important.

Chaos definitely exists in the equations of classical physics. But does it exist in the real world? Recall that Lorenz *approximated* the full set of weather equations to just three equations that then exhibited chaos. What about the full set of equations? Do they also exhibit chaos? All equations, be they for the weather, a fluid flow, or the human heart involve approximations, so we cannot be certain that the chaos was not introduced through the approximation. Furthermore, the search for chaos in the real world is compounded by the fact that experimental scientists are uncertain if the chaos is really inherent to the dynamical system they examine or due to some external random "noise" producing the chaotic effect. Also, as I remarked before, it is difficult to experimentally distinguish between true chaos and complicated quasi-periodic motion.

While such doubts were once expressed, most physicists are now convinced deterministic chaos exists in the real world. The first experiments were done by Jerry Gollub of Haverford College and Harry Swinney of the University of Texas at Austin on circular Couette flow—the flow of a fluid between two concentric cylinders with the inside one rotating. As the rotation is increased, the velocity field of the contained fluid becomes periodic with the period doubling until chaos sets in. The experimenters focused on the delicate transition between periodic behavior and chaos. While their results were highly suggestive of true chaos, it was difficult to distinguish the appearance of chaos from the quasi-periodic case.

The first unambiguous experimental evidence for chaos came not from the study of fluid flows, but from the study of oscillating chemical reactions in a 1980 experiment by J.-C. Roux, A. Rossi, S. Rachelart, and Christian Vidal. By carefully monitoring and altering the concentrations of the reacting chemicals, the chemical oscillations became truly nonperiodic—chaos set in. Later experimental work by J. L. Hudson, J. Mankin, Roux, and Swinney on such reactions showed conclusively that the irregular oscillations were due to a strange attractor.

Are there other kinds of attractors besides the ones we have discussed? We think so. Attractors are properties of nonlinear equations, and such equations, we believe, describe the real world in all its complexity. We can imagine such equations describing the behavior of the stock market, the international economy, organs of the human body like the heart and the brain, and human behavior. Such systems, since they are described by nonlinear equations, are also subject to the various attractors—the fixed point, the limit cycle, the quasi-periodic cycles, the strange attractor, as well as other attractors that may be mixtures of these types or ones yet to be discovered.

Some people have even gone so far as to speculate that attractors in the nonlinear equations describing neural networks can represent the mental states corresponding to thought. Memories might correspond to limit cycles. Other scientists have fruitfully applied these ideas to many fields, such as evolutionary theory, molecular evolution, population theory, game theory, and animal behavior, including foraging, fighting, and sexual behavior. Ants (in particular their foraging behavior) provide a telling example of the application of nonlinear mathematical models to social insects. It has been shown how the random generation of foraging strategies helps the colony to survive by providing diversity and adapting to new conditions in food supplies. A group of scientists associated with the Center for Non-Linear Studies at Los Alamos and other institutions, the "chaos cabal," as it has been nicknamed, has been organizing meetings and conferences that testify to the diverse applications of nonlinear dynamics. Several such meetings have been run under the auspices of the Santa Fe Institute, a new center for the study of complexity.

No one today doubts the existence of deterministic chaos in the equations of classical physics. This discovery brings to an end the ideal of predictability in classical physics—an ideal held out by the Newtonians and even in this century by Einstein. But there are several ironic elements in this beautiful new development. The first is that the chaos has structure—the geometry of the strange attractors. Chaos isn't just a meaningless jumble. In fact, it may be possible to detect the statistical regularities in chaos provided that chaos is used as a probe.

The second irony is that while classical physics, usually the image of determinism, now contains chaos, the equations of quantum theory (which have an inherently statistical interpretation) have so far not revealed any chaos. The central equation of quantum theory, the Schrödinger equation, is an equation for a probability amplitude. Yet the Schrödinger equation itself is a completely deterministic equation for the time evolution of a probability. The fact that the equations of quantum theory such as the Schrödinger equation do not reveal chaos is very puzzling to many mathematical physicists because the equations of quantum theory in some suitable approximations should reduce to the equations of classical physics, equations that do exhibit chaos. So where is chaos in the equations of quantum theory? A solution to this outstanding unsolved puzzle may provide a deeper understanding of the relation between the quantum and the classical world.

Chaos, once viewed as something uncontrollable and terrible, is becoming friendlier. Out of chaos comes order, and out of simplicity emerges complexity.

Even while some researchers were discovering the structure of chaos in nonlinear equations, others, about two decades ago, found equally remarkable new structures, unanticipated orderly solutions called solitons. Like the discovery of chaos, the discovery of solitons reflects amazing properties of nonlinear equations, properties that correspond to features of the real world that the equations describe. Solitons can be thought of as nonlinear solitary waves—lumps that can retain their shape as they move along in space. The nonlinearity of the self-interactions of the soliton is what holds the lump together and prevents its dissipation.

Although the existence of nonlinear waves was already known in the nineteenth century, they were thought to be rather special and peculiar, so the area of research remained a kind of mathematical backwater. The first recent hint of the existence of solitons in nonlinear systems came shortly after the Maniac I computer was built at Los Alamos in the early 1950s. Enrico Fermi, J. R. Pasta, and Stan Ulam decided to use the new computer to model the behavior of a spatial matrix of sixty-four particles connected by nonlinear springs. They thought that this system, once it was set off vibrating in one place, would soon exhibit random vibrations of all the particles. Instead they found that the system returned almost periodically to its original configuration. This unanticipated behavior was one of the first clues about the existence of the pulselike solitons moving like waves through the matrix of particles connected by springs.

Back in the 1960s two mathematical physicists, Norman Zabusky and Martin Kruskal, first examined on a computer what would happen if two such solitons were allowed to collide. Most people would have guessed that they would fragment or dissipate, turning into nothing. Instead, Zabusky and Kruskal discovered that the two solitons passed right through each other as if nothing had happened. Solitons were very robust.

Today we know that solitons show up in a vast variety of nonlinear equations describing physical processes. They are found in equations describing DNA and alphahelix proteins, gigantic ocean waves, and complex laser-plasma interactions. Some people have found solitonlike behavior in the equations that describe neural nets. In order to account for its centuries-long duration, scientists even suspect that Jupiter's great Red Spot is an example of a soliton. Magnetic monopoles, quantum particles that have a unit of magnetic charge, are predicted by a variety of quantum field theories and are solitons (these monopole-solitons were discussed in my book *Perfect Symmetry*). Solitons as stable lumps of field energy have been observed in many dynamical systems. Their existence bears witness to the riches of nonlinear dynamics.

Nonlinear dynamics is in its infancy. This discovery of deterministic chaos and solitons in nonlinear equations is probably just the tip of the iceberg. New and wondrous things remain to be uncovered. Descartes's dream that the world could be mathematized is being realized today, but the mathematics is highly nonlinear. Scientists are just beginning to face up to the immense challenge of nonlinearity, and it will occupy them well into the next century and beyond. Nonlinear dynamics is at the forefront of the emerging sciences of complexity.

None of this would have been possible without the computer. While traditional mathematical analysis is, and will continue to be, of utmost importance in gaining deep insight into the nature of nonlinear equations, the computer has provided the motivation to push forward because it can numerically solve equations where conventional analysis fails. This was foreseen by John von Neumann in his remarks at McGill University in 1946:

> Our present analytical methods seem unsuitable for the solution of the important problems arising in connection with nonlinear partial differential equations and, in fact, with virtually all types of nonlinear problems in pure mathematics . . . really efficient high-speed computing devices may, in the field of nonlinear partial differential equations as well as in many other fields which are now difficult or entirely denied of access, provide us with those heuristic hints which are needed in all parts of mathematics for genuine progress.

Von Neumann, the principal architect of the programmed digital computer, welcomed the computer into mathematics. He felt equally at home in pure or applied mathematics. However, at that time many mathematicians, while recognizing the practical importance of applied mathematics, felt that pure mathematics should remain aloof from the computer. Some even felt that the computer introduced a corrupting influence on young mathematicians. However, it seems odd that pure mathematicians who would accept the idea of the proofs generated by the Turing machine—an imaginary computer—would resist the idea of a proof by a real one.

Computers in mathematics are best thought of as elaborate blackboards on which to try out ideas and do calculations. Maybe there were mathematicians long ago who resisted the introduction of blackboards and felt one had to do everything in one's head.

While the movement toward abstraction in mathematics is still very strong, the use of the computer reflects a return to the constructive outlook of nineteenth-century mathematics, a down-to-earth approach far removed from abstract set theory, existence proofs, and the like. The computer is the primary instrument of the new discipline of "experimental mathematics."

Experimental mathematics sounds like a contradiction. Isn't mathematics, even applied mathematics, supposed to be free of empirical constraints? Indeed it is. Yet there is an important and growing role for computer experiments in mathematics. Some equations and problems in mathematics are so difficult and complicated that in order to gain insight into them, numerical analysis, done on a computer, is essential. Once mathematicians have acquired that insight they can go on to formulate and prove general theorems, which is what they are really after.

Experimental mathematics is going to be essential if we are to solve the problems of nonlinear science. Applied and pure mathematicians are going to work with computer scientists and specialists in the various branches of the natural and behavioral sciences. This kind of interdisciplinary teamwork is needed in order to begin to push back the frontier of complexity.

New facilities are being created to meet this challenge. Research scientists need access to supercomputers—mainframes that can manage massive amounts of data, that are highly interactive and have good graphics capabilities. Such facilities might also provide the researcher with experts who can build special dedicated computers—devices built from existing hardware but made to solve just one problem at remarkable speed.

Back in the 1930s, Joseph Stalin asked one of his advisers in what area of science the Soviet Union excelled. The answer he got (a correct one) was nonlinear mathematics and dynamics. A Soviet scientist who was then an international leader in this area was lecturing in Paris, but Stalin called him back and set up, under his leadership, a major institute for the study of nonlinear problems. The Soviet Union has been strong in this important area ever since, although Soviet scholars have not taken full advantage of the advent of the computer until very recently because the use of information transmitting and processing equipment is under strict state control.

In 1985, under the leadership of Steven Orszag from Princeton University and Kenneth Wilson of Cornell University, the National Science Foundation agreed to set up five major supercomputer centers in the United States. Previously supercomputers were not available for many university researchers. In fact, some

U.S. university researchers had to go to Europe to use the super-computers that had been given to European laboratories by the U.S. government as a political favor. U.S. scientists in the big national labs had access to supercomputers. "Anyone else," argued Wilson, "has to scrounge time wherever they can find it." That's going to change now. The new supercomputer centers distributed across the United States can be used by a consortium of regional universities via a direct link between the university and the center. Wilson, now director of Cornell University's Center for Theory and Simulation in Science and Engineering, remarks about the power of such computers: " . . . an astronomer with a telescope can observe the universe over perhaps fifty years—the length of his scientific career. But an astrophysicist with a super-computer can 'see' for a billion years. Computer simulation is therefore a theoretician's experiment." These supercomputer facilities will become major "experimental mathematics" centers working on a variety of problems, many of them in nonlinear science.

In the next chapter we will have a look at some of the kinds of problems that are going to be worked on at these and similar facilities.

Chapter 5

Simulating Reality

Do not lose your faith. A mighty fortress is our mathematics.
—STAN ULAM

Why do we model reality and represent it as myth, metaphor, or scientific theory? Why not just take it as it is and let our experience be its own best simulation? Why does our mind recast its own experience in terms of symbols, symbols whose meaning we often do not understand ourselves?

Undoubtedly there is evolutionary survival value in our representing the world in terms of myth, metaphor, and scientific theory. We are evidently unique among species in our symbolic ability, and we are certainly unique in our modest ability to control the conditions of our existence by using these symbols. Our ability to represent and simulate reality implies that we can appropriate the order of existence and bring it to serve human purposes. A good simulation, be it a religious myth or scientific theory, gives us a sense of mastery over our experience. To represent something symbolically, as we do when we speak or write, is somehow to capture it, thus making it one's own. But with this appropriation comes the realization that we have denied the immediacy of reality and that in creating a substitute we have but spun another thread in the web of our grand illusion.

In this chapter I will be examining a number of simulations of reality produced by the sciences of complexity. These simulations all have something in common—they are all done on a computer.

Computer modeling grew up with the computer and is one of its primary applications as a research instrument. Like the microscope and the telescope did in a previous age the computer opens up a new window on reality. Or does it, in fact, create that reality?

I was always struck by the fact that Galileo, when he first used the telescope, performed many experiments to convince himself that the instrument only magnified objects; it did not create new objects or distort existing ones. He wanted to be sure that he could answer any critics who might claim that his telescope created a reality rather than simply clarifying an existing reality. How then can we tell whether the reality revealed by computer simulations isn't just an artifact of the computer?

Remember the adage, at least as old as the computer, "Garbage in, garbage out"—a computer performs only as well as the input data and program we use? The input data and the program are surely human artifacts—they are gathered and created by the scientist. Computers (at least all existing computers) are ultimately "dumb" machines, just like telescopes and microscopes, and we cannot abrogate human judgment about the data and programs in deciding if a simulation is valid or not. We must view the computer as a scientific instrument in human hands, not a magical "black box" that creates a reality beyond our ken. Otherwise we will surely confuse the computer simulation with reality.

Usually in computer modeling scientists are trying to model a rather complex system (otherwise why bother to use a computer). The fundamental hypothesis behind simulating complex systems is that the apparent complexity of the system one is trying to model is due to a few simple components interacting according to simple rules that are then incorporated in the program. In a certain sense, the complexity of some systems, while real enough, actually has a simple explanation. To be effective, computer modeling must use a program that is simpler than the system one is modeling. Otherwise one is trying to blindly mimic the system on a computer, without any understanding.

This is the reductionist hypothesis of scientific explanation expressed in the language of computer modeling. It is important to recognize that the hypothesis refers to the program, not to the data, and that the hypothesis is independent of whether the system is simulatable by a system simpler than itself or not.

As an example, consider the Lorenz case of modeling the weather. The computer program represented his three equations, and these equations were rather simple. The output of the computer beginning with some set of initial data was "deterministic but not predictable"—the detailed output of the equations representing the weather could not be simulated. Yet there was order in this chaos; the underlying pattern of paths in state space was not arbitrary but had an explicit geometry—the shape of the strange attractor that was a consequence of the simple program. One should therefore not confuse the property of unpredictability (unsimulatability) with underlying intrinsic complexity. The system can be unpredictable, and yet the underlying program is simple.

In the natural sciences the hypothesis that the underlying programs modeling real systems are simple has been profoundly vindicated. This simply reflects the fact that for physical and biological systems there exists a simple invariant order—material processes that are present in the world. Irrespective of whether the scientist is trying to model the behavior of quarks inside a proton, the transmission of proteins across a cell membrane, or the heart-lung system, there is a *there* there.

Behavioral scientists have a greater challenge in making computer models because they lack a deep theory of social or psychological phenomena. There is the danger that the computer model becomes confused with what it is supposed to be a model of. The computer model, instead of being an instrument to study reality, becomes the reality (this can happen to natural scientists, too).

The impact of the computer on the behavioral sciences is immense, enabling these scientists to deepen their descriptive understanding of psychological and social behavior. This impact has less to do with the existence of a deep theory of behavior than with the capacity of the computer to manage and analyze lots of data. We are getting a better picture of what social, economic, and psychological behavior is; we are establishing correlations between different phenomena and building what are called "phenomenological models" rather than "deep models." A phenomenological model accounts for and correlates the data in a quantitative, descriptive way without going into the deeper reason why such correlations exist. Such models are the first step toward a deeper understanding.

In this chapter we are going to take a look at several computer models—simulations of reality—to give the reader an idea of the range of what is possible using this technique. However, this will be a limited view, as I cannot hope to report on even a fraction of what is being done in computer modeling.

Simulating Intelligence

Ever since computers came into existence their capabilities have been compared to those of humans, especially with regard to mental abilities. These comparisons are rather facile because human beings and computers are very different; it is like comparing a screwdriver to a human hand. Nonetheless such comparisons stir our emotions because the computer, in simulating intelligent behavior, challenges the very conception we hold of ourselves. And because the issues are easily grasped, they have a lot of popular appeal.

Most people who have thought about simulating intelligence see no obstacle, in principle, to building a true artificial intelligence, a machine that would pass the "Turing test" of being able to fool people into believing it was a thinking and feeling human. The argument among scientists and philosophers is not over whether this can be done in principle, but rather how this can be accomplished in practice and how it cannot. Can a digital computer, appropriately programmed, simulate true human intelligence? The computer, at every moment of its operation obeying well-defined rules, would respond to some intelligent input with an intelligent output. Could one have a spontaneous and stimulating conversation with it?

No one has built a machine or designed a program that comes close to this capability. Whether this is a problem in principle, as some philosophers insist, or simply a problem in practice, as artificial intelligence proponents insist, will be debated for a long time. The debate, however, is sterile—it produces no insights into how to proceed to build more intelligent machines, something that even the most critical philosophers think is possible.

The future of intelligent machines, I believe, lies less with the artificial intelligence (AI) experts or philosophers than with the computer engineers and scientists—hardware and software designers—who, oblivious to the debate, will go wherever technology and scientific understanding can lead them. The capability of computers to perform intelligently surely will improve, until someday in the distant future we will have remarkably intelligent machines. The way they exhibit and use their intelligence will probably be very different from the human way, and they will possess capabilities and limitations all their own.

I sometimes fantasize what those first intelligent machines will be like. One could probably hold a good discussion with them, provided one didn't get into deeper issues. They would be terrific at knowing all sorts of things, storehouses of knowledge, like knowing the telephone numbers of all one's friends and the rivers in Tibet, incredible at computational mathematics, but poor in mathematical "intuition." They might even have "personalities" comparable to that of household pets and develop a knowledge of their owners' personal habits. Such an intelligence would be good at presenting options for decisions but poor in judging between them. It would have the moral sensitivity of a cat.

Businesses, industries, and nations would strongly compete to build better intelligent machines. With such competitive pressure they will improve rapidly. So advantageous will these machines become to their possessors that aspects of their design will be kept secret lest they fall into a competitor's hands.

The existence of these machines would also put an end to much discussion about the mind-body problem, because it will be very hard not to attribute a conscious mind to them without failing to do so for more human beings. Gradually the popular view will become that consciousness is simply "what happens" when matter is put together the right way into a neural network, the same way that a working television set is "what happens" when electronic components are put together the right way. Some people will probably argue that artificially intelligent life should also be protected by law for its own sake—an AI bill of rights. That will be a sign that true AI has arrived.

Up until the last five years the attempt to build intelligent machines was dominated by people who might be called "the artificial intelligence community." This is a rather loosely defined community of groups that differ from one another yet hold a number of characteristics in common. First, members of this community grew up with the digital, programmed computer so that most of their thinking about thinking machines is associated with that particular computer architecture. Second, they hold the view, shared with cognitive scientists, that the program is the essence of mind. They favor high-level symbol manipulation and believe that a serially organized terminal search is the essence of intelligent behavior.

This AI approach has had a number of significant successes in the area of theorem proving, backgammon, checkers, and chess-playing programs, expert systems, and other applications in robotics. If one looks in detail at these AI programs, one learns that they have little or nothing to do with how we know humans do these things. That, however, is not a criticism. But the design of such intelligent programs is enormously time-consuming; a new program is needed for each task, and if the program is asked to do anything ever-so-slightly outside of what it was designed to do, it fails miserably.

The dissatisfaction with the AI, digital, serial approach to intelligence simulation has caused computer scientists to look elsewhere for principles in designing intelligent machines. Today the emphasis is on connectionism—a new development that is inspired by the brain's neural network, the evolutionary system, or the immune response. The idea here is that massive parallelism, distributive information storage, and associative interconnections, all inspired by biological systems, are the key to progress in simulating intelligence. I will devote the entire next chapter to "connectionism."

Gian-Carlo Rota, a mathematician from MIT, recounts a story about the late Stan Ulam, a mathematician at Los Alamos, who held strong critical views about the AI approach. Rota and Ulam were walking along the streets of Santa Fe talking about the big problem of building truly intelligent machines—how to "crack the cognition problem," how to get computers to grasp meaning, a hot topic already at that time in the early 1970s. Ulam argued: "Philosophers and logicians, from Duns Scotus in the twelfth century to Ludwig Wittgenstein only yesterday, have done a lot of clear thinking about all this stuff. If your friends in AI persist in ignoring their past, they will be condemned to repeat it, a high cost that will be borne by the taxpayer."

Rota challenged Ulam to say something positive about "the barrier of meaning." Responding to the challenge, Ulam suggested they play a word game on how the word "key" is used. What they will discover by playing this game, Ulam said, is "that what you are describing is not an object, but a function, a role that is inextricably tied to some context. Take away the context, and the meaning also disappears. . . . When you perceive intelligently, as you sometimes do, you always perceive a function, never an object in the . . . physical sense. . . . Your Cartesian idea of a device in the brain that does the registering is based upon a misleading analogy between vision and photography. Cameras always register objects, but human perception is always the perception of functional roles. The two processes could not be more different. . . . Your friends in AI are now beginning to trumpet the role of contexts, but they are not practicing their lesson. They still want to build machines that see by imitating cameras, perhaps with some feedback thrown in. Such an approach is bound to fail, since it starts out with a logical misunderstanding."

"But if what you say is right," Rota responded, continuing to challenge Ulam, "what becomes of objectivity, an idea that is so definitely formalized by mathematical logic and by the theory of sets, on which you yourself have worked for many years of your youth?"

"Really?" Ulam shot back. "What makes you so sure that mathematical logic corresponds to the way we think? You are suffering from what the French call a 'deformation *professionnelle.*' Look at that bridge over there. It was built following logical principles. Suppose that a contradiction were to be found in set theory. Do you honestly believe that the bridge might then fall down? . . . Logic formalizes only very few of the processes by which we actually think. The time has come to enrich formal logic by adding to it some other fundamental notions. What is it that you see when you see? You see an object *as* a key, you see a man in a car *as* a passenger, you see some sheets of paper *as* a book. It is the word 'as' that must be mathematically formalized, on a par with the connectives 'and,' 'or,' 'implies,' and 'not' that have already been accepted into formal logic. Until you do that, you will not get very far with your AI problem."

Rota said it sounded like an impossible task, but Ulam assured him, "Do not lose your faith. A mighty fortress is our mathematics. Mathematics will rise to the challenge, as it always has."

Ulam began walking away, just what, Rota was reminded, Descartes, Kant, Charles Saunders Pierce, Husserl, and Wittgenstein had done at a similar junction. He was changing the subject.

Simulated Annealing

In shifting from the subject of simulating the mind to simulating annealing—a physical process in which a crystalline substance is melted and then allowed to cool—we are shifting from the transcendent to the mundane. Yet our understanding of the mundane processes of annealing may in the end teach us something of far greater generality, perhaps even how the transcendent mind is materially supported.

Imagine taking a crystalline substance and heating it to high temperature until it melts, turning into a fluid of atoms. A fundamental question in the statistical mechanics of such a state is what happens as the temperature is lowered? Does the substance remain a liquid, or form a crystal with many defects, or form a glass with no crystalline order? In careful annealing the temperature is lowered to just about the freezing point and left there for a long time. This gives the atoms lots of time to form a "best fit" to one another and form a true crystal as the temperature is finally lowered to the freezing point. The true crystalline configuration of atoms is close to the lowest energy configuration, what is called the "ground state" of all the atoms.

This annealing process can be simulated on a computer using a special algorithm devised by Nicholas Metropolis of Los Alamos National Laboratory. The Metropolis algorithm provides an efficient simulation of a collection of atoms in equilibrium at a specific temperature—a random jumble of atoms moving about. Applying this algorithm to the annealing processes is a good idea. Buy why bother with something so mundane as the annealing process?

Scott Kirkpatrick and his collaborators C. D. Gelatt, Jr. and M. P. Vecchi at the IBM laboratories first grasped the deeper implications of the simulated annealing process: it provides an approximate solution to some of the most intractable optimization problems in mathematics. Recall the traveling salesman problem that we discussed in conjunction with computational complexity

—we want to find the shortest route for a salesman making a tour of N cities, each city to be visited once. All known ways of solving this problem require an amount of time of a computer that grows exponentially in N, the number of cities. For a thousand or more cities, the computing time required to exactly solve the problem is simply enormous. Solving this problem seems to have nothing to do with annealing. But it does.

In the simulated annealing process one starts out with a random collection of atoms. But the atoms, being only mathematical, can be replaced by other things—for example, a randomized collection of different routes for the traveling salesman. The amount of randomization is controlled by the "temperature," here just a variable that one can adjust in the computer program. As the fluid of atoms is allowed to slowly cool the atoms form a crystal—the optimum lowest energy configuration. It may not be the absolutely lowest energy configuration—a perfect solution—but it is close enough. Likewise for the traveling salesman problem. As the "temperature" controlling the randomization of routes is lowered, the routes "crystallize" around a configuration that is close to the shortest optimal configuration. Rather than finding the perfect, exact shortest route, one settles for a route that is probably not much longer. The advantage of the approximate solution over the exact one is that we can actually find it in a rather short amount of computing time.

Simulating annealing thus leads to a new attack on previously intractable problems. It improves on previous methods of problem solving—the "divide and conquer" method (breaking a big problem into subproblems and then trying to solve those simpler problems) or the iterative improvement method (guessing a solution and then, by degrees, trying to improve upon it). Simulated annealing, in contrast with these conventional methods, has a random element to it, and when the randomness stops it locks on to an approximate solution.

Interestingly, this algorithm for complex problem solving was inspired by imitating an actual natural process. First we learn how nature does it and then try to imitate her accordingly. The process of natural selection is another example of how nature does it—in this case selection and pattern recognition. In the sequel we will examine the modeling of such selective systems.

Finding algorithms, like simulated annealing, is not just an intellectual pastime; it has been used to save millions of dollars.

Simulated annealing has been used to help determine the solution to the complex problem of designing computers—in particular how to organize and connect the chip circuits in an optimal way. It can be used for routing global airline traffic and other similar routing problems. Furthermore, as Kirkpatrick and his collaborators note, "it provides an intriguing instance of 'artificial intelligence,' in which the computer has arrived, almost uninstructed, at a solution that might have been thought to require the intervention of human intelligence."

When I first heard about simulated annealing it caused me to think about how I solved problems, rarely through a rationally deductive process. Instead I value a free association of ideas, a jumble of three or four ideas bouncing around in my mind. As the urge for resolution increases, the bouncing around stops and I settle on just one idea or strategy as the best. Likewise when I feel my actions are in a rut, I introduce a chaotic element—undertake a random action, like seeking out a new person, group, or meeting, without trying to justify it in terms of my existing values. It is usually a learning experience, if for no other reason than to show me that I am not in a rut after all. Adopting metaphors from science for our own life can change the way we think and act.

Cellular Automata, Artificial Life, and Computational Biology

The mathematical theory of cellular automata was created by John von Neumann back in the 1950s. A cellular automaton is a set of cells (one might imagine a grid like a checkerboard, each square being a cell). Each cell can be in a number of states (as the square on the checkerboard could be either a black state or white state). The entire automaton can change in time according to predetermined rules. For example: surrounding every two-dimensional square cell there are eight other cells, so a rule might require that whenever four or more of the surrounding cells are white, then the central cell changes in the next time step. There are lots of rules that one can invent, and each set of rules leads to a differently evolving cellular automaton. The idea of a cellular automata is simple . . . deceptively simple.

Cellular automata were mostly mathematical curiosities until

Edward Fredkin got interested in them. Fredkin is one of the divine madmen of modern computer science and one of a rare species—the self-taught scientist-inventor. He has an undisciplined but highly creative intelligence that lets nothing get in its way. A dropout from Cal Tech, Fredkin went in the air force where he met his first computer of substance. It was a relationship that has endured. Fredkin subsequently started up his own computer company that made image-processing equipment, and he became a millionaire in short order. Secure in his wealth, he then became a professor at MIT and confounded the faculty with his unacademic style. He rarely publishes his ideas because once he has solved a problem to his satisfaction, he is done with it and feels no need to write it up. While some scientists are interested in simulating natural processes in the universe, Fredkin has gone them a step better. He is possessed by the vision that the entire universe *is* a computer.

How can the universe be a computer, in particular a cellular automaton? Fredkin, as well as others who have toyed with cellular automata on video screens, was impressed by the fact that if you set up the right rules, a cellular automaton can generate waves and other kinds of motion observed in nature. Can nature, then, be a cellular automaton? Maybe space and time are not continuous at the microlevel but discrete (in spite of the fact that the most powerful high-energy accelerators of today do not reveal any such granularity). If space and time are discrete and divided into little cells, then the universe might be viewed as a cellular automaton—in short, as a computer. Fredkin is looking for the grand rule that will make this space-time cellular automaton function the way our real universe does. So far he hasn't found it. I doubt that he will.

Fredkin has spent a lot of time talking to physicist Richard Feynman (Feynman was best man at Fredkin's wedding). I don't know what has transpired during those conversations, but I can guess. Feynman probably told Fredkin that a computer cannot reproduce quantum particle behavior, called "long-range quantum correlations." Quantum particles do not obey the laws of classical physics; they are weird. They are so weird, in fact, that one can prove (this is known as Bell's theorem) that no local, mechanical system can reproduce the long-range quantum correlations that are, in fact, observed in laboratory experiments with quantum particles. In other words, you cannot account for quantum events by any mechanical picture. Cellular automata, at least the *conventional* ones, are local mechanical systems. Hence a universe built out of such cellular automata cannot be our quantum universe. The problem one runs into here is that a computer (and a cellular automata is a computer) is essentially a classical physics device and hence cannot simulate quantum phenomena. Perhaps a more general notion of a computer—a "quantum computer"—could do the job (see the discussion at the end of the chapter "Warriors of the Infinite"). Fredkin, I'm sure, is not so easily stopped by such an argument and will come up with an answer to this criticism.

Some years ago he assembled a group of computer scientists and physicists who shared his passion for fundamental computational problems on an island he bought in the Virgin Islands. The point of the meeting was to have a free-ranging discussion among a handful of experts. One of the people who attended that island meeting was Steven Wolfram. And one of the things that happened at that meeting was that Wolfram got interested in cellular automata.

Stephen Wolfram is typical of the new breed of intellectual entrepreneurs. He started out his career as a theoretical physicist working on the problems of quantum field theory. In the course of this work he became heavily involved in computing and even developed his own computer language, SMP, which can manipulate mathematical equations. He quickly became a convert to the new computational view of physical processes—the laws of nature are algorithms, and physical processes are seen as computational systems that process information much as a computer does.

Now a leader of the recently created Center for Complex Systems Research at the University of Illinois, Wolfram has been at the forefront of the new sciences of complexity. He sees complexity as arising out of simplicity. "Nature," says Wolfram, "provides many examples of systems whose basic components are simple, but whose overall behavior is extremely complex. . . . Complexity in natural systems typically arises from the collective effect of a very large number of components. It is often essentially impossible to predict the detailed behavior of any one particular component, or in fact the precise behavior of the whole system. But the system as a whole may nevertheless show definite overall behavior, and this behavior usually has several important features."

Wolfram, following Fredkin, has developed the study of cellular automata as an example of this view of physical processes. A good way to visualize a cellular automata (as Wolfram actually does in practice) is to imagine a video screen—a regular matrix of pixels. In this simple system a pixel can either be lit on, "1", or off, "0". These pixels are the component cells of the automata. Initially we assume that the first row of cells (here fourteen units long) has some specific form, for example,

$$01011010100110$$

Next we must pick a specific rule by which this initial configuration evolves. The rule we pick is very simple: If there is a 0 with a 0 to its right, do not change the 0; if there is a 0 and a 1 to its right, then change the 0 to a 1; if there is a 1 and a 0 to its right, do not change; if there is a 1 and a 1 to its right, then change the 1 to a 0; if there is nothing to the right (like at the right end), assume it is a 0. This rule can be put into the form of a table:

00	01	10	11
0	1	1	0

This tells us how to construct the next row given the previous row. In short, our cellular automata can evolve in time by constructing row after row. Starting with the initial row given above and the rule we just gave, we see how the automata develops:

$$01011010100110$$
$$11101111101010$$
$$00110000111110$$
$$01010001000010$$
$$11110011000110$$
$$00010101001010$$
$$00111111011110$$
$$01000001100010$$
$$11000010100110$$
$$01000111101010$$
$$11001000111110$$
$$01011001000010$$

And so on. Depending on the initial row and the rule we use, a very complex pattern, replete with complicated geometrical figures, can develop. Wolfram has lots of examples; in fact, he has made postcards of some of the more intriguing patterns. Cellular automata are a beautiful example of how complexity can arise out of underlying simplicity.

A number of interesting questions about such automata immediately come to mind. For example, does a particular automata eventually terminate (a row of 0's eventually comes up) or become periodic (the initial row shows up as a subsequent row), or does it go on forever? If it does go forever, is it simply repeating the same stable pattern, or is it a complicated unpredictable pattern? How can we answer such questions?

Some cellular automata stop, others are periodic, and others go on forever. In some cases (very simple ones) we can mathematically predict that they are going to quickly terminate or develop a stable pattern. In these cases, we have an example of "simulatable complexity"—there is an algorithm that is simpler than the calculations represented by automata and tells us in advance what is going to happen. In cases of "unsimulatable complexity" there is no such algorithm, and the most efficient way to establish what is happening is to actually run the automata program: the automata is its own best simulation. There are thus automata for which Turing's halting problem—the problem of predicting whether a specific computation is going to stop or not—is undecidable and others for which it is decidable. Cellular automata, in spite of their apparent simplicity, get one into deep computational issues of simulatability and decidability.

The classification of the behavior of cellular automata is similar to that of dynamical systems in terms of their various attractors (a cellular automata *is* a dynamical system). First there is the "fixed point" behavior—the automata stops. Second is the "limit cycle" in which the automata simply undergoes periodic behavior. The third class is chaotic behavior. Fourthly and finally is the most interesting class, in which there is a quasi-periodic behavior along with propagation of various structures. This fourth realm exists just before the onset of chaos and is the true realm of complex behavior.

Cellular automata can exhibit a very rich behavior. The cellular automata we described above was only fourteen units long. On larger scales with lots of pixels, so that the pixels are very small compared with the scale at which one is observing, automata can exhibit continuum features like wave motion, long-range interactions, randomness. Some cellular automata are known to be identical to universal Turing machines and hence can simulate anything that can be simulated on a Turing machine. In short, cellular automata are universal computers.

The mathematician John Conway, even before Wolfram got involved with cellular automata, devised a particularly intriguing cellular automata called the Game of Life. It is really not a game but an example of artificial life. There are two known forms of artificial life—robots that move about in real space and time and computer simulations, life forms that exist only in a computer's software. Conway's Life is an example of the latter.

Instead of just an initial row of pixels, Life uses the whole two-dimensional video screen. For every unit of time there is a whole new screen so that one can see the entire configuration change. Again, there are rules that dictate which pixels are lit and which are blank depending on the pixels that surround them during the previous unit of time. Conway invented the rules that perpetuate interesting patterns. With his rules one quickly discovers that there are all sorts of objects that appear on the screen that seem to have a life of their own. Some objects called "gliders" move across the screen at forty-five-degree angles; another object, "the beehive," goes through a periodic behavior. The various objects collide on screen and either annihilate, form other objects, or move off screen. There is quite an inventory of life forms, and hackers are occasionally discovering new ones.

No one knows what the limits of the Game of Life are. Many configurations simply dissipate into uninteresting, predictable configurations, but some go on and on generating more "life." Conceivably, if the area of interaction was large enough, rather than just a computer screen, this artificial life could go on forever, perhaps creating more and more complex forms. It is amazing to see how a handful of simple rules can generate such complexity. Likewise, it is impressive how the rules of atomic combinations in the real world can generate the complexity of living things—the real game of life.

The fact that simple rules governing cellular automata can give rise to patterns as complex as those exhibited by living organisms has fascinated many people. Back in 1975 R. Laing proposed artificial molecular machines that would interact with one another by reading and writing each other's tapes. Christopher G. Langton at the University of Michigan has carried these ideas quite far. In his words, he has decided to "explore the possibility of implementing the 'molecular logic of the living state' in an *artificial biochemistry*, based on interactions between *artificial molecules*. These artificial molecules are modeled as *virtual automata*, which are free to roam around in an abstract computer space and interact with one another. We show that cellular automata are capable of supporting virtual automata that are equivalent to Turing machines and can thus perform any computable task. On this basis, we propose that the notion of the 'molecular logic of the living state' can be captured by the interactions of virtual automata and thus that the existence of *artificial life* within cellular automata is a distinct possibility."

Researchers like Langton are not interested in creating life in a test tube. They want to create it in a computer. Should they succeed, it causes one to wonder what the eventual moral and ethical implications might be.

What is of special interest to Langton is emergent behavior in cellular automata—by adjusting the parameters that control the development of automata, new and complex behavior can emerge. Langton implemented his ideas through the creation of an artificial insect colony. He was inspired to do this in part by Herbert Simon's observation in his *Sciences of the Artificial*: "An ant, viewed as a behaving system, is quite simple. The apparent complexity of its behavior over time is largely a reflection of the complexity of the environment in which it finds itself." Langton was also inspired by E. O. Wilson's ideas about social insects. Wilson has identified aggregate behavior in ant colonies—mass communication—what he calls "the transfer, among groups, of information that a single individual could not pass to another."

Langton has made an artificial ant that he calls a "vant"—a small bunch of colored dots on a video screen. It does not look like an ant. What it is is a cellular automata that can move about on the video screen. When it hits other objects in its environment, including other vants, it has programmed rules that tell it how to behave. Langton's vants cooperate in building trails and through that cooperation create aggregates that represent a higher-order behavior—just like real ants. In spite of their limitations, vants can exhibit "emergent" behaviors. One wonders how more complicated vants might perform. Can life really be a kind of video game?

Langton has also been exploring self-reproducing automata.

Surely one wants reproduction to be part of the simulation of life. Once one has reproduction programmed, it is possible to study evolution. A step in this direction is to first study molecular evolution that is stimulated by catalytic agents. Remarkably, cellular automata can mimic catalytic activity. Ultimately one wants to simulate what the chemists Manfred Eigen and Peter Schuster call hypercycles—multilevel hierarchies of cyclic catalytic reactions that may provide the basis for molecular evolution. These cyclic reactions may be viewed as the limit cycles of nonlinear molecular reactions. Should they appear, this would be a signal that the rules for the artificial biochemistry one is using are indeed correct and could lead to true evolution.

The computer has also opened the door to direct models of real evolution—organisms interacting with the environment and each other in a complex ecosystem—rather than trying to deduce it from artificial biochemistry. These ecosystems are very complex, and their evolution depends on the development of many subsystems that lead to diverse new forms. In real time these changes take aeons, and experiment is impossible. The only way to see evolution in action is to make computer models. Mateen Rizki and Michael Conrad, two computer scientists, have made such models, and they comment: "Computer technology has opened up a new approach to the problem. It is now possible to construct detailed models of the theory of evolution that capture the essential features of ecosystem organization. Implemented as simulation programs, these models serve as a new type of laboratory for the study of evolutionary processes."

While some people are studying the complexity of evolution well *after* the advent of the first replicating molecules like DNA, others are examining the difficult problem of the origin of life—what happened *before* the first replicating molecule. DNA is a complicated molecule. Once we have a replicating molecule like DNA we can see how life evolved. But how did that first replicating molecule get built? Random combinations of simpler molecules to produce DNA is simply too unlikely. It had to be produced in some other way.

This puzzle—the puzzle of prebiotic molecular evolution—is now being investigated by many people using computer models. The basic idea is that one starts with a soup of amino acids and other small metabolites that are the building blocks of DNA or RNA and tries to work one's way up to a chain of chemical reactions to complex proteins and nucleic acids. J. Doyne Farmer, Stuart A. Kauffman, and Norman H. Packard describe their particular work as follows: "The possibility we study here is that the origin of life came about through the evolution of autocatalytic sets of polypeptides and/or single stranded RNA. By *autocatalytic set* we mean that each member is the product of at least one reaction catalyzed by at least one member. Our central thesis here is that templating is not required to achieve an autocatalytic set. Instead simple polymers can catalyze the formation of each other, generating autocatalytic sets that evolve in time to create complex chemical species whose properties are tuned for effective collaboration with each other. The system thus bootstraps itself from a simple initial state to a sophisticated autocatalytic set, which might be regarded as a precursor life form." They find that such a scenario is indeed possible. Once the concentration of simple polypeptides exceeds some threshold, an autocatalytic network is triggered, resulting in a rich "soup" of proteins. While such computer studies are never completely conclusive, they hold out the hope that we will understand the origin of life on a chemical basis.

Some researchers like Stuart Kauffman and Robert Smith at the University of Pennsylvania use automata to simulate the evolutionary process. They devise adaptive automata in which they identify the "genotype" with the specific rules governing the various elements of each automata and the "phenotype" with the dynamical properties of the resulting automata. This is an attempt to imitate real life, in which genes govern protein synthesis and the construction of cells while the behavior of the resulting organism defines its phenotype. Mutations for these automata are random changes in the genotype or rules. Selection by the environment acts on the phenotype, thus changing the distribution of genotypes in the next generation. All these features are part of the computer program. The adaptive automata are then allowed to interact with a "fitness landscape," and one can see from the simulations how the "fittest" automata survive in the course of one hundred generations or so. One surprising thing such simulations reveal is that the automata often *do not* get trapped in the optimal configuration for survival, especially as the complexity of the entity is increased. A second finding is that even if a population is driven to an optimal attractor, selection in the face of constant mutation may be too weak to hold it there.

What such studies imply for real evolution is unclear. But adaptive automata are an example of learning behavior and pattern recognition. In other words, simulations of evolution not only may teach us something about biological evolution, they also realize an example of artificial learning. Understanding artificial life may someday enable us to design it appropriately and put these new life forms to work for us solving complex problems. They will, in effect, become our computational slaves.

The work of people like Kauffman, Langton, Farmer, and Packard exemplifies a new approach to the problems of biology, an approach that has been dubbed "computational biology." This is biology done on a computer rather than in a laboratory or in the field. Traditional biologists may look askance at computational biology, yet it is an approach that can deepen our understanding of many profound problems in biology.

Stuart Kauffman's own work at the University of Pennsylvania, for example, indicates that natural selection may be only part of the story of evolution—a view which, if correct, will have major implications for biology. Kauffman remarks that he "had spent more than a decade exploring the idea that much biological order might reflect inherent self-organized properties of complex systems, even in the absence of natural selection. Since Darwin, of course, we have come to view natural selection, sifting our rare useful mutations from myriads of useless ones, as the sole source of order in biological systems. But is this view correct?"

Kauffman has done extensive computer studies (such as the automata study described above) of large-scale genomic systems to try to answer that question. He finds that such systems with only 10,000 genes, with each gene regulated by two others, tend to spontaneously settle down into only a few stable patterns. These patterns have nothing directly to do with natural selection. "More generally," he concludes, "the fact that randomly assembled model genomic systems exhibit marked order even roughly reminiscent of that found in organisms strikes a blow at our worldview, in which selection is the sole source of order in biology. I think that view is wrong. Complex systems exhibit far more spontaneous order than we have supposed, an order evolutionary theory has ignored. But that realization only begins to state our problem. . . . Now the task becomes much more trying, for we must not only envision the self-ordering properties of complex systems but also try to understand how such self-ordering interacts with, enables, guides, and constrains natural selection. It's worth noting that this problem has never been addressed. Physics has complex systems and spontaneous order, for example in spin glasses, but need not consider selection. Biologists are fully aware of natural selection, but have never asked how selection interacts with the collective self-ordered properties of complex systems. We are entering virgin territory."

With such challenges confronting scientists it seems likely that computational biology is here to stay. Already, the first workshop on computational biology was held in 1987 under the auspices of the Santa Fe Institute.

Modeling Molecules

If we turn from modeling artificial molecules to modeling real ones, we have a new challenge—how well does the model fit the reality? For artificial molecules there is no such problem. However, by modeling real molecules the payoff, both in theoretical knowledge and commercial application, is great because computer modeling of real molecules gives us a control of detail otherwise inaccessible, a control that enables us to directly design useful molecules and drugs.

Before the advent of computers chemists used to make rod-and-ball sculptures of large molecules. Different-colored balls representing the atoms were linked together by rods representing the bonds. Using these molecular sculptures, scientists could establish the interatomic distances between atoms and the angles between the bonds and in this way establish a correlation between the data (gotten by scattering X rays from a crystal made of the molecules) and the model. This was the way James Watson and Francis Crick determined the structure of DNA—a mixture of using X-ray data, rod-and-ball model building, and brilliant guesswork.

The impression one gets from looking at such a molecular sculpture is that of a complex, static entity. This impression, long held by scientists, is now known to be false. Molecules move. They are dynamic entities, stretching and twisting about. The fastest movements are the basic bond-stretching librations, at a frequency of about a thousand billion vibrations a second. Slower movements are twists about a bond axis, and slower still are mass movements of parts of the molecule. The X-ray studies only revealed the *av-*

erage position of the atoms in the molecule, and hence one got the impression of a static entity.

These conformational changes and fluctuations in large biomolecules are an important part of their biological function. This observation has given rise to the new theoretical discipline of protein dynamics, initiated by Martin Karplus (now at Harvard) and his co-workers at Digital Equipment Corporation in a watershed paper of 1977, "Dynamics of Folded Proteins." "These fluctuations," says Karplus, "must have been taken into account in evolutionary development." The new field of protein dynamics is a direct consequence of the computer's ability to model the complexities of molecules.

Computer modeling of large molecules is a small industry today, a success story based on a number of factors. First there is a growing body of good experimental data upon which scientists can test their models. Second, available computers have the calculational power, and new algorithms can simulate the detailed dynamics of the moving molecules. Finally, the field of computer graphics has made giant strides so that researchers can see the results of their labor in three dimensions and color (for distinguishing different parts of molecules). The molecules hang in space on the video screen and can be rotated and magnified for maximum display potential.

The first important use of computers for modeling molecules came in 1964 when Cyrus Levinthal, a protein chemist, and Robert Langridge, a physicist, working at Harvard, managed to display molecules in 3-D on a screen. Langridge is now at the University of California at San Francisco, where he directs the computer graphics laboratory and studies the interactions of complex molecules, and Levinthal, now at Columbia, continues to work on protein dynamics among his many other interests. Levinthal is especially excited by the new possibility of using parallel processors —a new computational technique—instead of serial computers to mimic molecular dynamics. He explains, "If you think about what's really happening when a protein sits in water, an ensemble made up of, say, five thousand atoms, it's obvious that the interactions among all those atoms are happening at the same time, not sequentially, not one after the other, as we've had to treat them. If we had a machine that could calculate these interatomic interactions simultaneously, all in parallel, all in real time, then we could get to be almost as fast as a real protein." The advent of new massive parallel machines will transform the molecular modeling industry.

The fundamental problem in protein structure is understanding how these long molecules fold up into a specific three-dimensional structure. A protein molecule can be visualized as a chain, the links of which are amino acids. What we know about most protein molecules is the precise sequence of the twenty different amino acids laid out along them. If we could imagine laying this chain down on the table and then letting it go, we would see something quite remarkable. The chain would twist and contort until it was all wrapped up on itself. First the chain would coil up like a loosely wound spring (the secondary structure), and then the resulting spring would twist up upon itself, forming a complicated 3-D object (the tertiary structure). Certain parts of the original chain might protrude, others would be all twisted up. Most of the molecule might be relatively inert, and only one part that sticks out would be the active site that interacts with other molecules. That active site may have a specific three-dimensional structure that is crucial to its biological function. The problem confronting molecular modelers is how, given the sequence of amino acids on the chain, can we predict the final three-dimensional structure? No one understands the complete answer to this question, and until we do progress in "molecular engineering" and "designer molecules" will be quite limited.

What physical law determines the configuration the molecule ultimately folds up into? Presumably the answer is that it picks out the minimum energy state. The trouble is that for complex proteins there are dozens, if not hundreds, of different configurations, all of which have an energy that is within a few percent of the true minimum. Finding the true minimum is like finding a needle in a haystack.

This is a problem before which even molecular modelers are humbled. Because there are so many energy states near the minimum and because the energy of the molecule depends so critically on the precise model—how we model the force laws, the torsion in the bonds, the electrical attraction or repulsion between atoms —if we made a slight error in the model or chose to ignore some force we think is negligible, then we will have picked the wrong energy minimum and hence the wrong 3-D configuration. These problems become compounded when we study the interaction of two molecules. To this day the problem of determining the 3-D structure of complex molecules remains unsolved. When it is solved it will be a major breakthrough.

Molecular modelers are interested in molecules other than proteins. Arnold Hagler of the Agouron Institute has been studying peptide hormones as well as proteins. The peptides are a gonadotropin-releasing hormone (GnRH, which stimulates ovulation and sperm production) and vasopressin (which restricts blood vessels), both of which are biologically important. Hagler wants to understand why these hormones are so powerful by identifying their active sites and receptors. Then he wants to build a molecule that can block their activity without "side effects."

Peptides are a lot more labile than proteins and flop about a lot. That makes them hard to study because their activity depends on their shape. By looking at mutant molecules that resemble the peptides but are less floppy, Hagler hopes to isolate the essential active components of the peptides to design an antagonist. Already he has come up with a design for a GnRH antagonist.

The world of computer molecular modeling has opened a window on the microcosm never before seen. It isn't the real world, but it has the singular advantage that we can manage and manipulate it. And because of that facility we enhance our power to manage and manipulate the real world of molecules.

Expert Systems: Modeling Skills

Once, at a small informal talk I attended at the Reality Club, Edward Feigenbaum, former chairman of Stanford's computer science department and founder of Teknowledge, held up an advertising page of a local San Jose newspaper. He pointed out that on that day carrots could be gotten for $.89 a bunch, hamburger was on sale for $1.59 a pound, and some special microchips were on sale for $1.89 apiece. This, he pointed out, was the true signal of the computer revolution. The microchip, whose design required the input of scientific thinking of more than a millennium, the engineering skills of thousands, all the power of modern technology, was selling at prices comparable to fruits and vegetables.

Feigenbaum, a leader in computer science and artificial intelligence, wasn't selling microchips that day; he was telling us about expert systems—computer programs that embody and manipulate useful information about the world, information that is often identified with the skills of a human "expert." Expert systems are computer programs intended to assist people in their work.

The first expert system was DENDRAL, initiated back in the 1960s by Feigenbaum and Joshua Lederberg, a biologist and Nobel Prize winner, and later worked on by Bruce Buchanan, all then at Stanford. DENDRAL's job was to enumerate possible structures for organic molecules after being given data from mass spectrometers (which gave information on the mass of the molecules) as well as user-supplied constraints on the molecular structure (these constraints incorporated the experts' knowledge). In order to get the program to incorporate plausible constraints, DENDRAL's designers went to real experts—the chemists who had been struggling with the problem for their entire careers. The chemists had lots of rules—hand-me-down skills—based on knowledge and guesswork. All this chemical knowledge and intuition was algorithmically organized and associated valences (how strong the guess might be) assigned to the connectivities in the program components. Over the years DENDRAL became more and more expert at guessing the structure of organic molecules given data from the mass spectrograph. And significantly, it was soon used as an aid by the very people it was intended to serve—the chemists. At least twenty-five papers have been published with results that credit DENDRAL's assistance.

The success of this expert system soon led to many others. MYCIN, started by Edward Shortliffe, is a medial diagnostic assistant for blood and meningitis infections. PROSPECTOR serves as a consultant to geologists searching for ore deposits. MACSYMA does symbol manipulation of algebraic equations and can do elementary integration symbolically, thus assisting scientists and engineers in their work. There are even expert systems that are attempting to automate scientific research being developed by Peter Friedland at Stanford's Heuristic Programming Project. The goal is to develop an expert system in molecular biology that will collaborate with scientists in order to make sense out of experimental data and suggest new hypotheses to test. Bruce Buchanan is now looking into how the structure of three-dimensional folded proteins can be deduced from nuclear magnetic resonance imaging and other chemical data.

Expert systems are one of the successes of AI. They involve sequential search programs that utilize the memory capacity of modern computers to represent the knowledge. Expert systems don't, of course, understand what they are doing any more than an adding machine understands addition. But in conjunction with a skilled human user they are like dynamic handbooks of knowledge and skills and as such are very valuable. Expert systems are used to guide investment strategy or check a creditor's background. They can also be used as teaching tools. A novice can learn a lot of organic chemistry with DENDRAL being used as a teacher's text.

This completes our brief, and very incomplete, survey of computer modeling. I tried to give the reader some sense of the diversity of computer simulations, and even that survey is incomplete. Some of the more mundane applications that don't catch the public eye deserve mention. For example, a computer model of the U.S. electorate made back in the late 1950s tested the response of the electorate to social issues, and these findings were put at the service of John F. Kennedy's successful political campaign for the presidency. Computer models of the national and international economy aid decision makers. Game theory can be implemented in programs, and this is helping to understand the negotiation process (viewed as a game) and how to avoid deadlocks and even war. But there are other, more direct, uses of computer models in negotiations.

For example, the Law of the Sea Treaty used computers in an important way. Elliot Richardson, hero of the Saturday Night Massacre during the Watergate crisis, was the chief U.S. representative and negotiator for the treaty (which the United States, ironically, did not sign, although 130 nations did). Richardson told about the treaty negotiations at a large meeting I chaired on computer culture in 1981, which was sponsored by the New York Academy of Sciences. One of the sessions, chaired by Donald Straus, president of the Research Institute of the American Arbitration Association, dealt with computer-assisted negotiations.

The stumbling block for an important part of the treaty had to do with deep sea bed mining operations for metallic nodules that lie on the bottom of the ocean. There is no international authority in such regions. Industrial nations had the know-how and capital to carry out such mining operations, but the less developed countries wanted to share the revenue as the price for their political cooperation. In 1970 the U.N. General Assembly, without opposition, declared these nodules the "common heritage of mankind." Without an international treaty on the mining operation, banks in the industrial countries would not risk an investment. So people were highly motivated to work out an agreement.

Dan Nyhart and others at MIT had previously developed a computer model that incorporated much that was known about the economics of deep sea bed mining. The U.S. government as well as others were interested in the commercial viability of such a new mining operation and supported the development of the model. Jim Sebenius, then working for Richardson at the Department of Commerce, heard about the MIT Deep Ocean Mining Model at about the same time he was becoming involved in the law of the sea negotiations. He grasped the value of such a model in getting 150 different nations of diverse cultures and values to come to an agreement. Tommy Koh, the ambassador from Singapore, headed the working group that dealt with the mining questions and he too grasped the value of a complex computer model for the negotiation process.

The key to eventual success of the negotiations was that these and other leaders convinced the representatives of the many nations of the computer model's credibility. The fact that some political advisers to commercial mining companies were critical of the model helped, ironically, to establish its credibility with representatives of third world countries. Using the model, the economic particulars of the treaty on the deep sea bed mining operations, which was to be done by an international agency, were worked out.

It would be helpful if such computer models could be used for arms control negotiations. But the problems of establishing weapon equivalencies are too difficult to overcome, and a computer model cannot be easily agreed upon by the different parties. Nonetheless computer modeling can play a role in many kinds of negotiations.

Computer modeling is a powerful new tool in the workshop of science. By simulating reality, we come to understand it. In the next chapter we will examine what is undoubtedly the greatest challenge to computer simulation, modeling the most complex piece of matter in the known universe, the human brain.

Chapter 6

Connectionism/Neural Nets

It is widely believed that the "computer of the future" will be highly parallel and highly fault-tolerant. However, designing such a machine has proved surprisingly difficult, and we might have given up long ago, except that the brain is living proof that fault-tolerant parallel processing is possible and powerful.

—JOHN S. DENKER, 1985

People have long had the dream of flying, and birds were the living proof that flying was indeed possible. It was therefore not surprising that our first attempts at flight sought to imitate the birds. There is the early legend of Daedelus. But one of the first historical attempts at flight used Leonardo's ornithopter—mechanically operated wings. Such precise imitation of the birds was not the way to achieve flight, as we all know. Instead humanity first took to the skies in balloons, which have nothing to do with birds, and later in aircraft. Planes do, in fact, imitate the birds in part—they have wings and tails. But they also have propellers and mechanical engines. While we can learn much from nature, a compulsive adherence to its imitation is likely to fail.

People also have the dream of building an artificial brain, and if, as the above quote from John Denker of the AT&T Bell Labs indicates, we did not have living proof that the brain does what it does, we might think that the dream was indeed impossible.

Nature has certainly been generous to us with her many fine examples of what can be done. I wonder how we will proceed in the future when we have exhausted this remarkable source of challenges. Someday we may exceed nature. However, for today, nature exceeds what we can do in many areas, especially in intelligent, adaptive behavior. The challenge of building an artificial brain or intelligence is at the frontier of the new sciences of complexity. Again, it is the advent of the computer that has opened this frontier.

Computers and brains, although they are sometimes compared, are very different—as different as a horse and a locomotive (the "iron horse"). The basis for the comparison is that digital computers and brains both process information, but the way they do it is extremely different. Brains are characterized by their diverse capability, the fact that their function is adaptive and context dependent, and they have enormous generalizing power. Computers cannot really do any of these things very effectively (if at all), but they can compute and manipulate signs far faster than any brain.

There are other differences. Unlike computers, the brain is self-assembled; it evolved in an environment as rich as the world itself. Not only are no two brains alike, no two neurons are alike, even in identical twins. Brains understand what things mean, how they function; they are sensitive to semantics. Digital computers just obey rules or syntax; that's why they are such good calculators, but poor at the things in which humans excel. Unlike a computer's "world," the real world is unlabeled, and yet our brain can organize its experience, memorize and recall parts of it. Brains evidently do have pattern recognition hierarchies. In the visual field they organize textons (perceptual "atoms") into objects, objects into scenes, and these into abstract concepts. Existing computers can do none of this.

If we examine the brain anatomically, we also see how vastly different it is from any existing electronic computer. In spite of the fact that we do not know the detailed architecture of the brain, we do know the scale of its operations. There are on the order of 10^{11} to 10^{12} neurons in your brain, and each of these has anywhere from a few to several hundred thousand synapses making connections to other neurons, with a few thousand being a typical number. So there are about 10^{15} synapses in your brain, and assuming that each of these could be chosen in at least two states (inhibitory or excitatory), we would conclude that here are $2^{10^{15}}$ possible brain states. This enormous (but finite) number represents the total number of possible distinct brain states and suggests that there is indeed a limit to different experiences that a human being can have. This number is far larger than the estimated number of atoms within the horizon of our universe and far, far larger than the number of states in a big supercomputer.

Not only do computers and brains differ in terms of the number of units, but also the speed at which these units operate. Microcircuits in a computer operate on a time scale of nanoseconds—10^{-9} seconds—while the typical neuron operates on the time scale of milliseconds—10^{-3} seconds, a factor of a million slower. Yet in about 100 milliseconds, 100 steps in neuronal firing time, the brain does remarkable, definite things in perception, hearing, and thinking. How can the slow brain compete with a fast computer? It does so by *massive parallelism*—billions of neurons functioning in parallel, simultaneously. A serial computer, in spite of its speed, does its computations only one step at a time. Even Dan Hillis's *Connection Machine*, a state-of-the-art parallel computer with over sixty-five thousand processing units functioning in parallel, does not approach the parallelism in the brain.

The brain is fault-tolerant. No operation in the brain depends on a single neuron—in fact, thousands of neurons die every day, and we seem unaffected (maybe this even has a salutary effect). By contrast, if a single circuit wire breaks, an entire serial computer can fail. The brain, we know, is highly redundant as a consequence of its massive parallel architecture, while most computers are not.

In short, the brain is a network, most computers are serial hierarchies. Computers have central processing units; if the brain has an executive authority, it is distributed throughout the network. Computers have programs that tell them what to do. By contrast, networks are not so much programmed as they are designed. While networks can do computations, they do not do them the way a serial computer calculates, one step at a time.

So brains and serial computers are very different. Some purists might insist that a serial computer can, in principle, precisely simulate physical processes, including those in the brain. Any parallel computation can also be done serially. However, if one examines what is involved in such a precise simulation it is in practice impossible, certainly in real time. To effectively simulate on a huge serial computer one millisecond of the brain's operation—how every neuron functions, every synaptic vesicle or ion moves—could take thousands of years.

In view of the differences between real brains and real computers, the notion that a brain (or mind) has an internal program like a digital computer seems bizarre. This view—that the essence of mind is a program and can be understood independent of its material support—seems odd today. Yet this was the central hypothesis of cognitive science only a few years ago (see the chapter "Waiting for the Messiah"). In its more radical forms this hypothesis seems to me to be unsupported by any evidence. All current evidence suggests that knowledge in the brain is not represented by a program—a set of instructions for manipulating signs—if anything, it is more likely to be represented by a network of connections. The purpose of this chapter is to explore this connectionist idea.

With the wisdom of hindsight we can see how the advent of the digital computer triggered a "fashion industry" in new ways to think about the mind and how to build learning machines. The contemporary history of this intellectual industry is instructive, not only to see how reasonable people were led astray in the past, but also to try and see how we are being led astray today (which is much harder to do). This brief history will also provide some background perspective with which to see the new development of connectionism within computer and cognitive science and its specific realization in parallel distributive processing.

When scientists first began thinking about what computers could and could not do in simulating intelligence back in the 1940s and 1950s, they were already divided into at least two camps—what I will call the "computationalists" and the "connectionists." Computationalists saw the essence of cognition as computation—the kind that can be done on high-speed serial computers. The paradigm of such computation was the Turing machine. Computationalists were also committed to the notion that the simulation of intelligence could be accomplished principally by manipulating signs according to a set of rules.

Connectionists, by contrast, saw the essence of cognition as the response of a neural or electronic parallel network to input stimulation. The paradigm was the brain. Connectionists rejected the notion that rule-governed sign manipulation can simulate complex intelligent action as not being a very useful idea. Instead they saw intelligence as a property of the design of a network.

Although I have tried to exaggerate the distinction between the computationalists and the connectionists, their views are not always, in actual practice, so distinct. First, neural nets can and do compute as do serial computers. They simply do it differently from the way it is done on a serial computer. Second, any kind of parallel network can *in principle* be simulated on a serial computer —it's just very difficult to do so, and the simulation will be incredibly slow. So from a mathematical, *in principle* viewpoint, the two outlooks are equivalent. Why then all the fuss?

One must distinguish between strategy and tactics. The strategic objective of both the computationalists and connectionists is the same—to simulate intelligence in all its richness. The tactics, however, are quite different, as we see from the contrasts given above. When two groups are competing for research funds, the differences between them become exaggerated, and in spite of the shared strategy the tactical differences are aggravated.

While the intellectual competition between these groups has been intense in the past, it is diminishing today. I don't want to minimize the differences between their views, however, for the idea they hold of how the mind and intelligent behavior is realized is quite different. The fact that *in principle* the two views are equivalent is not a practical consolation.

Back in 1943, Warren McCulloch and Walter H. Pitts convinced people that neural networks could compute; they could do logic. While this seems obvious today it was viewed as an important accomplishment back in 1943. This insight opened the door to further challenges. One question was, how could such networks learn? The first glimmerings of an answer came from the work of Donald Hebb in his *Organization of Behavior* in 1949. It was clear that for a machine to support learning there had to be some kind of physical change in the machine to represent the fact that learning had taken place. Hebb made an explicit suggestion based on biology now known as Hebb's rule: If two units on each end of a connection were simultaneously activated, then the connection between them would be strengthened. This rule reflects the reasonable assumption that the more a connection is used, the easier it becomes to use it again. But how can a machine learn using Hebb's rule?

Imagine a network connecting a set of processing units (neurons) that also has an input and an output. The units are all the same except that each one responds slightly differently to an input, and the strength of a unit is limited by some sort of cutoff. Finally one allows the units to compete with each other for responding to the input. This can be implemented by Hebb's rule—the more a connection is used, the stronger it becomes. When presented with some pattern for the input, the machine's units will adjust the strength of their connections to it, and this is reflected in some definite output. Similar input patterns have similar outputs so the machine "learns" to recognize patterns. A device built on these principles is called a "competitive learning machine." While it is not difficult to get such a device to learn easy things, it is very difficult to get it to learn difficult things. For example, while human beings find it rather easy to recognize two different photos of the same face, no learning machine can yet do this.

Back in 1951, Marvin Minsky, then a graduate student in mathematics in Princeton and soon to become a leader in AI research, and Dean Edmonds, a fellow student, went up to Harvard to build *Snark*, a learning machine with funds gotten them by George Miller. In Minsky's words:*

> [*Snark*] had three hundred tubes and a lot of motors. It needed some automatic electric clutches, which we machined ourselves. The memory of the machine was stored in the positions of its control knobs, 40 of them, and when the machine was learning, it used the clutches to adjust its own knobs. We used a surplus gyropilot from a B24 bomber to move the clutches. . . . We are amazed that it could have several activities going on at once in this little nervous system. Because of the random wiring it had a sort of fail safe characteristic. . . . I don't think we ever debugged our machine completely, but that didn't matter. By having this crazy random design it was sure to work no matter how you built it.

Minsky went on to write his Ph.D. thesis on a problem related to learning. Later he went to MIT and attached himself to Warren

---

* Reported by Jeremy Bernstein in his *New Yorker* profile (vol. 57, pp. 50–126, 1981).

McCulloch and Oliver Selfridge, two leaders in the nascent area
of what would be known as AI research. When John McCarthy
joined the MIT faculty, he and Minsky founded the Artificial Intelligence Project. Later, in 1963, McCarthy went to Stanford to
start an AI lab there. Soon another was started at the Stanford
Research Laboratory and this plus the existing AI lab at Carnegie-
Mellon University set up by Allen Newell and Herbert Simon
made up four AI facilities working closely together, a formidable
force for the development of the computational viewpoint. The
basic idea was that the essence of mind could be captured as a
program that manipulated signs. The driving material force behind this intellectual viewpoint, we can see in retrospect, was the
fact that digital computers, whose principles of operation were
congenial to this viewpoint, actually existed, worked, and could be
put to use.

Like any new enterprise, there were successes and failures.
While learning is certainly a characteristic of intelligence, a machine does not have to be able to learn in order to exhibit intelligent behavior. What it needs is the right program. Programs were
written that could prove theorems, manipulate objects, play games
like checkers, backgammon, and chess. But it was also clear that
the way the programs did this—by massive serial search—was very
different from the way humans did it. Also, the limitations of this
approach became apparent. Nowhere was this so apparent as in
the attempt to develop programs that could translate languages.
The problem of the context dependence of the meaning of words
became apparent. People understand things in terms of how they
function (see the discussion between Stan Ulam and Gian-Carlo
Rota related in "Simulating Reality"), and programs have no way
of representing such meaning except the brute force method of
serially listing all the ways a word can be used, thus defining a
word's meaning by how it is used operationally. This approach has
had limited success because the operational definition of meaning
is itself brutally limited. The ways in which a word can be used
grows extremely rapidly with the context—the "explosion of
meaning" problem.

In order to come to grips with the problem of the context dependence of meaning, several AI researchers decided to limit the context—create a little artificial microworld in which all the terms and
operations referred to each other. They tried to isolate the context

and thus avoid the "explosion of meaning" problem. These methods go by the name of "frames," "scripts," and "schemata." For example, Roger Shank of Yale University has developed a restaurant script, a restaurant being, presumably, an isolated context. Various aspects of the restaurant, the table, menu, waitress, check, and service can be represented as signs in a program along with the logical relations between them. The problem comes if something happens out of the narrow context of the restaurant microworld. For example, the customer gets a headache and asks the waitress for an aspirin. The program has got to pull in another script—the "headache script"—and "realize" that in a good restaurant aspirin is available to customers. Signs representing "menu" and "waitress" are manipulated according to the rules in the program. The programs are thus very inflexible; once something new is introduced, the program can't handle it.

AI, independent of its successes and failures, has introduced a new way of thinking about the mind—a set of rules for manipulating signs that refer to concepts and objects. Once in a discussion with Marvin Minsky I asked him why he and McCarthy chose to call their enterprise "artificial intelligence" rather than "cognitive science," which I thought more appropriate. Marvin replied characteristically, "If we ever called it anything other than artificial intelligence, we wouldn't have gotten into the universities. Now that we're in and the philosophers and the psychologists know that we're the enemy, it's too late." Minsky has given a stimulating exposition of his views in his eclectic yet brilliant new book *The Society of Mind* (1985), and anyone interested in the AI viewpoint should have a look at it.

Back in the early 1960s a debate broke out between Minsky and Frank Rosenblatt (who were classmates at the Bronx High School of Science in New York) about the nature of learning machines. Rosenblatt invented the *perceptron*, a simple neuronlike learning device. It had a set of inputs from a "retina"—a spatial array of sensing units—which were then processed by a set of binary threshold units computing some function of the inputs from the "retina." The results of these computations went to one or more decision units that analyzed them, modified the connections to the threshold units, and then produced an appropriate output. The hope was that the perceptron could "perceive"—learn to recognize patterns. As Rosenblatt put it in his book *Principles of*

Neurodynamics (1962), "Perceptrons are not intended to serve as detailed copies of any actual nervous system. They're simplified networks, designed to permit the study of lawful relationships between the organization of a nerve net, the organization of its environment, and the 'psychological' performances of which it is capable." Rosenblatt showed how one could simulate such neural-like networks on a serial, digital computer (rather than building them out of hardware) and also advanced the mathematical analysis of such networks.

He went on to develop perceptrons that exhibited what he called "spontaneous learning" and became quite excited about their capabilities, an excitement, it turned out, that was misplaced. What got him into trouble with the AI community, however, was his overblown claim that perceptrons were superior to computers, a claim that is rather odd in view of the fact that Rosenblatt himself simulated perceptrons on conventional computers. He felt that perceptrons, because of their statistical properties, were somehow different from ordinary serial computers.

Rosenblatt was also extremely critical of the AI notion that the intellectual powers of the mind could be captured by sign manipulations. In tune with the connectionist viewpoint, he thought that the only way of achieving the intellectual powers of the mind was to imitate the way the brain does it. Minsky, McCarthy, and other members of the AI community did not care *how* the brain did it; they were only concerned with simulating *what* the brain did.

Rosenblatt overstated his case. During the 1960s Minsky, in a fruitful collaboration with Seymour Papert, did a mathematical analysis of perceptrons and showed rigorously what their limitations were. The same problems that confronted workers using the serial computers, like the combinatorial explosion of patterns, also appeared in the network of perceptrons, but they appeared as network rather than serial problems. Their book *Perceptrons* (1969) effectively killed research on perceptrons. Rosenblatt died in a solitary boating accident that may have been a suicide.

It seemed as if the computationalists had triumphed. Work on neuronlike networks effectively stopped. But it was a temporary victory. The negative results about perceptrons derived by Minsky and Papert only applied to the most elementary single-layer perceptrons. The work of Minsky and Papert does not apply to the multilayer networks of perceptrons or those that contain "hidden units" (whose inputs and outputs do not connect to external units). Minksy now reassesses the impact of his book with Papert. "I now believe the book was overkill. . . . So after being irritated with Rosenblatt for overclaiming and diverting all those people along a false path, I started to realize that for what you get out of it . . . it is such a simple machine that it would be astonishing if nature did not make use of it somewhere." Rosenblatt, although the most controversial proponent of connectionalism, was not the only one. Connectionist research was going on throughout the 1970s and began to emerge full strength as the problems with the traditional computational view became apparent even to its protagonists.

In 1955, at about the same time Rosenblatt was developing his perceptrons, Oliver Selfridge created *Pandemonium*, a computational example of perception utilizing dynamic, interactive mechanisms. The mathematical analysis and models of S. Grossberg in the late 1970s led to insights into the properties of neural nets and competitive learning machines. J. A. Anderson and Longuet-Higgens independently espoused neural-net models and insisted on distributed rather than local representation of knowledge in the network. David Marr and T. Poggio created a model of stereoscopic depth perception in 1976, which was congenial to the connectionist outlook. In 1982 J. A. Feldman and H. Ballard, first using the term "connectionism" to describe their work, made explicit many of the organizational principles of the new approach. Douglas Hofstadter, author of *Gödel, Escher, Bach* (1979), emphasized the importance of a subcognitive realm—the view that symbols and concepts are really complex composites.

Like a river that had been driven underground in the 1960s only to reemerge full strength in the 1980s, the connectionist view is now the dominant approach to simulating intelligence. Under the rubric of parallel distributive processing (PDP), it is attracting many of the brightest youngsters. The leaders of the PDP outlook, David E. Rumelhart, James L. McClelland, Geoffrey E. Hinton, and thirteen others, have formed the PDP Research Group. While centered at the Institute for Cognitive Science at the University of California, San Diego, the PDP Research Group comes from a variety of U.S. institutions. In 1986 the MIT press published the two-volume collection of papers by this group, *Parallel Distributed*

Processing, volumes that are having a dramatic impact on the direction of research. (Much of the material reported in this chapter appears in those volumes.)

Other research groups have also emerged—part of the pattern of the rising sciences of complexity. We already mentioned the Center for Complex Systems Study at the University of Illinois and the Center for Non-Linear Studies at Los Alamos. Many university computer science departments have also shifted their focus and in some cases universities created new centers like the Institute for Non-Linear Science at the University of California, San Diego. Corporate laboratories like those at AT&T Bell Labs and IBM are part of this venture, as well as many smaller corporate labs. The Neurosciences Institute at the Rockefeller University and the Salk Institute, headed by Gerald Edelman, is a sort of brain trust for studying the brain. Other nations are also moving in this direction. In Japan the Fifth Generation Project, headed by Kazuhiro Fuchi, is experimenting with new computer architectures.

Parallel Distributed Processing refers to a set of computer models. As the name implies, these are parallel systems rather than serial, and their processing of information is distributed throughout the network rather than at a local site as in a microcircuit switch. "These models," say McClelland, Rumelhart, and Hinton, "assume that information processing takes place through the interactions of a large number of simple processing elements called units, each sending excitatory and inhibitory signals to other units." They are inspired by the architecture of the brain in developing their models because "people are smarter than today's computers . . . the brain employs a basic computational architecture that is more suited to deal with a central aspect of the natural information processing tasks that people are good at."

In order to get an overview of the new connectionism, or PDP, I thought it would be useful to simply outline some of its main themes. I will also describe a number of definite models—Hopfield networks and Boltzmann machines, the immune system, classifier and evolutionary models—and critique this development.

The first and central theme of connectionism is *the inspiration from neural architecture* for network design. While it is impossible to precisely imitate the brain because no one knows enough about the brain to do this, connectionists often take their general design clues from the neurosciences. In contrast with the computation-alists, who reject the brain as an exemplar, Rumelhart and Mc-Clelland believe "that an understanding of the relationships between cognitive phenomena and brain functions will slowly evolve. We also believe that cognitive theories can provide a useful source of information for the neuroscientist. We do not, however, believe that current knowledge from neuroscience provides no guidance to those interested in the functioning of the mind. . . . Rather we have found that information concerning *brain-style* processing has itself been very productive in our model building efforts."

For example, the fact that the brain is organized into neurons, with axons and dendrites that connect them, is used by connec-tionists in their brain designs. The neurons correspond to the "units" and the axons and dendrites to the connections. Not all neurons connect to either inputs and outputs. Some simply con-nect to other neurons, and these correspond to the important "hidden units" of PDP. Brain signals can be both inhibitory or excitatory, and these two possibilities are also reflected in the de-signs of the connectionists. Learning, likewise, is reflected in mod-ifying the connections, much as the chemical properties of neural connections are altered by an organism's learning.

In short, it is the connections, the very design of the network, that is the key to its functioning, not some internal program like those in a conventional computer.

It is important to note, however, that while PDP designs are inspired by the brain they do not, indeed cannot, imitate it exactly. These designs use "neuronlike" devices, not neurons or anything approaching the biological complexity of actual neurons. Many of the networks and systems used by PDP researchers have no analogues in actual neuroanatomy. In spite of these differences connectionists believe that they are far closer to building net-works that resemble those in the brain than was previously at-tempted.

Consistent with this neural outlook is *the emphasis on parallel processing* rather than serial processing. The brain is a massively parallel network and this implies that it has great redundancy and fault-tolerance. Furthermore, parallel systems more easily trans-form information in special ways that seem desirable to simulate intelligent behavior.

The new view of the representation of knowledge is another theme: *knowledge is distributed throughout the network*; it is not localized in a specific magnetic memory core or the position of a microswitch. The representation of knowledge, according to connectionists, is distributed among the strengths of the connections between the units. The network models we describe in the sequel will show how this can be done. While neural nets can do computations like ordinary computers, this image is somewhat misleading. Networks don't quite so much compute a solution as they settle into it, much as we subjectively experience our own problem solving.

There has been a long running controversy among neuroscientists (which is still ongoing) about whether memory is localized or distributed in the brain. The idea that there is one memory engram stored in each neuron is certainly wrong. Yet so is the idea that memory is distributed throughout the entire nervous system. In the nineteenth century the view was often expressed that highly localized parts of the brain did specific things. The brain was viewed as a machine with different parts; some parts corresponded to memory, others to motor functions, and so on. Neuroscientists like John Hughlings Jackson and Karl S. Lashley in the United States and Aleksandr R. Luriia in the Soviet Union pointed out the difficulties of accepting such a view as strictly localized neurofunction and argued forcefully (and with much overstatement in Lashley's case) for a distributed function. The debate today is over *how much* localization versus *how much* distribution.

One of the outstanding problems that distributed systems may have alleviate is *the problem of constraints*. In dealing with real-world problems, rather than made-up mathematical problems, we find that there are many constraints, some only implicit, on acceptable solutions. In routing airliners around the world to different cities, one must constrain them to fly near the surface of the earth and not through it. That's an example of an explicit constraint. The fact that in ordering a hamburger one expects it to be served on the table and not on the floor is an example of an implicit constraint. Standard computers have algorithms, such as the recent Karmarkar algorithm, which are rather good at solving problems in which the multiple constraints are all explicit. But human beings are good at solving problems in which the constraints are implicit or ambiguous; in fact, they excel at this. The problem of implicit constraints is closely related to the problem of context-dependent meaning—knowing how things in the world function, like a hamburger about to be served up. Furthermore, constraints change in time with the context of the problem—the constraint problem is dynamic, not static. One of the hopes of PDP is that it will design systems that are closer to human capabilities in dealing with constraints.

The connectionist viewpoint is committed to *understanding cognition at the subsymbolic microlevel*. This contrasts directly with the computational, AI viewpoint. We recall that one of the early ambitions of AI research was to simulate intelligent behavior by manipulating symbols that directly represented concepts and objects. For example, the words of language are symbols that refer to concepts and objects, and if we could only find the rules that correctly manipulate those words, then we would be simulating intelligent linguistic behavior. While words do obey certain rules, we cannot capture the totality of their meaning in this way because of the context dependence of their meaning as well as the fact that to use words correctly we must also refer to how concepts and objects function, not just to the concepts or objects themselves. The attempt to find a macrolevel symbol manipulation program that could simulate language behavior did not succeed.

Evidently such macrosymbols as words and concepts and objects to which they refer are supported by another level; macrosymbols are composites, not the "atoms" of cognition. Hence PDP researchers take another step down the reductionalist ladder (although they describe their work as "interactionalist" not "reductionalist"). Paul Smolensky, in contrast with Allen Newell and Herbert Simon's physical symbol hypothesis, invokes what he calls the *subsymbolic paradigm* "in which the most powerful level of descriptions of cognitive systems is hypothesized to be lower than the level that is naturally described by symbol manipulation." Macrosymbols, according to Smolensky, emerge from a subsymbolic level that is really the network of connections. A description of how macrosymbols emerge from a more elementary level is beautifully articulated in Douglas Hofstadter's two popular books —*Gödel, Escher, Bach* and *Metamagical Themas* (1983).

These are the major themes identified with connectionism. Next, let us look at some of the models that have been both inspired by and have inspired these themes.

Hopfield Networks

In 1982 John Hopfield, of Cal Tech, wrote an influential paper in which he set forth a set of equations that described the dynamics of a model neural net.

Hopfield's model neural net can be viewed as an electronic system of which the key element is a model neuron, an elementary circuit consisting of just a capacitor that has an input "dendrite" and output "axon." The axon of one neuron is connected to the dendrite of another neuron by means of a "synapse," represented in this model by a resistor. One can imagine thousands of these model neurons all connected to one another with resistors, and this forms a network. All of the connections between one neuron and another are described by what I will call the "connection matrix," which specifies the strength of the synaptic connections between the dendrite and axons of different neurons. One can furthermore imagine that an electric current is set flowing in each neuron and then ask what happens to the network. Hopfield showed that something rather remarkable happens—this simple model network can exhibit memory and learning. Furthermore, specific memories are distributed throughout the network and not localized in any one place. It is not difficult to see how that happens.

There are as many equations describing the operation of the Hopfield model as there are "neurons" in the network. Let us suppose that there are a million neurons. These million equations cannot be solved exactly, but Hopfield was able to show that in the simplifying case when the connection matrix was symmetric (so that the strength of a dendrite connecting to an axon is the same as that axon connecting to that dendrite—not a neurologically realistic assumption), the solutions to the equations were fixed points in the neural state space (state space and fixed points were described in our previous chapter, "Life Can Be So Nonlinear"). That means the current flowing in the network can achieve a variety of different steady states, each state corresponding to a different fixed point.

According to John Denker, who described an analogue to the Hopfield model, we can visualize this complicated electronic system because the Hopfield network equations, although they are for an electrical network, have an exact analogue in classical mechanics—a marble rolling up and down a surface of hills and valleys. In order for this mechanical analogue for the Hopfield equations to be precise, it turns out that the marble must be massless, so it has no inertia, and must be moving in a viscous fluid like honey. This marble moves along a surface, but instead of being a surface of just two dimensions, the hills and valleys are in a million dimensions, where we suppose a million is the number of neurons. The position of the marble in this million-dimensional space is specified by a million coordinates—which also specify the state of the system. So a valid way of thinking about the dynamics of a Hopfield model is as a massless marble moving through honey in a million-dimensional space!

Now it is easy to see what is going on in the Hopfield network because if we release the marble at some position in the million-dimensional space, it will move to the lowest point of the nearest valley—a minimum. It can't overshoot the minimum because it is massless in this viscous fluid; it just oozes to the bottom. The marble at rest at the bottom corresponds to a fixed point of the system. This fixed point (there may be lots of them in the multi-dimensional space) has a specific basin of attraction. Release the marble anywhere in that basin of attraction, and it will roll to the associated fixed point and stop.

Clearly the important feature of this system is the multidimensional surface of hills and valleys. The shape of this surface, it turns out, is controlled by the connection matrix that specifies the strength of the connection between the various neurons. By suitably choosing a connection matrix, one can set up the fixed points of the system—where the marble will come to rest in the multi-dimensional space. But what does all this have to do with memory and learning?

The positions of the fixed points can represent stored information or memory. For example, suppose you wanted to have a Hopfield network store a list of your friends' names and telephone numbers. The names and numbers could be coded so that each letter of a name and each number is represented by a distance on a coordinate in the N-dimensional space. By suitably choosing the connection matrix, each name and number will then correspond to the coordinates of a minimum or fixed point. When one sits at a fixed point, one simply reads off its coordinates and decodes them into a name and telephone number.

Suppose now you want to recall a friend's number but can't

remember all of it, only the first few digits corresponding to the exchange, say, 874. Furthermore you can't remember your friend's last name, only the first, John. Using this information, you can set the position of the marble in the multidimensional space corresponding to what you do know—"John" and "874"—and the other coordinates, corresponding to information you don't know, you pick randomly. Well, it is highly likely that even with this partial information reflected in the initial coordinates of the marble it will be positioned somewhere in the basis of attraction of the correct fixed point and roll down to it. At the fixed point one reads off the coordinates corresponding to the full stored memory: "John Brockman, 874-0500." This is an example of a "content addressable memory," or CAM (associative recall). You need specify only part of the content of a memory to get all of it.

Interestingly, this memory of names and phone numbers is distributed throughout the network. One can show that eliminating part of the network only causes the basins of attraction to shift about—the system is robust. If one tries to store more information in the network than can be safely coordinated in the multidimensional space, the fixed points become "fuzzy"—they start to overlap. No one pretends that this model realistically models actual neurofunctions, yet it has many of the properties that might be expected of the brain.

Mathematically, the Hopfield model, here a description of neural nets, is identical with another model, the spin glass, which makes its appearance in the entirely different field of condensed matter physics (which, not so remarkably, is what Hopfield worked on before he became interested in neural nets). Spin glasses are substances in which the spins of neighboring atoms or molecules interact in a special way. The equations that describe the interactions between the neighboring atomic spins turn out to be identical with those of the Hopfield neural model. One of the side effects of Hopfield's work was that many theoretical physicists working on spin glasses became overnight experts on the properties of neural nets. Some of them, like Hopfield, switched fields.

The Hopfield network can also learn. This can be done by implementing the Hebb rule—one strengthens the connections that serve to deepen the minima for the fixed points one wants to reinforce. New memories can also be added by creating new minima in the multidimensional space. One can, if one is not careful, create an obsession or idée fixe—a fixed point with a basin of attraction so wide and steep that all other basins drain into it.

The Hopfield model is not neurologically realistic. For one thing, neurons in the brain don't connect symmetrically. Once one no longer assumes a symmetric connection matrix, the precise mechanical analogy is lost as well as the fixed points. People who mathematically examine such generalizations of the simple symmetric model suspect that other kinds of attractors come into play —limit cycles and strange attractors.

In spite of its limitations, the simple model provides a new metaphor for the mind—a multidimensional surface of hills and valleys. This surface is continually changing its shape as a consequence of learning from new external experience and internal processes, thus creating new attractors (never a true fixed point because that would imply thinking has stopped). All the complexities of a human mind could, in this view, be represented by the bumps and valleys on such a surface, a kind of latter-day phrenology (the nineteenth-century pseudoscience that correlated bumps on the head with human character).

It is possible to further develop these ideas about Hopfield networks. For example, Alan Lapedes and Robert Farber have divided the search for minima in N-dimensional state space into two parts —a master and a slave. The master network has a symmetric connection matrix so that it has definite fixed points. The slave network has a nonsymmetric connection matrix so there are no fixed points, and the system moves about cyclically in a region of attraction. The master net, however, controls the slave. According to its proponents, "Our formulation thus naturally involves two nets— the first net optimizes, or 'programs,' the second net, and then the second net does the job. We refer to this relation between the two nets as a master/slave relationship. This optimization method of neural programming provides for merging two basins of attraction together (and separating them again), weighting certain components of a fixed point so that it attracts more strongly ('sculpting' the basins), and the division of neurons into inhibitory and excitatory subpopulations." Lapedes and Farber go on to formulate a definite model that realizes these ideas and show how its action as a CAM is superior to that of a single net.

An exciting possible relation of these models to the real world is provided by Bill Baird's and W. J. Freeman's work on pattern recognition in the rabbit olfactory bulb. The electroencephalographic data from the olfactory bulb in the rabbit's brain indicates that when the system is inactive, the signals in the bulb are random oscillations. When the rabbit takes a sniff this randomness changes, and one observes both coherent oscillations and a regular spatial pattern in the activity of the bulb. These patterns can be correlated with specific odor recognitions.

A mathematical neural-net model can be made of the rabbit olfactory bulb, and this resembles a Hopfield learning network. There are equilibrium states, basins of attraction, and limit cycles corresponding to the observed physiological data. When the rabbit sniffs, the system is driven out of equilibrium and becomes unstable. Various instabilities compete with one another until the system settles into a limit cycle—the odor has been recognized. There is thus a remarkable relation between abstract neural-net models and a real pattern-recognition system in a mammalian brain.

Boltzmann Machines

In a previous chapter we described the annealing transition, how a computer model of a dynamical system could be used to solve difficult optimization problems. The main idea was to introduce a temperature and then allow the elements in the system to have a random motion that freezes into an optimal configuration as the temperature drops. Simulated annealing could be used to find approximate solutions for difficult-to-solve problems like the traveling salesman problem. With this method the problem is not so much solved as it is settled into.

Because of its facility in optimizing difficult problems with lots of constraints, simulated annealing can be used to construct a learning algorithm for Hopfield networks. This approach has been taken by Geoffrey Hinton and Terrence J. Sejnowski in constructing their Boltzmann machine and by Paul Smolensky in an equivalent development called Harmony theory. The Boltzmann machine is aptly named after Ludwig Boltzmann, the nineteenth-century physicist who first mathematically described the statistical mechanics of gases and formulated the probabilistic basis of the second law of thermodynamics. The Boltzmann machine learns by simulated annealing.

Imagine, once again, a neural network. This time, however, some of the units (neurons) will interact directly with the environment, which we suppose possesses some definite pattern. These sensing units will be called "visible units." Other units, in general a large number, do not interact directly with the environment but do connect to the visible units and each other. These are called "hidden units." Now we want to train the machine to recognize the pattern that is sensed by the visible units. This requires finding the best landscape—the multidimensional surface in state space that represents all the neuronal connections—and the one that corresponds to the given input pattern from the environment. Finding this surface, in general, is a very difficult problem because it requires adjusting the connection matrix of not only the visible units, but the hidden units as well.

One can solve this difficult problem of finding the best connection matrix for the network by using simulated annealing. Hinton and Sejnowski in their mathematical construction of the Boltzmann machine specify a "learning algorithm." They show that allowing the units to have stochastic properties like a gas of molecules, by first randomizing the connection strengths between them, and then "cooling" the network down so that when it settles it finds an adequate solution for the connection matrix is subject to the input constraints of the given environmental pattern. The net thus "learns" to recognize a pattern. It finds the best multidimensional surface that corresponds to a given input pattern—an internal representation for the pattern has been learned.

This kind of learning is characteristic of PDP models. McClelland, Rumelhart, and Hinton note that they "do not assume that the goal of learning is the formulation of explicit rules. Rather, we assume it is the acquisition of connection strengths which allows a network of simple acts to act *as though* it knew the rules. Second, we do not attribute powerful computational capabilities to the learning mechanism. Rather, we assume very simple connection strength modulation mechanisms . . . based on information locally available at the connection."

There is an interesting twist on these ideas about learning. Francis Crick and Graeme Mitchison have speculated that dreaming in mammals (REM sleep) may be a form of "reverse learning." Usually people think that dreams are mentally important and represent deep symbolic aspects of our unconscious life. Crick and Mitchison suggest just the opposite—dreams are our way of getting rid of useless information. In terms of our grand multidimensional surface representing the states of the mind (our modern phrenology), there may be lots of little extraneous bumps and valleys that confuse our ability to recognize the really important terrain corresponding to significant memories. Dreams, according to this unlearning theory, are represented by the process of removing those unneeded bumps and valleys, getting rid of the mental rubbish, and keeping only the important parts of memory. If these ideas about dreams being an unlearning process are right, they ought to be testable. I wonder how this theory accounts for recurrent dreams (trash that just won't dump?), serial dreams, or the symbolic content of dreams? This somewhat heretical idea deserves exploration.

The Immune and Evolutionary Systems

Our bodies, and those of all mammals, have a highly evolved immune system whose purpose is to identify and destroy invading foreign molecules, or *antigens*. It does this in a matter of a few days after exposure to an antigen. In order to do this without also attacking our own bodies, it must be able to recognize our own molecules and not destroy them. The immune system, like the evolutionary system, is thus a powerful pattern-recognition system, with capabilities of learning and memory. This feature of the immune system has suggested to a number of people that a dynamical computer model, simulating the immune system, could also learn and have memory. J. Doyne Farmer, Norman Packard, and Alan Perelson are one group studying this model, while another group, with somewhat different starting assumptions, consists of Geoffrey Hoffman, Maurice Benson, Geoffrey Bree, and Paul Kinahan.

The immune system, it seems, has nothing directly to do with how the brain learns or with neural nets. Neither does the evolutionary system. Yet, as is emphasized by Gerald Edelman, each of these three pattern-recognition systems, the brain, the immune system, and the evolutionary system, may be essentially the same, if viewed in terms of abstract principles; only the time scale on which they function is different. The evolutionary system works on the time scale of hundreds of thousands of years, the immune system in a matter of days, and the brain in milliseconds. Hence if we understand how the immune system recognizes and kills antigens, perhaps it will teach us about how neural nets recognize and can kill ideas. After all, both the immune system and the neural network consist of billions of highly specialized cells that excite and inhibit one another, and they both learn and have memory. How, then, does the immune system do it?

The primary regulatory components of the immune system are lymphocytes (the white blood cells made in your bone marrow at a rate of about a million a second), antibodies (molecules associated with the lymphocyte), and specific T-cell factors (the action of which we will not discuss for reasons of simplicity). Each B-lymphocyte has on its surface about one hundred thousand antibodies, which can be visualized as little molecular keys sticking out of the lymphocyte cell body. All of the antibodies on a particular lymphocyte are identical, but they differ, ever so slightly, from lymphocyte to lymphocyte. Each antibody has an active site called a *paratope*. The paratope can be thought of as the notches on the "key" so that each B-lymphocyte has all these thousands of keys, each one identical, sticking out of it.

Each antibody, as well as the antigens that it attacks, also has another active site, called the *epitope*, which functions as a "lock." Once an antibody's key fits an antigen's lock, the antigen is destroyed; that is how the immune system does its work of getting rid of antigens. Furthermore once an antibody key finds a lock it fits, it then triggers a manufacturing process in which millions of clones of its associated B-lymphocyte get made each with its set of identical keys, made to order for destroying that particular antigen. In this way the body mobilizes its defense.

However, the antibodies, besides being keys, are also locks— they have epitopes. Hence antibodies can recognize and destroy other antibodies within its own immune system. In this way the immune system can attack itself. If it did so, we would have a massive autoimmune response and quickly die. In fact, the immune system usually does not attack itself, and the way it regulates itself was first described by Niels Jerne in his "idiotype network theory." According to this theory, a specific antibody is enhanced if its "key" is used a lot and suppressed if its "lock" is used. So even if self-destructive antibodies get made, their number is regulated (and suppressed) by other antibodies. Like the evolutionary system, there is a "struggle for survival" for each antibody in an environment of other antibodies.

Each clone of a specific lymphocyte thus simulates or suppresses a fraction of the production of all the other clones. Also, the immune system is maintained by replacement of about 5 percent of the lymphocytes every day, as well as by the natural death of an equal number.

Mathematical equations for the numbers of each of the N clones can be set up to describe this process. One finds that this dynamical system can be described in terms of an N-dimensional state space. In this state space there are a large number of attractors corresponding to stable states of the immune system, which correspond to the "memory" of the system. Learning in this system corresponds to finding a more stable state with a higher survival value. So the mathematical model of the idiotypic network seems to have the same recognition, memory, and learning properties of the actual immune response. But what does this have to do with neural nets?

The conventional view of learning in neural nets is that learning corresponds to modifying the strengths of the neural connections. In the immune response those connections between neurons would correspond to the affinity of specific keys and locks, and this is *not* subject to modification. What does change in the immune system is the numbers of clones, and these could be analogous to the numbers of neurons. But neurons do not kill each other off. So instead of killing off neurons, what may happen in the neural network is that the firing rate of groups of neurons is altered, and that effectively reflects learning (this goes against the conventional view). The idea that groups of neurons compete with each other —a "neural Darwinism"—has been developed in detail by Gerald Edelman. The analogy between the immune response, evolution, and the neural network may be difficult to maintain, yet it is suggestive.

Whether or not the immune system can tell us about neural learning may be an open question. But it does tell us something directly about another learning and problem-solving system—the *classifier system* of John Holland of the University of Michigan—at least in the model of the immune system devised by Farmer, Packard, and Perelson. They have shown that in spite of superficial difference, the essential dynamics of the immune system and classifier system are the same.

Holland's classifier system has been used for everything from regulating gas flows in pipelines to playing poker. According to Farmer and his colleagues, "The system can be divided into two parts, a set of *rules* or *classifiers*, and a *message list*. The rules contain information giving possible responses of the system, while the message list constrains the inputs from the external environment and provides a forum for the rules to communicate and interact with each other. . . . The classifier rules consist of multiple parts: one or more *conditions*, an *action* and a *strength*. . . . The conditions allow the classifier to 'read' the message list by searching for matches of the conditions against the messages posted on the list. When a match is found, and if certain criteria are met, a rule is allowed to post its action part as a new message on the list. Some rules have a special role as *effectors*, meaning that their action parts cause external outputs. . . .

"The *strength* is a number associated with each rule which is designed to indicate its value to the system. This forms the basis of learning. If a rule helps bring about useful responses, it gains strength, and otherwise it loses it. Strong rules are given more influence than weak rules in determining the overall response of the system."

We can now see the analogy between Holland's classifier system and the immune system. The classifier rules function as antibodies, their conditions as the epitope "locks," their action as the paratope "keys," their strength as the numbers of a specific clone, and so on. The learning and memory in both systems is similar. We can say, without exaggeration, that the principles of the immune system can regulate gas pipe flows and tell us how to play poker.

Holland sees a major challenge in the study of such adaptive systems: "At the core of areas of study as diverse as cognitive psychology, artificial intelligence, economics, immunogenesis, genetics, and ecology, we encounter nonlinear systems that remain far from equilibrium throughout their history. In each case, the system can function (or continue to exist) only if it makes a continued adaptation to an environment that exhibits perpetual novelty. . . . The task of [the] theory is to explain the pervasiveness of these features by elucidating the mechanisms that assure their emergence and evolution. The most hopeful path seems to be a combination of computer modeling and a mathematics that puts more emphasis upon combinatorics (that branch of mathematics dealing with combinations) and competition in parallel processes."

I have alread mentioned the analogy between the immune system and the evolutionary system. Evolutionary learning is a way of searching out a set of behaviors using random variation followed by selection. Michael Conrad and his collaborators have built computer models for the evolutionary process that exhibit this kind of learning. They say they introduce a *"parallel random search* where a finite ensemble of systems undergoes random mutations. If there is a fitness function . . . parallel random search uses it only to halt the learning process when the performance is within some tolerance of the ideal. In all other senses, this search is blind" (like evolution). In other words, selection of a random set according to some criteria of fitness is an algorithmic learning procedure.

All of the systems we have considered here—the immune response, the classifier system, and the evolutionary system (and perhaps the brain)—recognize and learn according to the same general principles. Gerald Edelman of the Rockefeller University has dubbed them "selective systems" and identified their general operational principles as "random repertoire," "the selective principle," and "amplification."

"Random repertoire" means that these objects all differ slightly from one another, like the paratope "keys" on millions of different antibodies or the color of butterfly wings in a population of butterflies. The "selective principle" means that a criterion selects only a few of the "fittest" objects out of the random repertoire; the rest of the objects are suppressed or eliminated. Finally, "amplification" is a way of increasing the numbers of the selected objects, like the cloning of the right lymphocytes or the reproduction of the fittest butterflies. These three steps constitute a pattern-recognition or learning algorithm. We can see these same principles at work in the Boltzmann machine, which also utilizes randomness and selection.

Perhaps our thinking exemplifies a selective system. First lots of random scattered ideas compete for survival. Then comes the selection of what works best—one idea dominates, and this is followed by its amplification. Perhaps the moral of this selective system model is that you never learn anything unless you are willing to take a risk and tolerate a little randomness in your life.

In this very brief survey of models that implement some of the new ideas about memory and learning I have omitted a lot of interesting work done on speech production, sentence processing, social and behavioral models, and even other neurological models. But I have tried to provide the reader with an impression about the nature of distributed memory and learning systems and why they differ from the computational view of the earlier generation of cognitive and computer scientists.

In 1987 more than two thousand people met at the "First International Conference on Neural Nets," an exciting meeting that, among other things, revealed the enormous commercial potential of these new ideas. New companies, as well as older ones (meaning five years old!) have sprung to the fore ready, or almost ready, to go to the market with neural network devices. Neural nets are different from conventional computers and computer programs like AI expert systems that just do precisely what they have been programmed to do. Neural nets *learn*. That feature will in itself create a new industry. As Esther Dyson, who has followed these developments, puts it in her newsletter *Release 1.0*, "Yes, neural networks are self programming; they can 'learn by themselves,' as the ads will no doubt claim. Yes, the results are more than you could ever hope to achieve with 'more' programming, or with explicit rules, but that doesn't mean there's no work. Even after someone has built the learning system, the neural net itself, the user (or reseller) must develop the 'training materials,' properly configure the input and output data, and hook the system up to its environment—other computers, input devices, pc screens. These seemingly trivial problems—managing the training, data preprocessing, and systems integration—will remain a challenge for users and an opportunity for entrepreneurs even as engineers build cheaper and more powerful neural net software and enabling hardware."

The attitude of the new generation of scientists working on connectionist ideas and PDP is quite different from those of some AI researchers a decade or more ago. The hyperbolic claims are absent (unless the proponent has a financial interest in a company). They do not speak about solving the problem of the mind or cracking the cognition problem tomorrow. They don't talk about their machines as "thinking" or having human capabilities. People who work in this area are for the most part humbled by the enormous challenge confronting them. They are also excited by it. But progress will be slow.

It is not difficult to find reasons why this new approach to the problem of cognition will fail. The workers in the field are themselves keenly aware of these criticisms.

A major criticism is that the connectionists' models are not neuronally realistic. The difference between a real neuron and the model neurons in connectionist models is like the difference between a human hand and a pair of pliers. Neurons fire a series of spiked impulses, are both inhibitory and excitatory, and for the neuronal network the parallelism is truly massive. Model neurons, by contrast, respond in an off or on manner, are often all excitatory, and the network is only modestly parallel. Maybe the connectionist models have nothing or little to do with the brain, and their claim that they are inspired by the brain's function is misleading. Just because the brain does all the wonderful things it does is no guarantee that the connectionists' models will imitate it.

Even if they are imitating the brain's structure—building airplanes and not balloons, as it were—how do we know that the neuronal network is really the key to the brain's function? Maybe the neuronal network is a visible but only auxiliary part of the brain, and the key to its operation lies in complex biochemistry and the action of neurotransmitters. Maybe the neural network only serves a regulatory function on what is basically a chemical system. This view is a sort of a heresy, yet the fact that it can be scientifically maintained at all is an indication of how ignorant we are of the brain's overall operation. In the face of such ignorance, why should we let ourselves be inspired by the little that is known? Connectionists being inspired by the neurosciences may be an instance of the blind leading the blind.

The connectionists are very proud of the fact that they have broken away from the computationalists' idea that the essence of cognition consists in manipulating symbols that directly refer to concepts and things. Indeed, they are committed to understanding cognition at the subsymbolic microlevel. But are they in fact doing this? If one examines their work in detail, one finds, for example, that words, referring to concepts and things, are directly represented as labels in a program—just like the computationalists were doing, only the connectionists do this in a parallel network rather than in a serial program. That is hardly the "subsymbolic microlevel" they are striving to achieve. In fact, no one knows how to represent a concept or thing on the subsymbolic microlevel, or even precisely what this means. If this ambition could be realized, it would come close to cracking the cognition problem. And no one is close to accomplishing that.

Another criticism that is easily made of the connectionists' program is that it is just a jumble of partial ideas and there don't seem to be any major guiding principles. As a result many of the problems are not precisely posed, and it is not clear where the program is headed. Perhaps, however, the program is still immature, and it is too soon to identify the main principles of this new science.

It is far easier to criticize this work than to undertake the challenge it presents. So far connectionists have created interesting models, and new ones are being mathematically explored. Ultimately one would like to see a machine, based on these ideas, that can recognize signatures, speech from several speakers, and ultimately human faces. Even with the connectionist program, as exciting as it is, we still have to impose our strict constructive demand—build a machine or write a program that actually does these things. The PDP proponents are aware of this requirement.

As Rumelhart and McClelland put it succinctly: "The real proof is in the pudding."

We shall see how it tastes.

Chapter 7

The Quick Buck Becomes Quicker

*The generally accepted view is that markets are always right—
that is, market prices tend to discount future developments accurately even when it is unclear what those developments are. I
start with the opposite point of view. I believe that market prices
are always wrong in the sense that they present a biased view
of the future.*

—GEORGE SOROS, 1987

During the Second World War, Albert Einstein at the urging of
Leo Szilard wrote a now famous letter to Franklin Roosevelt. This
letter, expressing Einstein's view that nuclear fission could be used
to build a weapon and that Germany might well be pursuing such
a direction, set in motion a chain of events which led to the Man-
hattan Project and the first and only use of atomic weapons by the
United States against Japan. The abstract subject of nuclear physics leapt to the foreground in people's thinking, influencing the
creation of foreign policy and the international order among nations. Some scientists who possessed the knowledge to build the
weapons were lifted out of the obscure world of academic research
into the public eye. What scientists thought could and could not
be done took on added significance. This scenario—the transfor-

mation of abstract knowledge into practical artifacts—is today repeating itself in an entirely new area.

The banking industry, long insulated from major technological change, has been hit by a revolution that will alter forever the way it does its business. This revolution is a consequence of improvements in telecommunications, data processing, and, of course, the computer. A new class of people who have mastered this new technology has sprung into prominence and in several instances risen to leadership positions in major financial institutions.

Institutional survival in a highly competitive banking environment can depend on advances in computer modeling of markets and the economy, and software and algorithms, as well as telecommunications, that supply data input. Banks, which have long been hiring experts in data processing, are now hiring computer scientists, engineers, and mathematicians to help design their equipment and algorithms. They used to depend on their vendors, computer and software producers, for their internal needs. But they soon realized that to maintain a competitive advantage they had to take on the research and development responsibility themselves. Major financial services institutions now have their own research staffs examining how they can improve their data processing performance by using new hardware and software. Abstract mathematics, sometimes developed to understand selective and adaptive systems, is now being applied to guide financial decisions. The sciences of complexity are impacting the business and financial world. And that impact is just beginning.

The real movers of the world economy today are the large international banks linked to each other electronically by a network that, seen as a whole, comprises the world's first global computer. In 1986 over $64 trillion was exchanged on this network, and that volume is still growing. (The other global computer, and second largest, is the U.S. military communications system.) The banking computer network is a parallel, not hierarchical, network, although it has hierarchical components. Within each financial institution the system is hierarchical, but globally no one is in charge, and there is no central, executive authority. In this sense it is a "free market." Some computer scientists are attempting to develop computer models of the world's first global computer to try and understand it better.

If we look back, we can see what events helped to bring about this global computer. A few decades ago the placement of the first satellites in orbit created a technological curiosity and a symbol of national accomplishment. Some people complained about the high cost of the satellites. However, satellites provided a highly reliable transcontinental and intercontinental communications link, and financial institutions quickly took advantage of them. Banks in London could release credit to banks in New York as the sun set in England and New Yorkers were still at work. Likewise, New York banks were able to communicate credits to the West Coast and thence to Asia. While people slept, their money worked. The satellite system enabled a "bulge" of credit to rotate with the daylight zone around the planet. Some people estimate that satellites increased the world credit supply by as much as 5 percent—hundreds of billions of dollars—much more than the entire cost of the satellite systems.

When optic fibers are deployed across the Atlantic and Pacific oceans by the end of this decade, many functions of the satellites will become obsolete. The increased bandwidth afforded by photonic systems will enable supercomputers on different continents to talk to each other. It is conceivable that European and Asian computers will be buying and selling on the U.S. markets (and vice versa). Already, effective international telecommunications and computations have destroyed the arbitrage market that makes money on small differences in currency exchange rates. The only advantage of having a local computer near the market is the one hundred milliseconds or so that it takes light to travel between continents. But that is a significant advantage if one has a fast algorithm. I recently spoke to a mathematician newly employed at a New York investment house who was developing sophisticated algorithms to determine buy-sell options. Why? So that his institution could get their orders in a millisecond ahead of their competitors.

It is well known that one of the most rapid forms of communications is a good joke. Businesspeople routinely leave their office in London with a fresh joke, fly to New York on the Concorde, only to find out at an evening cocktail party that everyone had already heard it. How is this possible? Banks and investment houses maintain open phone lines around the world in case there is a news break. The operators who maintain the lines often have no business information to transmit, so they trade new jokes.

That's how jokes circle the globe so quickly. They are still one of the fastest forms of human communication.

The introduction of high-speed computing, data processing, and innovative software has transformed the financial services industry. Leaders in the financial services industry, while keenly aware that such technology makes a difference today, were not always so aware. A decade ago the investment industry was hit by a technological revolution in the form of new electronic trading systems for stocks. Though suffering from an avalanche of paperwork (some called it the "paperwork holocaust"), the New York Stock Exchange delayed the installation of this innovative technology. They were too busy making money and thought they would lose orders during the change-over period. The exchanges in Tokyo and London, which were not so concerned about short-term profits, became electronic markets. By their understanding of where the industry was headed, they got a bigger piece of action. Even today a major problem is that as technology advances, systems quickly become obsolete and noncompetitive. How does one change over an entire network without bringing it down?

New skills are needed in order to manage the modern financial services industries—not just computer programmers, but high-level mathematicians who know how to design fast algorithms. In September of 1986 there was a "computer-assisted" slide of the market. One of the reasons for this slide was that the buy-sell programs for many investment and brokerage houses differed in such a way as to produce an instability in the system. While the first step in most houses' programs for buying and selling was the same, the second, third, and fourth steps differed. This can produce a positive feedback loop; when the market becomes unstable and before human beings can intervene, the market can drop precipitously, costing many people a lot of money. When I asked many stock analysts about "instabilities" or "singularities" in market behavior, they never heard of them. Most are not trained in even rudimentary modern mathematics.

What are the chances that we will ever understand economic systems? They are clearly examples of extremely complex systems, but there is lots of quantitative data to check one's ideas out on. Professional economists who bother to concern themselves with practical matters don't have an especially good batting average when it comes to predicting the future of the economy. They are smart, but they just don't have the right intellectual tools in their hands.

When I was in school learning about supply-and-demand curves, I asked my professor, "Where did those curves come from? Were they made up, based on data, or did they represent a theory?" The best answer I got, at least the one I remember, was that they represented the theory of economic equilibrium. The market, it was asserted, establishes an equilibrium, and the point at which the supply-and-demand waves intersect determines the price. This, reasonable as it seems, is of course nonsense.

The economic system, if it is anything, is a system far from equilibrium like the evolutionary system or the immune response. It is continually making adjustments to keep itself far from equilibrium (although there may be a local equilibria). Next to nothing is understood about dynamical systems far from equilibrium. Probably the various kinds of attractors—fixed points, limit cycles, and strange attractors—play a role in coming to grips with how a complex system like the economy functions. Some mathematical economists such as Stanford's Kenneth Arrow have expressed cautious excitement about the application of the new ideas about chaos to economic dynamics. Mathematicians and others are endeavoring to apply insights gleaned from the sciences of complexity to the seemingly intractable problem of understanding the world economy. I have a guess, however, that *if* this problem can be solved (and that is unlikely in the near future), then it will not be possible to use this knowledge to make money on financial markets. One can make money only if there is real risk based on actual uncertainty, and without uncertainty there is no risk.

As emphasized by the investment manager George Soros in his book *The Alchemy of Finance* (1987), human biases profoundly influence markets in a reflexive fashion. Because such biases are influenced by political developments and cultural factors it is probably impossible to make a reliable model of the international economy. Like the weather, the international economy is an unsimulatable system. Yet short-term prediction and seeing long-range global trends may be possible using mathematical models.

I remember that back in the 1960s popular intellectuals spoke about "the information age" and "the global village." Well, it has arrived, but not exactly in the form that these intellectuals anticipated. Felix Rohatyn, a New York investment banker and public-spirited citizen, recently remarked that we are now living in the "money culture," a development brought about by the new data processing technologies. By this he meant that the dominant form of commercial exchange between people is not goods and services, but money. Money is, of course, a form of information, and it can move at the speed of light. People can easily invest it, transfer it, and lend it. And lots of people are doing this, some accumulating great wealth.

Only a few decades ago, if one picked up American business magazines, the articles were about new products, industries that produced goods and services, and the people who made that happen. Today the big news stories are about *deals*, financial transactions, buying, selling, conglomerating, integrating, divesting, and destroying companies. Smart young people who want to enrich themselves are attracted by all these deals and want a piece of the action. Nothing is being produced, but wealth is seemingly created. This bubble burst with the collapse of the market on October 19, 1987.

One could even imagine a satire on the theme of the "money culture." People invest in the financial services industry, which, in turn, services their investment. Nothing but information is ever exchanged; no one produces anything; money, however, is always changing hands. The whole system bootstraps itself into existence —just money being exchanged and making more money based on the human confidence that it will continue to be exchanged. The image one gets is of an immense "chain letter" with promises of payments to all at a cost to none. Of course, it cannot work forever. At some point human confidence gets shaken, and a lot of people are hurt.

The real money culture, of course, invests in products and services. What has changed is the speed with which this is done. Speed, while a quantitative parameter, can, if dramatically increased, lead to qualitative changes—the changes we see in the global economy and, in particular, the large multinational corporations that play such an important role in maintaining it. In several such large corporations there has been a shift in both the leadership and the emphasis. The companies used to be run by traditional executives who understood the product and how it was produced and sold, whether it was automobiles or oil. But with the rise of the money culture many corporations, especially the oil companies, discovered that they could make more money investing and trading their surplus capital than doing what the company traditionally did—look for oil. Engineers and salesmen were re-placed by international money market analysts and accountants. These new people began to run the companies. Which, of course, causes one to wonder who's minding the shop.

In 1986 I met with a group of bankers and businessmen. I told them that I knew of a "computer nest" operating in Luxembourg or Switzerland that was using a new "massively parallel computer" built by hackers in collaboration with a group of bright young traders for the express purpose of recognizing patterns in the com-modities market. It had a learning capability similar to the Boltz-mann machine. The traders were pulling in between two and three million dollars a day and wreaking havoc on the European com-modities market.

My audience was stunned. "Who are they? What are they doing?" they asked, now on the edge of their seats. I told them that the story wasn't true, but could easily become true in the near future. This kind of "technical breakout" by an opponent, which is so often feared by military strategists, could also happen in the financial world.

Not only will advances in pattern-recognition systems influence financial decision making; so will the advent of detailed models of the global economy. There is an enormous amount of data gen-erated by the world economy, so much that one human being or even a team cannot digest it. But computers can use that data in detailed models of various national and international economies and analyze it. Far-ranging supercomputer models will become a powerful asset in the hands of their creators—crystal balls that may make economic forecasting more realistic. One can foresee the characterization of economic systems in terms of different limit cycles and strange attractors. The international economy is a nonlinear system and can be understood as such.

There are dangers in the operation of the global computer sys-tem. A major instability could result in an international economic crash far worse than that in 1987. Many people predict that this can happen—that the markets will not stabilize after the October 1987 crash. Since no one person or group understands what is going on in the world economy and there is no central executive control, the entire system could end up in the basin of attraction of a fixed point presenting very low economic activity. National governments would have to intervene to get the system started again, and new international institutions would have to be established, at a sacrifice of some national sovereignty, in order to prevent the recurrence of a crash.

In spite of all the advantages in computer technology it is not possible to abrogate human judgment in decision making. Much of this implementation of the new computer equipment, however, is designed to do just that. I find that distressing. Elementary decisions, lots of them, can and are made by computers. Perhaps in the future more complex economic decisions will be made by computers as well. But people, with their innate desire to control their destinies, would be foolish to abrogate such high-level judgments to computers.

The diffusion of responsibility incurred by computers is a major danger, too. Once, waiting for breakfast to be served at a fancy new hotel, and after a long delay, I asked the waiter what was wrong—where was my breakfast? "The computer is down sir," came the reply. I commented to my colleagues at the table that one will be hearing that excuse far more often in the future. My delayed breakfast was not the fault of the waiter or the cook. Not even the manager could be blamed. Only the computer manufacturer, programmer, or installer, all long since gone, could be responsible for the fact that my breakfast was delayed. The diffusion of responsibility serves certain interests, and it is important in each instance to identify them carefully. We are in deep trouble if we can't identify a human agent for these kinds of problems and hold them immediately responsible. But there are still other dangers.

Some intellectual prophets have declared the end of the age of knowledge and the beginning of the age of information. Information tends to drive out knowledge. Information is just signs and numbers, while knowledge has semantic value. What we want is knowledge, but what we often get is information. It is a sign of the times that many people cannot tell the difference between information and knowledge, not to mention wisdom, which even knowledge tends sometimes to drive out.

I've examined just one of the many impacts that the new sciences of complexity will have on the world—that in the financial services industry. There are other impacts—on education, medicine, and the legal profession. The computer, a new mode of production, has come into existence and created new classes of people, new jobs, and new forms of wealth. What I find especially interesting about this development is that abstract mathematics, sophisticated algorithms, and vanguard technology are going to determine the future of industries and professions long immune to such changes.

Someday, sooner than many people think, the sciences of complexity will impact on the legal system, not just in data processing but in actual decision making. Could an expert system replace an attorney or at least assist one? Probably a lot of mundane legal work can be done by computers, and lawyers will discover that they can serve their clients better by using computers. The use of content addressable memories, for example, would be a great aid in case work. Right now the impact of the new sciences of complexity on the legal profession is still minimal; but this will soon change.

A new salient of knowledge is being created, and our generation is privileged to see it unfold. Like all great changes throughout the course of human history, it provides challenge, opportunity, hope, and danger. We stand on the threshold of the human mastery of complexity—an agenda for science that may show us, for the first time, who and what we truly are.

Information, be it embodied in organisms, the mind, or the culture, is part of a larger selective system that determines through successful competition or cooperation what information survives. Information can be encoded in genes, nerve nets, or institutions, but the selective system that promotes survival remains similar. This insight is hardly original. Yet it remains a mystery to me why philosophers, psychologists, and social and cultural scientists have rarely grasped the import of the Darwin-Wallace notion of selection for their own work (this has recently been changing). A selective system is a pattern producing and recognizing system, be it the pattern of life on earth, the symbolic order of the mind, or the pattern of culture. A selective system manages complexity.

In the next part of the book I will take the reader on an intellectual journey through a forest of several philosophical issues that bear on contemporary science—the nature of material reality, the problem of cognition, the body-mind problem, the character of scientific research, the nature of mathematics, and the role of instruments in the conduct of inquiry. The issues form, in part, the framework of our thinking about the scientific enterprise, an enterprise that is now opening a new frontier—the frontier of complexity, exploring the very order of the mind, life, and nature.

Part II
PHILOSOPHY AND
ANTIPHILOSOPHY

Chapter 8

The Building Code
of the Demiurge

*Out yonder there was this huge world, which exists independent
of us human beings and which stands before us like a great,
eternal riddle, at least partially accessible to our inspection and
thinking. The contemplation of this world beckoned like a liberation, and I soon noticed that many a man whom I had
learned to esteem and to admire had found inner freedom and
security in devoted occupation with it.*

—ALBERT EINSTEIN
Autobiographical Notes

Back in the 1970s I met a group of people on the cliffs overlooking
the south coast of Big Sur, anticipating the imminent arrival of
extraterrestrial beings. The visitors from the other side of the galaxy were in a giant spacecraft hidden neatly behind the moon,
where it could not be detected. They had already sent messengers
to Earth, artificial human beings, assembled "molecule by molecule" to confound scientists. I wanted to meet one of them and
ask him questions about modern physics that were puzzling me;
but no one knew how to tell who they were.

Enrico Fermi, the nuclear physicist, when asked about the existence of extraterrestrials, responded that they are here already;

they are called Hungarians. Fermi was struck, like many of his colleagues, by the fact that the small nation of Hungary had produced so many brilliant scientists—the mathematician John von Neumann, the physicists Leo Szilard, Eugene Wigner, and Edward Teller—and that perhaps another, unearthly explanation was required for this intellectual excess. Whenever I think of the space behind the moon, I cannot help imagining all those Hungarians in their giant spacecraft, ready to come here and confound us with their genius.

I like the idea that the universe is teeming with benign life; it makes those vast empty spaces between the stars seem friendlier. I take comfort in the thought that there is no way to conclusively prove that life near other stars does not exist except by going there and checking, and that's unlikely in the near future. The most that scientists can do today is to assign rough probabilities for the existence of extraterrestrial life. They disagree rather strongly about those probabilities; they even disagree about what "life" means.

My opinion (and it is no more than that) is that even if my guess is right and there is lots of life in the rest of the galaxy, then it is extremely unlikely that such extraterrestrial life has either the capability of or any interest in contacting humanity. Given the vastness of space and the available differences in evolutionary times, the likelihood is that extraterrestrial life will either be too primitive to be able to contact us or it will be millions of years in advance of us, know the state of affairs rather well, and have little interest in us. My point is that it would be extraordinary if any other life in our galaxy had evolved precisely to the stage of our technological society today or to one just enough in advance of us that it possesses both the means and the interest in contacting us.

In spite of such arguments against our ever contacting extraterrestrial life, many people eagerly await the day when humanity first directly confronts an alien intelligence. That day, if it comes, would be perhaps the most exciting day in the long history of humanity; it would alter our view of our place in the universe and the future of our species.

Rather than simply passively waiting, some astronomers are actively planning to search for signals from outer space—this is the SETI project. SETI, an acronym for Search for ExtraTerrestrial Intelligence, is a proposal to use a radio telescope, tuned to receive signals at a propitious frequency, and to listen in on possible planets near local stars. The SETI astronomers hope to hear intelligent signals. Other astronomers think that we are alone in the galaxy and that any such search is a waste of scarce resources. It is hard to prejudge the prospects of SETI's success—the project is an exciting long shot in any case.

I'm not sure if looking for an alien intelligence in outer space is the only place to look. I think that there is One here already.

Imagine for a moment a creator, the Demiurge, much as most medieval Europeans did—a Being who made the universe as his personal creation. There is something comfortable and cozy about the belief in a creator God. Most scientists like myself intellectually reject this belief as hopelessly inadequate and without evidence. And so it seems to be. Even reflective religious people think that it is a sacrilege to look for evidence of God in the natural world. But we will entertain the notion of the Demiurge for the sake of our argument. After all, you don't have to *believe* in the Demiurge to *imagine* that a Being made the stars, Earth, and moon, the plants, animals, and us—surely a highly intelligent Being. For my purposes the Demiurge is a good model for the Alien Intelligence from whom we are currently getting intelligent signals. How does the communication system work? Let us first examine a simple example of the kind of communication system that I have in mind.

Suppose a group of archaeologists discover the ruins of an ancient civilization buried underground and covered by jungle. At first they know almost nothing—just the fact that the civilization existed. But as they clear away the ground and jungle they find buildings, temples, and tombs. Slowly, over a period of decades, from the artifacts and pictorial inscriptions, they begin to piece together the history of an ancient people—they are interpreting the information inherent in the ruins. The ruins may thus be viewed as a message, an intelligible structure, and the ancient people who built the civilization as the "alien intelligence" from whom the archaeologists are receiving the message. One does not usually think of artifacts from the human past as a communications link; but that is indeed one way they function.

Imagine now, instead of the ruins of an ancient civilization as the intelligible structure, that the material universe, the "ruins" of the hot big bang, contains a kind of message. The universe, after all, like the ruins, has a definite structure, it is intelligently organized, and that organization can be studied by natural scientists. The universe itself may thus be viewed as the communications link between the Alien Intelligence—the Demiurge who created it —and us.

Although the idea that the universe has an order that is governed by natural laws that are not immediately apparent to the senses is very ancient, it is only in the last three hundred years that we have discovered a method for uncovering that hidden order— the scientific-experimental method. So powerful is this method that virtually everything scientists know about the natural world comes from it. What they find is that the architecture of the universe is indeed built according to invisible universal rules, what I call the cosmic code—the building code of the Demiurge. Examples of this universal building code are the quantum and relativity theory, the laws of chemical combination and molecular structure, the rules that govern protein synthesis and how organisms are made, to name but a few. Scientists in discovering this code are deciphering the Demiurge's hidden message, the tricks he used in creating the universe. No human mind could have arranged for any message so flawlessly coherent, so strangely imaginative, and sometimes downright bizarre. It must be the work of an Alien Intelligence!

What about mathematics? Is there a "message" in the structure of mathematics such as the one I envision in the structure of the physical universe? Can we also view it as the work of an Alien Intelligence? Mathematics, after all, does not depend directly on observing the physical world to keep it honest; the demand for formal consistency suffices. In spite of obvious differences between mathematics and natural science, the way in which discovery appears in the two fields is not all that different.

Let us imagine that the Demiurge also has the power to create logic—the set of all consistent rules that lets us manipulate symbols. If there is a "message" in mathematics, then it seems to be even more alien than the one in the physical universe. The Demiurge really let his imagination go creating mathematics—lots of different kinds of numbers, infinite dimensional spaces, bizarre geometries, and strange algebras for which we see no relation to the physical world. The conceptual objects of mathematics often relate to one another and form a mental world. Mathematicians explore this alien world and examine its conceptual objects, which are by design coherent structures that all follow from simple axioms and definitions. But mathematics, in spite of the fact that it seems set up, can still be viewed as an alien message because sometimes its discovered content is so utterly surprising that it seems like a novel discovery, not a necessity.

One feature of mathematics that is being increasingly emphasized today is that mathematics is not produced out of nothing, it is a product of human brains or of computers. Mathematical thought does not exist by itself in a kind of logical space but must be embodied in a material structure like a brain. Material structures obey the laws of nature—the cosmic code—and perhaps this limits the kind of mathematics that can be produced. The connection between possible mathematics and the cosmic code may be more intimate than we think.

One of the odd features of the cosmic code is that, as far as we can tell, the Demiurge has written himself out of the code—an alien message without evidence of an alien. Pierre Simon de Laplace, the great nineteenth-century French mathematical physicist, was asked by Napoleon what role God played in his scientific work, *Celestial Mechanics*, a post-Newtonian account of the dynamics of heavenly bodies. Laplace replied that he had no need to make such a hypothesis. Many modern physicists, adopting the fantasy of a Demiurge, think that the Creator had no choice in creating the universe the way he did—there is no choice about the message in the cosmic code. Some scientists, contesting this view, think he may have tried out other universes with different laws, but because those laws did not allow for the existence of life, the receiving end of the cosmic communication link was missing in those universes. Consequently life can never know about those other universes. Our own universe is all we can ever know, and here there seems to be no evidence that God exercised any option in creating it. Still another view is held by many rationalists who respond, like the philosopher Spinoza, that the search for reason in the universe and the search for God are the same search—the message is God.

Whether God is the message, wrote the message, or whether it wrote itself is unimportant in our lives. We can safely drop the traditional idea of a Demiurge, for there is no scientific evidence for a Creator of the natural world, no evidence for a will or purpose in nature that goes beyond the known laws of nature. Even the evidence of life on Earth, which promoted the compelling "argument from design" for a Creator, can be accounted for by evolution (excellent recent accounts are Richard Dawkins's *The Blind Watchmaker* [1986] or any of Stephen Jay Gould's books about evolution). So we have a message without a sender. But what is important is how this message, as it arrives through the agency of scientific discovery, functions in reordering our world. For it is by deciphering the cosmic code that scientists learn the rules that govern the material universe, how matter is made and life is organized. This knowledge, in turn, forms the basis for new technology—medical equipment, electronic communications systems, biotechnology, nuclear power—technologies that profoundly alter the human condition and opportunities for social development. In a sense, then, the program of human historical development is already written in the cosmic code.

The general topic of this book is the future of science and, in particular, the rise of the sciences of complexity and what they portend for our world. In order to understand the future of science I think it is important to first understand what science is and what it is not. I should state from the outset that this is a personal account—a fragment of my experience and, in part, autobiographical—and that not all scientists and others who have thought about these matters will agree with me.

Let us step back from this metaphor of the cosmic code and our strange communications channel with the Alien Being and ask ourselves: What is going on in the activity of science? What is it that scientists are seeking, and why do they have any reason to expect success in their search? These are the questions, especially as they apply to the natural and the cognitive sciences, I will be answering in the remainder of this and the next chapter.

I began asking such questions when I was an undergraduate physics major at Princeton University in the late 1950s. I could not have asked for a better group of inspired and qualified teachers of physics. The department had a policy that required even their top professors to teach undergraduates, an investment in time that pays off in the future of physics. But if I learned a lot from my professors, I learned equally from my friends among the other physics majors. We were a spectacular class, full of confidence and ambitious to make a contribution to science.

My lab partner, Boris, was ranked first in our entire undergraduate class, a circumstance that provoked some jealous grumbling among other physics majors. We felt that his distinction was not entirely deserved because Boris only took courses in science and math, subjects at which he excelled and got perfect grades. Most of us also took courses in literature, history, art, and political science in order to broaden our education. In these subjects it was difficult to get perfect grades because the grade criteria were "more subjective." We challenged Boris and told him in no uncertain terms that his being first meant nothing to us unless he exposed his grade point average to the vicissitudes of a "humanist's opinion." Boris responded by taking a course in the art department, something like medieval or Chinese art, and walked off with a perfect grade, much to our chagrin. Confident in his capacity, he took some more art courses. He graduated as class valedictorian.

We physics majors spent endless hours intensely arguing about physics and math problems and the meaning of science; a good balance between competition and cooperation prevailed. I was reminded of these arguments when years later I met a friend, a physicist of Chinese ancestry who had been educated in the United States. In the late 1970s he visited mainland China, where he was born, and gave some lectures. When I asked him about his experiences, he sounded discouraged. After his lectures, he reported, each of the students would go off to study alone; the verbal exchange and argumentation among students that characterized his education in the West was absent. "I thought things had changed because of the revolution," he said, "but it was the same old Mandarin system." He knew, as I did not at that time, that the acquisition of a set of intellectual skills was viewed in China as a means of supporting oneself and one's family. One does not share knowledge if resources are scarce. It never occurred to me that the free exchange of ideas among us undergraduates, something we took for granted, was influenced by the material abundance of our society. Today, as American undergraduates again become concerned about future jobs, there is more competition and less cooperative free exchange.

The physics faculty was too engaged in *doing* and *teaching* physics to think *about* it. Thinking *about* science was what the philosophers of science did. So persistent undergraduates like my classmates and I audited or took courses in the philosophy department. The department was fortunate in having Carl Hempel, a

logical-empiricist from the Vienna Circle led by the philosopher
Rudolf Carnap, and Hilary Putnam, a philosopher with an abiding
interest in theoretical physics (now at Harvard). Taking philosophy
courses was a rite of passage for us physics majors—once our
intellectual curiosity about what the philosophers were up to was
fulfilled, we got on to the business of science research. In these
courses I was introduced to the philosophy of logical-empiricism,
the operationalism of Percy Bridgman, the Harvard philosopher of
science, expressed in *The Logic of Modern Physics* (1927), the views
on space and time of Hans Reichenbach, the Russell-Whitehead
program in logic, Wittgenstein's worldview, the views of Karl Popper expressed in *The Logic of Scientific Discovery* (1935), which
had major impact on our thinking, and much more. Many of these
distinguished philosophers devoted their thinking to the analysis
and interpretation of the special claim that natural science had to
truth. They wanted to make the methods of science rigorous, and
their efforts helped clarify my thinking. As a young scientist my
reading of these philosophers supported my conviction that I was
engaged in one of the great adventures of the human spirit.

But the relation between scientists and philosophers of science
is like the relation between successful politicians and political scientists—one is interested in being effective while the other is interested in understanding the basis of that effectiveness. My
contact with the philosophy of science reinforced my conviction
that what I wanted to do was science, not to think about why it
worked. I wanted to read the cosmic code. Philosophers of science, I discovered, when they attempted to *do* science, often bun-
gle their research rather badly. (I am convinced from reading
Popper's recent books on quantum theory that he does not understand the theory, probably because he was misled by his philosophical agenda. Remarkably, he asserted that he was surprised when
certain experiments failed to violate quantum theory, a conclusion
few physicists would have reached.)

The reason philosophers and others often fare so poorly when
they attempt to do scientific research themselves is that scientists,
because of their professional training, embody a set of cognitive
skills and attitudes. The same thing happens to scientists, like myself, who undertake philosophical investigations. These skills and
attitudes, which the scientist-philosopher Michael Polanyi calls
"tacit knowledge," are not readily communicable. An example of

that tacit knowledge is the knowledge possessed by anyone who knows how to ride a bicycle. No amount of reading books or attending lectures on bike riding will train you to ride a bicycle—you will fail in your first attempt to ride. Likewise with certain cognitive and intuitive skills; they are implicit skills learned by your "silent partners" during a long training. The implicit skills of a scientist, like the skill of a bike rider, a dancer, or an actor are essential for his work. Other professionals, such as philosophers, do not have easy access to such implicit skills; they already have acquired their own cognitive skills appropriate to their professional tradition. My subsequent experience as a research physicist only confirms my earlier view that the nonverbal cognitive and intuitive component of scientific inquiry—an area about which little is known—is critical to its creative success.

The philosophers of science are right when they insist on rigor in scientific method; indeed scientists themselves insist on it. But this misses the main reason for the success of science. The success of scientific inquiry does not depend on scientists' rigorously adhering to some set of rules laid down by philosophers, scientists, or anyone else. Scientific inquiry is successful because it is, like the evolutionary process, a powerfully selective system. Scientific theories, by design, are always vulnerable to destruction just like a species, subjected to environmental pressure, is subject to extinction. Because of that vulnerability, scientific truth has the strength that comes of survival in a challenging environment. The skills of the scientist (adherence to rigor being but one of them) are practiced in the arena of intense criticism and experimental test—they are vulnerable to challenge and challenged they are. Even when scientific theories fail to survive, as most eventually do, their evolutionary progeny carry the best "genes"—the ideas that still work —of the previous theory intact. Ironically, it is the willingness to risk everything, even existence itself, that is the guarantor of survival. Welcome to the world of the scientific method—red in tooth and claw! I will devote a subsequent chapter to "the scientific method" (such as it is). But what is the end purpose of scientific inquiry?

Ultimately, all scientific activity—the thinking, observation, and experimentation—is devoted to the search for a coherent, conceptual representation of reality—a theory or picture of reality. Once one has such a picture of reality or even a partial picture, it has a rich implicative structure, not only for science, but for culture, technology, and commerce as well. Such pictures of reality show us new aspects of the building code of the universe, creating a mental picture that goes beyond anything we can grasp directly with our senses or instruments. And the motivation behind finding these theories is the scientist's desire to know what in heaven and hell is really going on.

A scientific theory can be thought of as a map, which, like an ordinary road map, shows us how to get around and describes the territory and the rules it obeys—rules like those that require that rivers on maps flow around mountains, not over them. Like real road maps, scientific theory "maps" work because there really is a territory "out there" in our shared experience that corresponds to them. There are grand, all-embracing maps like Einstein's theory of relativity or Darwin's theory of natural selection. But most maps that scientists use daily are smaller and more detailed, like the theory of metals or the theory of protein synthesis. Of course, the metaphor of a map will break down at some point because a map is a spatial entity, while a theory is a conceptual entity; nonetheless I find it is a useful metaphor.

Every major theory of the natural world postulates a law or hypothesis that is the conceptual kernel of the theory. For example, the laws of Newton in classical mechanics or the hypothesis that information goes from DNA to proteins and never vice versa in molecular biology are such postulated laws. In the metaphor of the map these laws simply reflect the general rules we use in making up the maps. Occasionally the scientific discovery of a new territory requires that the very rules for making maps have to be modified. Still, for every good map there is always a set of definite rules.

What do the natural laws correspond to in the world, and in what way do they exist? They are, as I will argue, following the Enlightenment philosopher Immanuel Kant, the organizing principles that render our experience of the natural world intelligible and coherent. These organizing principles are incorporated into a coherent logical framework called a theory. A theory thus provides a logical picture of the natural world, a picture that is, in part, a product of our minds and culture. But there is a part of a theory, in fact the most important part, which is *not* a product of our mind—what I will call the "invariant structure" of the theory. The "invariant structure" of a theory corresponds to those features of a theory that are independent of our specific description of the territory of nature and the rules it obeys. Not all theories possess such an "invariant structure," and historically such theories are terminal theories—dead ends in the evolution of scientific knowledge. For example, the theory that heat is a substance—phlogiston—had no invariant structure because heat is not a substance. But if the invariant structure of a theory exists in the natural world, then it cannot be removed by simply changing our theory. The invariant structures of theories are the building codes of the Demiurge.

Theories are pictures of the world and the relation of these pictures to their invariants reminds me of a telling story about the painter Pablo Picasso. He painted pictures rather than devising scientific theories, but he grasped the point I am making here, as the following story reveals. Picasso was riding in a train compartment with a stranger, who, recognizing Picasso, asked him why he didn't paint pictures of people "the way they really are." Picasso asked the man what he meant by "the way they really are," and the man pulled out of his wallet a snapshot of his wife and said, "That's my wife." Picasso responded: "Isn't she rather small and flat?" Theories are pictures made by people. But in both Picasso's paintings of people and the snapshot there is a human body—the invariant structure—that is being represented.

While it is clear that we, in part, *create* the maps, the descriptions of nature, the subjects of the maps, the territory, and its rules, which are not created by us, must by contrast be *discovered*. Think of two people playing chess and suppose you do not know the rules of the game. At first you notice the playing board and the differences between the pieces—the "territory" of the chess game. Then, upon observing how the people play, you discover the rules of the game—how it is started, the different moves of different pieces, and so on. The rules are clearly not given with the "territory" but specify how it can change. The rules and pieces thus define the game. Perhaps after a long time we find that our knowledge of the rules is incomplete—we observe one of the players "castle," a new rule. Likewise, our knowledge of the rules of nature may change in time. And, like the rules of chess, the rules of nature correspond to something "out there."

It matters not if you believe that the Earth rests on the back of a giant tortoise or is a planet orbiting the sun; in either case your theory is *about* the real world, the Earth and its motion. Gravitational theory is about gravity, atomic theory is about atoms, genetics is about DNA and its expression. This "furniture" of the scientific world constitutes what I will call the "repertoire of reality" and becomes reflected in the "invariant structure" of the corresponding theory. Atoms, bacteria, and genes may have been mere hypotheses at one time—guesses intended to correlate data and promote a research program. But if they are indeed there, they become part of the repertoire of reality. To be sure, the theoretical description of these entities may be constructed by our minds and are "regulative principles" we invent to render the world intelligible. Also our understanding of the repertoire of reality may change over time—atoms once thought to be indivisible can be split, the relativity of all motion turns out not to apply to the motion of light. Yet the recognition of a repertoire of reality implies that there is something independent of consciousness whose existence cannot be explained or "theorized away." While historically the objects of scientific investigation may begin as hypotheses, and while the demarcation between what is and is not an object is not always clear (a demarcation that can itself be examined), it seems to me that one cannot deny their existence without denying the existence of an objective world and the possibility of science in the first place.

We can carry our image of chess one step further. As we observe the different pieces and rules they obey, after a while we develop "a theory" of the game. The rules, we conclude, are not being exercised by the players in an arbitrary way but a very purposeful way—to win the game by capturing the opponent's king. This "theory" provides an overview of what is actually happening—why certain moves are being taken. The theory thus provides a coherent account of the action.

Likewise in science. If we apply the chess image, we could suppose that the pieces of chess correspond, for example, to atoms. The rules of the chess pieces correspond to the rules we see atoms obey—the rules governing the quantum jumps that produce the spectral lines. Finally the theory—in this example the quantum theory—provides a quantitative, coherent account of the rules and territory—an overview.

We thus have the objects of the world—the repertoire of reality

—the rules they obey, and finally, the grand theories, the pictures in our minds that integrate these components into a coherent whole. We have to describe the objects and rules somehow, and this description I will call a "representation"—the language of our theories. Some theories may appear different because they use different languages or representations. But they are in fact the same if they have the same "invariant structure." To see this let us examine the relation between representations and invariants in more detail.

The relation between an invariant and its representations can be easily grasped if we imagine a tree, or better still look at a real one. The tree can be represented or described in the English language—what kind of tree, the color of its leaves, its height, and so on. This is a linguistic representation, in the English language, of the tree. Likewise we can describe the same tree in Arabic or Chinese. These are different representations. The invariant structure, however, corresponds to those deep unchanging properties in the description of the tree that do not change with the language. Similarly, in order to express the invariant structure of a theory we must always use some representation—a specific language, often mathematical—but the invariant is really independent of that specific representation. A Frenchman and an Englishman will describe the pieces and rules of chess differently. Likewise, Newton's laws can be expressed lots of different ways, but the essential concept—the invariant concept—remains unaltered. In short, the rules for making maps may be expressed in different ways, but if we can translate one set of rules into another, they are, in fact, equivalent.

The invariant structure expressed by a theory is something that can, in principle, be checked by anyone because it corresponds to something in the world and not just in our minds. If these ideas are right, it is possible to do the following "thought experiment." Imagine that we establish contact with an extraterrestrial intelligence—a thinking crystal on some faraway planet that uses some kind of language. People have studied the problem posed by extraterrestrial languages—how do you communicate with an intelligence that has no knowledge of your language and culture? How to create a lingua franca for the universe? Clearly one must appeal to "common" experience. It would be possible to send the number for π—the ratio of the circumference to the diameter of a circle—

in a binary code (the simplest code) because probably even thinking crystals know about geometry—it's logical. In this way the
common language of mathematics could eventually be established. The next step in communication would be to appeal to the
existence of invariants—the deep structure of the material world.
We could try sending Maxwell's equations for the electromagnetic
field as a starter. Even thinking crystals ought to know about those
laws because they refer to entities—electromagnetic waves—
which are invariant structures even in a thinking crystal's world,
although they may represent those laws very differently from the
way we do. By contrast, if we tried to communicate our feelings or
emotions, these might not translate into anything that a thinking
crystal can comprehend. Only the invariant elements of the repertoire of reality and its rules stand a chance of being communicated. In this respect, the findings of natural science resemble
those of pure mathematics.

Kant was the first person to clearly articulate the relation between theories of the natural world and the world itself. While
today some of his ideas are museum pieces of eighteenth-century
thought, the essential framework of his philosophy remains intact;
every modern philosophy of science is deeply influenced by it.

Kant, in my view, created a great schism in the world of knowledge and between the people who think about it. The schism was
the separation between those who *think about* and *experiment*
with the natural world (today called scientists) and those who *think
about* how scientists think about the world (today called philosophers of science). While this distinction certainly existed before
Kant, after him it became a true schism. Due to Kant, the philosophical emphasis shifted from the world and what was in it to
how we know that world and the nature of our knowledge about
it. Kant thus launched a philosophical research program in understanding science that continues to this day. The program is called
the "philosophy of science," and its adherents talk mostly to themselves and have had little influence on science as practiced by
those who do it. Scientists, for their part, are often "antiphilosophers" (like the physicist Richard Feynman). They feel that you
express your "philosophy of science" by actually practicing it. All
the great scientists have created their own philosophy—their
work. But it is not easy to master modern science well enough so
that you can practice it, and this difficulty also aggravates the
schism between scientists and philosophers.

Kant's philosophy about how we comprehend the world, expressed in his *Critique of Pure Reason,* is very complex and difficult, but the central ideas can be simply presented in terms of a "Kantian cartoon"—a picture of how Kant saw the relation of the world to the mind. Imagine four concentric spheres that represent the transition from the outer to the inner world. The outermost sphere represents "the thing in itself," and it is dark—we have no way of knowing what it is. Things in themselves for Kant are not objects, they do not exist in space and time, and notions such as singular and plural do not apply to them. Moving inward, the next sphere, in our cartoon, is the sphere corresponding to the natural world. That sphere is illuminated—we certainly have experience of a world that exists in public space and time. This sphere corresponds to the territory in our map metaphor. The next sphere inward represents the knowing mind—the cognitive world of our mental representations, our experience. It also possesses the internal sense of time. This sphere is illuminated because we have access to the contents of our knowing mind. This is the sphere in which our maps of the natural world exist. Finally the innermost sphere of this cartoon model of the Kantian ego is also dark. It is the ultimate source of our cognitions and thoughts and is inscrutable. According to Kant, neither the outermost sphere, the thing in itself, or the innermost sphere, the mind in itself, are researchable. This accords with Kant's view that a science of psychology (as distinct from neurophysiology) is really impossible—we cannot have direct access to the source of our thoughts. We can, however, examine the empirical or phenomenal self.

Let us provisionally accept this Kantian model of the mind and of reality. How then is it possible to have coherent, invariant maps of reality? After all, everyone lives in their own world of experience; my experience is different from yours, and both of our experiences of the world differ from that of an ancient Egyptian. What we think of the world is historically conditioned. A thousand years from now our current conceptual universe, our view of reality, may seem archaic and odd. It seems as if everyone lives in their own privately constructed world—a possible world. These "possible worlds" reflect the differences between cultures and societies, professional interests and personalities—in short, human intention.

Kant's position on the question of the historical and social conditioning of knowledge is quite clear—it does not apply to our knowledge of natural objects. There is one shared, public natural world, and it is studied by science. But some contemporary philosophers take issue with this.

The contemporary philosopher Nelson Goodman has especially espoused this view—that there is no aboriginal natural reality, just a plurality of realities. The world of appearance is "created" by the mind, and there is no ultimate reality "out there," a construct of our minds, with a privileged status. Goodman's philosophy—a philosophy of understanding that pays passing tribute to Kant—has had some influence on contemporary psychologists (interestingly they have never succeeded in creating a coherent map of the mind just as Kant suggested), but no influence that I know of on nautral scientists. Jerome Bruner, a distinguished cognitive psychologist, has echoed Goodman: "I have argued . . . for a constructivist view of reality: that we cannot know an aboriginal reality; that there is none; that any reality we create is based on a transmutation of some prior 'reality' that we have taken as given. We construct many realities, and do so from differing intentions."

While such views may help some people come to grips with the plurality of human experience and may speak to the philosophical needs of some psychologists, they do not console the natural scientist with his or her ontological commitment to the existence of an aboriginal reality. While our minds, on the basis of our experience, may indeed "construct a reality"—make a map—of the natural world, this does not mean that such maps are *arbitrary* constructs. The maps of the natural world incorporate those "invariants" that are independent of the specific representations that we do, in fact, construct. By "an aboriginal reality" I do not mean the Kantian "thing in itself" (which is inscrutable), but the territory of our shared experience, the world of appearance. Any competent individual is invited to check their experience, their "construction of reality," to see if it indeed conforms to a scientific map.

A theory of the natural world builds on a previous theory, a "prior 'reality' that we have taken as given." But it builds on a previous theory by incorporation of what works and rejection or modification of what doesn't work. Scientific knowledge, like the evolution of life, is a selective system. Theories of the natural world evolved from the organic-divine construction of the Middle Ages, to the mechanistic universe of Newton, to the quantum universe of today. And today's view is surely not the final answer —we will discover more. Like an evolving species, there is no final "perfection," no final picture of reality that is valid for all eternity. Yet the theories we have invented today correspond to what we experience and observe, incorporating the known repertoire of reality, an invariant order that is independent of our representation of it and which will surely form the basis of a future theory. In short, the "aboriginal reality" is the invariant structure of the world as revealed by the historical progress of science. Theories of the earth, the stars, the brain, living cells, or atoms may come and go, but these entities remain.

I can sympathize and identify with the intent of the natural philosophers of centuries, even millennia, ago as they struggled to comprehend the universe into which we are all born, seeking an invariant order beyond the welter of experience and feeling. That *intent* to comprehend the universe has been a persistent theme since the earliest time, a continuous motive to read the message of the Demiurge and to discover the repertoire of reality. As Edwin Hubble, the American astronomer, remarked, "The urge is older than history. It is not satisfied and it will not be suppressed."

I would submit that the invariants we find in the natural world are most easily understood as being implicit in the actual organization of the material world, just as the organizational principles of a building are implicit in its actual structure. While the pluralistic "possible worlds" view of Goodman may apply to the world made by men and women—the world of art, literature, law, and history—it does not apply to the natural world. The "possible worlds" view is only possible, in my opinion, because there is actually only *one* public natural world. And that is why the "possible worlds" of other people and other cultures are even intelligible. In short, what the Demiurge has put together no man can take apart, but what man has put together he most certainly can (and will) take apart.

While I do not share Goodman's view about the natural world (I have been called an unreconstructed "naive realist," maybe even a "scientific fundamentalist"—bad character types for philosophers), I do find his views very important for educational philosophy and useful in exploring, understanding, and empathizing with other cultures, beliefs, and conditions of life. I like to spend hours, even days, exploring other worlds by adopting the belief that I am, for example, an automaton without "free will," a political rightist or leftist, a woman, or a person, of another race and culture. (Readers may try this at their own risk.) Good actors, and novelists, are adept at this. While it is easy to get carried away in such role playing because my suppressed silent partners are finally getting their say, this psychological technique does give me access to other "possible worlds" to see how they are indeed constructed and what feelings and values hold them together from within. Sometimes, not always, I return to my own world enriched if for no other reason than that I have affirmed my limits. We are all actors; but most of us only know one role.

Scientists play a "communications game" with the territory of their experience—they try to extract as much information about reality as possible and score a point every time a more coherent and complete theory of reality on the basis of that information is constructed. Scientists want to find these theories because they show them a conceptual reality, a deep logical structure, that is otherwise hidden and that renders the world comprehensible. That comprehension not only relieves the frustration of the searching that preceded it, but reveals, for the first time, what is really going on. The main *feeling* I get from new theories is the same feeling I get from a wondrous revelation—the awe an infant feels upon discovering that a hidden order, a new world waiting to be discovered, exists beyond the house door, and *that's* why things within the house are the way they are.

It's important for us to understand what scientific theories are because they help define what a science is and establish its peculiar and limited claim to truth. But before outlining the properties of theories, I should summarize my own overall viewpoint. The invariant order of nature that is expressed in our theories—the cosmic code—is possible because the material world is actually organized in that way. While our theories are free inventions of our minds, the invariants they express not only inform the coherence of our experience, they reflect the actual material structure of nature as well. Or to say the same thing, the invariants are there in the natural world. I will argue (not prove!), first, that this natural invariant order is the *only* universal, coherent order, and, second, that anything else for which a scientific theory can reasonably be expected to exist is a consequence of that invariant order. Other forms of order such as those created by human beings—law, religion, the economy, society, literature, and art—are not primarily a consequence of the material order of nature, and we have no reason to expect that there is a hidden invariant order represented in a scientific theory that describes them. This humanly created order has a history (unlike the natural order which is eternal) that reflects the changing intentional system of human consciousness —belief, desire, thought, and feeling. It is an order created by human beings and, therefore, understood by them. Interestingly, our modern world embodies the clash between the consequences of the recently discovered material order of the universe and the older and still ongoing humanly created order, a clash that lies at the center of the intellectual dialectic of our time. But first, what are the properties of a scientific theory?

The main properties of scientific theories that postulate an invariant structure are that they be logically coherent, universal, and vulnerable to destruction. Let us examine these features in turn.

Scientific theories have got to be organized according to the canons of logic. If they are logical, then we can check that each theory is internally consistent, and different theories, covering overlapping regions of reality, cannot contradict one another. We don't even have the option of checking consistency if the theories are not logical. From an inconsistent theory one can prove anything (and its contradiction; so such a theory is useless). One way of making sure that theories are logical is for them to piggyback, in part, on the logic inherent in mathematics, although that is not necessary. A scientific theory need not be quantitative, as was Darwin's original formulation of the theory of evolution, or even mathematical, but it must be logically precise.

Scientific theories, because of their logical coherence, let us explore new territory with confidence, and if they are good theories, we can explore *deep* into the territory of reality. Because of their coherence power, scientific theories have an implicative structure—they point to new regions, unanticipated things to be discovered. This predictive capacity of theories is most impressive. When experimental physicists at the high-energy accelerator at CERN recently discovered the quantum particles W and $Z°$ with their masses right on the values predicted by an abstract mathematical theory, it impressed even the discoverers. The vindication by experiment is rare but exciting and is the signal that we really have a very good theory in our hands.

What distinguishes scientific theories from the pictures of reality provided by religion, culture, or politics is the intention of their creators that they be useful theories independent of their user's religion, culture, politics, sex, race, personality, feelings, or opinions. This is perhaps the most socially and culturally distinguishing feature of science—it is universal in the sense that its truths are true for *everyone*.

There is another sense in which scientific theory is universal— it is true for *everything*. Like the numbers, a scientific theory is universal; it applies indifferently to everything within its domain. It can stretch from an earthbound lab to the most distant galaxies. The discoveries about proteins or properties of membranes in a cell are true for all such cells.

This universality is precisely why scientific theories are interesting to some people and uninteresting to others. Some people are interested in indifferent, universal knowledge, others in historical, often personal knowledge with a narrative quality.

Here is a story that illustrates the differences in attitude that people have to universal versus particular knowledge. Once I was a guest at a New York City dinner party with a group of well-educated people. They were writers, editors, and intellectuals; not a scientist in the group except for me. Somehow the conversation got around to *The New York Review of Books*, a fine book review magazine that went well beyond just reviewing books—it effectively had essays and reflective articles of high intellectual quality. The *Review*, more than perhaps any other contemporary magazine, helped foster rapid intellectual communication at a very high cultural level. I avidly read and liked it (although it was a bit too Anglophilic for my American taste).

But I went on to describe my problem: I couldn't remember anything that I read in it. The information went into short-term memory storage and never got into my long-term memory. The reason for this, I had decided, was that in spite of the consistently brilliant style of writing, and the quality of the narrative, all that was being expressed in effect was one person's opinion about another person's thinking or actions. It is difficult for me to remember people's opinions (even my very own). What I remember are concepts and facts, the invariants of experience, not the ephemera of human opinion, taste, and styles. Such trivia are not to be considered by serious people, except as intellectual recreation.

Silence followed my brief remarks, and I felt isolated. The rift between the two cultures—science and humanism—widened considerably. I realized that in my blundering I had violated the sacred precincts of the other guests' high temple. Those people worshiped in that temple which was dedicated to political opinion, taste, and style, to a consciousness dominated by self-reflection, belief, and feeling, and intellectual gossip and activity for its own sake, only loosely bound by the constraints of knowledge. I tried to think of a joke to extract myself from an awkward situation but could not. Instead I made a few mollifying remarks to the effect that the expression of opinions was probably important in the political arena even by people who understood nothing of the political decision-making process if for no other reason than to preserve the sense of their intellectual freedom.

Scientists constitute numerically a small component of our culture, but one that is continuously growing in influence. Much of what calls itself "science" (the word is much abused) in fact is not. Most people, even educated people, do not yet grasp the fundamental character of scientific knowledge and the implications of our yet tenuous hold upon it. They may think it is a matter of opinion, reflects class interests, and is somehow "political," even anticultural or antireligious. The primary motive force behind science does not depend on such social factors (although they are important). It is the demands that the objects of investigation place on the investigator that move science. The public does not always see this motive because the objects of investigation seem so abstract. To be sure, the quantum theory or the theory of molecular genetics seem very abstract and removed from immediate human experience; but they have the supreme virtue of being true for anyone who chooses to examine them closely. And that is why such universal knowledge is both rare and important and will continue to transform the human condition.

Finally, theories must accord with experience and experiments. If a theory accords with the experience of all competent investigators, it is "right"; otherwise it is either wrong or not a scientific theory. Although the founding principles on which a theory is based cannot be directly checked against experiment, these principles logically imply statements that *are* directly testable. For example, Schrödinger's equation, which describes the dynamics of quantum particles, may be viewed as a founding principle. One can't test the equation directly. But one can rigorously deduce lots of results, like the energy levels of atoms and nuclei from Schrödinger's equation, and check these results against experiment. This is called the application of the theory. If the application fails, and the result is logically connected to the principle, then the principle must fail as well. If it succeeds in one application, we cannot, of course, conclude that the equation is right. But if it succeeds in application after application, again and again, scientists in fact go on to develop such confidence in the correctness of principle—the Schrödinger equation, in this case—that they accept it, too, as "right." The decision to accept a principle as "right" is made on the basis of consensus and judgment and not a strict logical procedure. While a theory must be logically rigorous, the decision that it is "right" is not.

This application procedure brings out a unique feature of scientific theories—they contain the recipes for their own destruction. A theory can't be right if it can't also be wrong. At any time some clever person may find a new application, usually in some new previously unexplored territory of reality, that will bring the theory down and destroy the consensus. Theories of the world or the mind provided by religion or psychoanalysis are not scientific because they can't self-destruct; they have been created that way. But that doesn't mean they are unimportant and not helpful; they are simply not scientific. Every truly scientific theory goes around with a bomb, ready to go off, strapped to its side. This vulnerability to destruction means that scientific theory is the result of a self-selected system like the evolutionary system. Any theory that makes it, like a species that makes it in an ecological niche, has got survival power in its assigned territory of reality.

Now, what reason do we have to expect such theories exist?

To answer this difficult question I have found it useful to examine what mathematicians say about the existence of mathematical objects. Interestingly, they disagree about what constitutes an existence proof of such an object. One group of mathematicians —the formalists led by David Hilbert earlier in this century—accepted proofs that logically demonstrated that a mathematical object, let's say a six-dimensional space with specific properties, had to exist even though they did not explicitly construct the space. This was called an existence proof. Another group—the intuitionists, led by L.E.J. Brouwer—was more tough-minded and only accepted such proofs if the object was actually mathematically constructed. This was called proof by construction. Constructive proofs are usually far more difficult to find than existence proofs, and that's why most mathematicians follow Hilbert's tack; they want to make rapid progress.

I am attracted to this constructivist demand, not so much for mathematics (for which the formalist methods are sufficiently rigorous), but as a requirement for speculative science and philosophy. Nothing destroys a poorly-thought-out idea faster than the requirement of detailed design or construction. While creative speculation is essential to the conduct of inquiry in its initial stages, inquiry cannot end in speculative fantasy. That is too easy. The end result must be a construction—a definite logical model, material apparatus, or experiment that implements the initial speculation. With the sole demand of construction, all of speculative thought is reduced to what it usually is—an intellectual fantasy having little to do with the actual world.

When it comes to the complex and ambiguous question of deciding whether a scientific theory can exist, I see no alternative to being tough-minded and demanding that it actually be constructed. In the natural sciences they do exist; we have them in hand. They are the quantum and relativity theory, evolutionary theory, genetics, chemistry, biochemistry, molecular biology—a vast, interlocking, and interacting set of theories. Because we have these theoretical maps we have a much clearer picture of material reality than we did in the past. The maps are continually being revised and edited; they have not yet described vast unknown territories—the origin of the universe and of life, brain function, to name a few. But the idea that scientific theories exist and work the way we expect them to is a fact. And they exist only if we can construct them.

How are such maps of reality possible? On the face of it, it seems a miracle that they exist—a logic behind reality, a cosmic code regulating the structure of everything in the universe! Kant thought that they were possible because the logic of nature and the logic of the mind accorded with each other. I don't disagree with Kant, but I think that the accord between the mind and nature is less of a miracle if one accepts the premise that the human mind itself is a biological phenomenon and therefore is itself subject to the rules of nature—the cosmic code.

To illustrate this accord suppose I give you a text written in a language you have never seen before. I teach you the language and after a while you are reading, with comprehension, the foreign text. Next I give you a text that looks like a foreign language but is really just random gibberish. No amount of teaching will ever get you to learn that language because there is nothing there to learn. Why was the first text intelligible and the second not? Surely the fact that you have a mind that already knows one language and can learn another language and can also comprehend order is critically important. But equally important is the fact that one text had a comprehensible order while the other did not. Likewise, the order of nature that we perceive—the cosmic code—is there because the material world is really organized that way.

I believe that the natural order is the *only* coherent, universal order, and that anything in the universe of mind and matter for which we can find a scientific theory or an invariant structure is ultimately a consequence of that order. Other scientists who explore the territories of reality that are not linked or contiguous to the universal material order of the universe have no reason to find an underlying theory—a cosmic code—such as I have described. I cannot even *imagine* how a theory of this kind not based on the material world order could exist.

It is important to emphasize that if this view is correct, then there may be no scientific theory of the kind that I have described for human intentionality—for beliefs, feelings, speech acts, or consciousness in general—except inasmuch as consciousness is subject to the conditions of the material world. In a sense consciousness is in part independent of, yet completely supported by, the material world.

As scientists search for the underlying theories of the natural world, a problem arises because the human mind is so remarkably well disposed to see patterns that it will find them even when there are none. Some people will see an order even in the random text. Maybe, they think, the text isn't random and contains a hidden message, and they make up a set of rules to interpret that text. That's pretty hard to do if the text is completely random, but suppose instead of random words it consists of random paragraphs, and they invent a theory of how the paragraphs relate to each other. It is extraordinarily difficult to convince people who want to believe in a deeper level of reality that there is no order in a set of random events. Often when they can't find a coherent order and think there must be one, they blame it on their method —they do not conclude the deeper representation simply doesn't exist. That's why it is necessary to be tough-minded when it comes to deciding if a theory describing a reality really has a claim to truth. Most do not.

It's very hard to find scientific theories of reality. To illustrate this difficulty I'd like to tell a short parable.

Once upon a time there was a philosopher-king in the fifteenth century who was a great lover of truth. He wanted to understand how the world worked, the stars and moon moved, the origin of the sun. For reasons of his own this king was dissatisfied with the physics of Aristotle and the cosmology of Ptolemy, the theories that held sway at that time. He called all his noblemen together and told them that they were charged with the holy duty of bringing to his court the twelve most brilliant men and women in the known world. These twelve geniuses were to meet in the court's map room and deliberate, pooling their knowledge, and come up with a new theory of the universe in one year. The king, a wise man, decided against richly rewarding the twelve for their work should they succeed or punishing them should they fail. Love of the truth alone should be their motivation.

The twelve were found, and they *were* the most brilliant people of the known world. They began their deliberations after being charged by the king to assume that all the current views might be wrong and "to begin again" (he was a very powerful king who could risk the wrath of the Church). At first the savants strongly disagreed with one another, but then, as they knew that the truth could only be one thing and not another, they began to cooperate and agree. At the end of the year they gave their report to the king at an impressive ceremony.

The report began conventionally. The savants said that the world was divided into substance and appearance—substance being how things really were and appearance how they seemed to be to our senses. Understanding the world of appearance required careful observation and sometimes experimentation. By contrast, the world of substance that lay beyond mere appearance could be known by reason alone; just as the truths of geometry were known by reason alone. In their report the savants proposed to focus on substance that could be known directly by unblemished reason, not appearance, which required the testimony of the doubtable senses.

The king, who had heard this before, interrupted the reading of the report and asked how the laws of motion could be deduced by reason alone. For example, how could he establish from reason alone that bodies of different weight had to fall at exactly the same rate under the influence of gravity, a fact he had demonstrated empirically by dropping cannon balls and musket balls from a tower? One of the savants stepped forth and gave the following argument.

He said assume, to the contrary, that heavier bodies fall faster than lighter ones. Then imagine attaching a chain between the heavy body and the light one and dropping the two bodies together. The heavy body, according to the assumption, would fall faster than the light one, and the chain would pull tight. The light body would, in effect, then be restraining the more rapid fall of the heavy body so that the two bodies, chained together, fall slower than the heavy body. But the two bodies taken together clearly weigh more than the heavy body alone and hence, according to the assumption, ought to fall faster than the heavy body. We have reached a logical contradiction—the joint system must fall both faster and slower than the heavy body alone—and thus the hypothesis we began with is false. The only logical possibility, concluded the savant, is that all bodies fall at exactly the same rate. (The reader who is convinced that the equal rate of fall is an empirical, not a logical, fact can have some fun finding the error in this reasoning.)

The king was very impressed with this logical argument (actually due to Galileo), which showed that there was no need to do experiments to determine the order of nature like dropping heavy balls from leaning towers. It was cited as a new "paradigm" of how science could and should be done in the future—careful logical deduction and argumentation uncontaminated by the flawed evidence of the senses.

The report went on. The savants concluded that the cosmology of Ptolemy with the Earth at the center of the universe, while it accorded with observation, was but mere appearance. The sun, the most magnificent of all heavenly bodies and free of earthly corruption, should be at the center of the universe. The heliocentric solar system was the substance that lay beyond the appearances. Thus they anticipated Copernicus's correct views.

But they went on. They divided the material world into six basic substances—earth, fire, air, water, ether, and magnetism. The mental or spiritual world was divided into five substances—satanic, demonic, human, angelic, and divine—which acted in different organs of the body. They went on to argue that Aristotle's law of motion, which stated that under a constant force a material body moved with a constant speed (as a block being pushed across the floor), held for perfect bodies such as the planets, which clearly had a constant speed in their orbits around the sun, and objects sliding on perfect surfaces.

When the twelve wise men ended their report, the king, very impressed, thanked them and gave each an unanticipated rich reward. They lived happily ever after.

We can see from our vantage point today that the twelve geniuses, although right about some things, were mostly wrong. The lesson of this parable is that in spite of the brilliance of people, if the right categories of thought, the instrumentation, and data are not available, they cannot produce a scientific theory. The methods for solving the problems that the twelve geniuses were charged with solving did not become available until three or more centuries later. We have the advantage of hindsight and know such theories are possible in the natural sciences—we have them at hand. But what about other sciences—the psychological and social sciences? Are there theories of the kind I described available? As Howard Gardner, a psychologist who has sympathetically but critically reviewed the cognitive sciences, has written: "By the middle of the twentieth century, two major mysteries of ancient times—the nature of physical matter and the nature of living matter—were well on their way to be unraveled. At the same time, however, a third mystery that had also fascinated the ancients—the enigma of the human mind—had yet to achieve comparable clarification." What are the grounds for believing such a "comparable clarification" is at all possible? Why do some scientists believe that there is an invariant structure to human cognition? In the next chapter I will explicitly focus my remarks on the cognitive sciences—a contemporary intellectual development within the purview of empirical psychology and computer science.

Chapter 9

Waiting for the Messiah

Sometimes truth comes riding into history on the back of error.
—REINHOLD NIEBUHR

Back in the early 1960s a major psychology conference was held on behavior. Researchers presented paper after paper on the learning behavior of rats—how they ran mazes with their brains monitored electronically or rats on drugs and so on. Then someone presented a paper on human behavior. In the question period that followed the presentation, a member of the audience asked the following question, half in jest: "This is a very interesting paper on human behavior. But what does it tell us about the *rat?*" The audience laughed, perhaps in nervous acknowledgment that the emphasis of psychology was about to change.

Cognitive science emerged in the 1950s and 1960s in part as a critical reaction to behaviorism—the view that one could study animals and humans as input-output systems, the input was sensory stimulation, reward and punishment, while the output was behavior—a view that dominated American psychology until then. Cognitive scientists thought that strict behaviorism with its theory of the reflex arc was too limiting and ignored important human mental functions such as language. They also thought it was conceptually wrong—that lots of behavior is not imposed from without but originates inside the organism.

The intellectual program of the cognitive sciences, an interdisciplinary effort, is extremely ambitious. Cognitive scientists may be psychologists, linguists, anthropologists, computer scientists, neuroscientists, even philosophers. They are going to need all the help they can get, for their ambition is to understand how any mind, human or artificial, works.

This is a rather large piece of mental territory by anyone's standards, so cognitive scientists deliberately deemphasize the role of emotions on one hand and the influence of social, cultural, and historical factors on the other. What they are primarily focused on is cognition, thinking, decision making, language, visual, auditory, or conceptual pattern recognition, or intelligent behavior in general. That is still quite a piece of mental territory. How do they approach it?

Cognitive scientists, in spite of their disciplinary differences, share one major assumption. They assume that there exist mental representations that can be analyzed independently of biology and neurophysiology, the brain's "wetware," on the microlevel of the neurons or the social or cultural context on the macrolevel of history. To put it crudely but simply, mental representations— pictures in the mind, concepts, and so on—can be thought of as existing independently of the real world. Put this way, cognitive science sounds like Platonism, a study of incorporeal mental objects that somehow exist in a mind. But they are not Platonists. They acknowledge that the mental representations of which they speak are necessarily materially supported, although the details of that support do not really concern them.

Many cognitive scientists get their inspiration from the electronic computer. They view the brain as a computer and the mind as a master internal program that manipulates information. The mental representations in this model are programs. In real computers the actual manipulations occur in "machine language," but it is the program, written by a person, which is translated into machine language that dictates how the machine processes information. The claim of some cognitive scientists is that the electronic signals in machine language, analogous to the signals in the brain's neurocortex, are really irrelevant to understanding how the program—the mind—functions. It is the program that captures the essence of the mind and mental representations. Their hope is to find and understand the program—forget about the brain—and that program will provide the long-sought-after map of the human mind. Finding such a deep theory of the mind would then "crack the cognition problem." The program, a set of rules for manipulating symbols, doesn't even need the brain to run it; it can be run on a computer and achieve artificial rather than natural intelligence.

In this chapter I will be talking about a critical look at the cognitive sciences, a view of an outsider looking in rather than an insider looking out. I should make it clear from the outset that my criticism of cognitive science is *not* focused on those descriptions of the mental world based on observation. There are a vast number of beautiful and exacting experimental observations on human cognition and animal behavior. What I am critical of is the premature attempts on the part of some cognitive scientists to find a *deep theory* of the mind, the way the quantum theory is a deep theory of atoms or molecular biology is a deep theory of genetics. The failure of cognitive psychology to find such a deep theory is telling. My own view, stated simply, is that a deep theory of cognition is unlikely to exist unless it is directly founded upon the actual material structure of the brain or the computer.

I see three major possibilities for the future of cognitive science (which are not exclusive or logically exhaustive). The first, and most exciting possibility, is that the material and organizational basis for cognition is indeed found—the cognition problem is "cracked." The question is at what level this cognitive organization is found and how simple or complex it turns out to be. There may not be any program for the mind short of the brain's neuronal network, no intermediate stage. If this view is correct, then the deep theory of cognitive science will beome incorporated in the future within either the neurosciences or computer science.

A second possibility is that cognitive science develops as a mathematical science—an exact theory of cognition based on logic. Cognitive science then becomes a special branch of mathematics and may have little or nothing to tell us about human cognition. However, a mathematical theory of cognition could be checked and tested using artificial intelligences and be very fruitful.

Finally, those for whom these directions are unpalatable and who think that the human mind can be studied independently of its material embodiment will find themselves drifting into something like narrative literature that is not a science at all, although it may be as interesting. Perhaps there is no solution to the "cognition problem," only a problem in how the brain works. The sheer complexity of the cognition mechanism will prevent a deep theory from being found, and cognitive science will become an interpretive, pluralistic intellectual activity.

To exemplify my view, take the puzzle of the human facility to produce language, a facility some cognitivists endeavor to understand independently of brain function even as they acknowledge that it is produced by the human brain. They think that by deeply analyzing human languages—sentences and speech, a form of behavior—they will understand the underlying machinery of language. While analyzing language is a valid and important task in its own right, in their wider ambition I think that they are mistaken.

Francis Crick once remarked, "We are deceived at every level by our introspection." I would extend this one step further: We are deceived at every level by our *behavior*. Behavior, of course, is real; but to understand it we must understand the details of its production in the nervous system and not treat the brain as a "black box" —an unknown input-output device. Language is produced by the brain in a manner as yet only dimly understood. When we understand the neurological basis for language, we will finally understand how humans produce the miracles of speech and linguistic thought.

The central postulate of cognitive scientists—that mental representations are programs—seems similar to those made in the natural sciences. For example, natural scientists will postulate that genes exist or that physical space and time is a curved Riemannian four-dimensional space. The method of its employment is similar also, what is called "Einstein's postulational method." Einstein, moving away from the strict empiricism of contemporary physics, described the method he used to create his general relativity theory to his friend, the philosopher Maurice Solovine. Einstein said that on the basis of nothing more than intuition based on experience, one makes a postulate (for cognitive science that is the postulate that mental representations are programs). The postulate cannot be directly tested, any more than the Schrödinger equation I described previously can be directly tested. But if the postulate is logically precise, one can rigorously deduce results from that postulate, and these *can* be tested directly. If the results fail, so does the postulate because it is rigorously tied to the results. If the results agree with experience, confidence in the correctness of the postulate is enhanced. Let us compare applications of this approach in the natural and cognitive sciences, for the differences are instructive.

Examples of the application of this method abound in the natural sciences. Classical genetics theory is a case with an interesting twist. On the basis of observations from plant and animal breeding, naturalists and biologists postulated the existence of genes. The genes, at least for the first decades of the century, could not be seen—they were an assumption—but they were expressed in terms of definite, discrete characteristics like the sex of animals or hair color. The observed regularity of these characteristics corresponded to the results deduced from the postulated genetic rules. But the overall genetic stability of living organisms suggested to scientists that genes had to be more than a postulated entity; they had to have a material basis. With the discovery that DNA was the genetic substance, the unraveling of its molecular structure, and the understanding of how RNA synthesized proteins, genes could be identified as segments of DNA or RNA molecules. From this example we see that the postulated entity, the gene, was not just a mathematical artifact, but a material object (more accurately, information encoded on a material object).

A telling example from the cognitive sciences can be found in linguistics, the core problem of which is: How is language possible? Human beings have an ability no other organisms have—they can speak and write language, logically express their thoughts with a facility that becomes an art in literature. How is this accomplished? Noam Chomsky initiated a linguistics revolution in the late 1950s and the 1960s by answering these questions in a new way and by putting linguistics on an axiomatic, rigorous basis. While his original specific ideas are not held by many linguists today, almost all of modern linguistics is a reaction to Chomsky's seminal ideas. An excellent and accessible review is to be found in Howard Gardner's *The Mind's New Science*, a history of the rise of cognitive science.

Chomsky assumed that the syntax of language—the grammatical rules that tell us how particular words can be used in a sentence —was autonomous, independent of other features such as semantics or pragmatics. He also assumed the autonomy of linguistics from other cognitive sciences—it was a field of research in its own right. These were really two heuristic assumptions, designed to liberate linguistics and syntactics from other concerns. By restricting the focus of linguistics, Chomsky hoped to discover something. And he did.

Chomsky was interested in how sentences could be generated. How out of all possible ways of putting words together can we guarantee that we will put together all and only well-formed sentences? First he showed that some of the old ideas (called "finite-state grammars") either could not work or were implausible. But he went on to postulate a new idea—the transformational grammar that did seem to work. The main assumption of a transformational grammar is that there exists a set of well-defined rules whereby one sentence can be transformed into another sentence. In short, there was an algorithmic procedure that could convert the abstract representation of one sentence into another. In this way, Chomsky asserted, all possible well-formed sentences could be generated. Chomsky went on to postulate the existence of a separate level in the mind—the transformational level—that carried out both the necessary and the volitional transformations of a sentence. This transformational level, a mental representation in the sense of cognitive science, could be viewed as an internal program for generating sentences.

Irrespective of the merits of this proposal, Chomsky's work created an impetus among linguists to adopt formal, rigorous methods in the study of language and invited psychology to do the same. Chomsky saw the mind as modularly organized with different parts relatively independent of one another. As this modular view of the mind suggests, he was committed to "mentalism," the belief that there exist abstract mental structures in the mind that are the reason that knowledge is at all possible. These organizational features of the mind were, in his view, primarily inborn and not acquired later through experience.

We can make a rough analogy between Chomsky's proposals regarding the production of language and the previous example from genetics. Like the early geneticists postulating the gene to explain the regular patterns of heredity, Chomsky postulates the existence of a transformational level to explain the patterns of language production. Geneticists, however, found that there was a material basis for the gene—DNA—while any neuroanatomical basis for the transformational level or the mental modules is lacking at this time. While such a discovery may come in the future, I doubt that it will resemble anything like the discovery of DNA and its implications for genetics.

Of course Chomsky and others do not assert that these mental representations are in the brain; they assert they are in the mind. How the mind is related to the brain is not known in sufficient detail to determine if the transformational level in the mind has a correspondence with the anatomy of the brain. This, however, does not evade the criticism I am espousing. Until the mind and its modules (if they exist) are understood on a material basis and thus pinned down, the models of the mind advanced by cognitivists and others will proliferate, shift, and slide with the tide of intellectual fashion and occasional new experimental findings and analysis.

I do not wish, by making this criticism, to diminish the extraordinary accomplishments of modern linguistics—they are very important for describing the complex phenomena of language. Linguistics, and Chomsky's work in particular, can really be viewed as a branch of mathematics—one of the directions that cognitive science might take. Chomsky's categories in his formal language theory have been fruitfully applied outside language theory—the "context-free languages" useful in specifying computer compilers, devices which translate the underlying machine language of a computer into programming languages used by people.

The work of linguists trying to understand actual human language reminds me of the work of the eighteenth- and early-nineteenth-century French and American "electricians" endeavoring to understand electrical phenomena. Their results were often contradictory (usually because they didn't recognize the influence of humidity on their apparatus), and it was decades before a unified account of electricity and magnetism was forthcoming. Likewise, I believe that the phenomena of language that linguists are uncovering today will be someday explained in terms of how the brain works and interacts with other brains. But that day is not yet here.

Not only is the problem of how people manage to *speak* an outstanding cognitive problem, so is the problem of how people *perceive*. The image of the outside world, focused on the two retinas on the back of our eyes, is continually changing as we move about. How is it possible that we perceive the images, in spite of their changes, as corresponding to single objects? How do we construct the unified and constant representation of the three-dimensional visible world that is in our mind from the welter of confusing information that is focused on the two-dimensional retinas of our two eyes?

David Marr, a researcher at the artificial intelligence laboratory at MIT, devoted himself to answering such questions until his untimely death in 1980. Marr postulated that vision involved the efficient symbolic representation of the image—in a sense there were programs in the mind that represented visual information. The model of vision he developed, like Chomsky's "mentalism," invoked modules in the visual system operating independently of one another and computing different features of visual information—orientation, global shape, stereoscopy, and motion. Marr developed specific and detailed models of vision implementing his ideas and which profoundly influenced the future direction of research. While he worked with and built computers, he was inspired by the brain and used many concepts from neurosciences. Marr cannot be described as a strict cognitivist, although he shared in some of their ideas. His intellectual commitment was to a highly computational view of vision; there was no predetermined correspondence between the perceiver and the object seen. The visual programs, in short, were primarily in the brain or the computer, not the world (although Marr did incorporate constraints based on features of this world). When his posthumous book appeared in 1984, the neuroscientists had already moved forward and rejected many of the concepts he had used in his work.

The fact that cognitive scientists do not seem to care about what is going on in the natural world, only about computations, mental representations and programs, be they in the brain or a computer, with its emphasis on disembodied mental representations, is very disturbing to many people. The battle lines between cognitive science and natural science with its materialistic orientation can sometimes be drawn quite sharply (when they cannot be drawn so sharply it will be, in my view, a sign of progress). The field of vision research brings the battle line into focus.

James J. Gibson, the vision researcher, and his followers challenge the computational and cognitive approach to vision. In their view the world already contains the information that is needed for perception. The world of visual objects and the logic of those visual objects is a program that is already there. We see the world as three-dimensional because it *is* three-dimensional. In spite of our changing sensations we see the constancy of the world because it is there. As Gibson wrote, "I am convinced that invariance comes from reality, not the other way around. Invariance in the ambient optic array over time is not constructed or deduced; it is there to be discovered." But how it is to be discovered is an open question—precisely the question that the computationalists are endeavoring to answer. To the cognitivists with their commitment to internal, not external, representations, Gibson's remarks are fighting words, and the battle rages. It will probably not subside until someone either builds a computer that can see—recognize faces and identify objects—or we understand how the brain does it. That may take a long time, and even then people will argue over the interpretations of that understanding.

The fact that we can see is something most people take for granted. But it is really a complete puzzle. What is going on in the brain when this happens? No one believes that there is a homunculus, a little man who sits in the brain and sees what is going on in the visual cortex. It is easier to state the fallacy of the homunculus than to avoid falling into the trap of this way of thinking. Like the geneticists who postulated genes, vision researchers postulate visual representations. But what is the material basis for these representations? The major insights into answering these questions, I believe, will come less from cognitive science than from neuroscience. The direction of future progress is exemplified by the awesome work of the neurobiologists David H. Hubel and Torsten N. Wiesel over the last three decades.

Unlike cognitivists with their "top-down" approach, Hubel and Wiesel studied from "the bottom up" how visual information is processed down neuronal pathways in an actual material structure —the mammalian brain. Their strategy is simply described by them: "Beginning, say, with the fibers of the optic nerve, we record with microelectrodes from a single nerve fiber and try to find out how we can most effectively influence the firing by stimulating the retina with light. For this one can use patterns of light of every conceivable size, shape and color, bright or dark, background or the reverse, and stationary or moving. It may take a long time, but sooner or later we satisfy ourselves that we have found the best stimulus for the cell being tested, in this case a ganglion cell of the retina."

By tracing the firing of individual nerves, Hubel and Wiesel discovered the remarkable fact that the striate cortex responds to specific orientations of forms in the visual field. The striate cortex consists of columns of neurons, and each column responds to one specific orientation in the visual field—a horizontal line activates one column, a vertical line another, and other columns are activated for orientations between the horizontal and vertical. This information is then sent out to other parts of the brain. Why the brain organizes its visual information this way remains unknown. Yet it is clear, they state, that "particular stimuli turn neurons on or off; groups of neurons do indeed perform particular transformations. It seems reasonable to think that if the secrets of a few regions such as this one can be unlocked, other regions will also in time give up their secrets." But so far, no deep secrets about vision have been unlocked.

Eric Kandel, a neuroscientist at Columbia University, and his collaborators have carried this "bottom-up" approach quite far by studying the nervous system of *Aplysia californica*, the simple sea snail. They are beginning to see the basis of learning at the molecular level. The behavioral changes in the animal, such as in the withdrawal response, are correlated with changes in the connection strength at synapses (both the number and activity of the vesicles containing neurotransmitters at the presynaptic junction are altered), which in turn changes the firing rate of the axon.

I think that the contrast between the accomplishments of neuroscientists and those of cognitive psychology is dramatic. I believe that someday language, in spite of the fact it is far more difficult to trace linguistic than visual information, will be understood in the same manner as Hubel and Wiesel have understood, in a small part, the problem of visual information processing. It will not be fundamentally understood by simply examining how people produce language, although of course that will be of immense help. However, understanding how visual or linguistic information is processed is a far cry from understanding vision or language. But it may provide the clues as to how such a deeper riddle can be answered.

We can see from the examples of language and vision research that cognitive scientists, supporting their postulate that mental representations are programs, like computer programs, have embarked on a very ambitious research project. Suppose we now return to our map room in the parable of the philosopher-king and his twelve savants and put twenty contemporary geniuses in it

(Herbert Simon, Allen Newell, John McCarthy, Marvin Minsky, Noam Chomsky, George Miller, Jerome Bruner, Jerry Fodor, Zenon Pylyshyn . . .) and charge them with creating a map of the human mind. I think the result of thirty years' work by the twenty geniuses would resemble the enterprise of their fifteenth-century colleagues—brilliantly correct in part, but overall a failure. And they would fail for rather much the same reason—the categories of thought are inadequate, and the available technology has not yet arrived to solve the problem at hand. More significant, they might fail because, unlike the case of the natural sciences, no such map exists. The internal representations they imagined existed in *their* minds and did not correspond to invariant structures in the material world. Some, despairing of the ultimate triumph of their science, will abandon their commitment to the notion of a unitary natural world, an aboriginal reality, and seek refuge in a pluralistic vision of many "worlds" and their "versions" advocated by Nelson Goodman.

It's easy to criticize cognitive science. For one thing the brain is not a digital programmed computer—the model for the brain is wrong. There is no evidence that the brain even has an internal program, like those in digital computers. According to some neuroscientists, the brain has no software "program"—it is all hardware (really "wetware"). The brain processes information, to be sure, but it does so without using a program. Other people, like the philosopher John Searle, have argued that if it did have such an internal program, it couldn't function the way it does. So the wonderful map—the internal program—of the human mind that some cognitive scientists seek may not exist at all—it is a sort of a mirage that disappears as one examines it closely. No model of human cognition has stood the test of time.

In spite of these criticisms (which only apply to the work of some cognitive scientists), I am optimistic about the future of cognitive science because it is focused on a set of problems that are simply not going to go away. And for this reason cognitive science is not just an intellectual fad generated by the advent of electronic computers. But if cognitive scientists seek a deep theory—an internal representation—of either a natural or artificial mind, then, I believe, it will have to be a theory about actual material things—brains and computers interacting with the world. If the kinds of programs that cognitive scientists claim exist and are the essence of mental representations, then they must be materially realizable, not just in theory, as some kind of model, but in practice. We must demand of cognitive science a strict constructivist requirement as we do in natural science. Some scientists might object because no "card carrying" cognitive scientist is an idealist, a Platonist; they are often materialists. Yet they often sound like Platonists living in a world of ideal models, unrealizable computer programs, a world of science fiction not science fact, at best a world of mathematical objects and relations that cannot apply to our world. The study of actual brains or actual computers interacting with the world—that is the future of cognitive science, if it is to have a future at all. Without a commitment to natural science and the grounding of cognitive science in the actual material order of the world, I fear that cognitive science will resemble empirical science less and less and drift off as a kind of narrative literature, a high-level but empty intellectual vision, at best a mathematical theory of the mind having nothing to do with either natural or artificial minds. In order to bridge the gap between the sciences and the humanities (as some cognitive psychologists have attempted), one should not, as a scientist, do this by casting off one's grounding in the natural sciences. No bridge can then stand.

In what follows I will briefly describe what I see as the future options of an empirical cognitive science—the study of brains and computers—in turn as if they were distinct areas of research and not overlapping (which they may well be). However, before describing the architectonic of the cognitive sciences, it would be useful to explain a couple of concepts that would help illuminate that description. The first concept is the meaning of the terms "top down" and "bottom up." Scientists and philosophers are always using them. The second concept centers on the distinction between "signs" and "symbols" or "syntax" and "semantics."

The terms "top down" and "bottom up" as used by scientists and philosophers refer to the direction they are trying to move in to solve a problem. The "top" for a material system means its macroscopic or global features, the "bottom" its microscopic or local features. For example, for the brain interacting with the body and the world, the "top" refers to the behavior or cognition on the part of the organism, "bottom" refers to the electrochemical events in the brain. Both the "top" and the "bottom" may exhibit regular, rule-governed behavior. The problem is to find the relation between the two. One can work as a psychologist from the "top down" or as a neuroscientist from the "bottom up" in attempting to solve this problem.

There is another, related sense in which these terms are used—to designate the causal relation of parts to wholes, the part being the "bottom" and the whole being the "top." Usually in the natural sciences the causal relation is clear: the behavior of the part determines the whole. That is why natural scientists are always trying to find the microscopic laws that govern the system they want to understand—the laws of the atoms to understand chemistry, the structure of DNA to understand genetics. Natural sciences have a "bottom-up" approach to explanation.

But in the cognitive sciences the situation is sometimes, but not always, reversed—the "top-down" approach for which the whole determines the parts seems to be the more fruitful. For example, for many years linguists attempted to follow a "bottom-up" approach to the problem of explaining speech and action. The approach was to start with the rules for making sentences, the sentences would in turn determine the pragmatics, and this in turn determined speech and action. But all attempts to move in this direction have failed because sentences are constructed by a speaker to fulfill a total context of meaning—an awareness of the entire situation by the speaker. The next time you speak, even if it is a single sentence, if you reflect on all that you presume in order to render that sentence intelligible—where you are located, your situation in life, the context you share with the person addressed and so on—you will see how richly context-dependent the meanings of sentences are. It seems clear that somehow, as speakers, we first grasp the total situation and then construct the sentences —a "top-down" approach. Unless a theory of speech and human cognition takes this into account, it must surely fail.

A similar "top-down" perspective is evident in the findings of Roman Jakobson and his Prague school of phonetics. They find that individual phonemes—the sound "atoms" of speech—do not have individual meanings; meaning arises from their combination. Again the context determines meaning.

A second concept that will illuminate the approaches people have taken to cognitive science is the distinction between "signs" and "symbols" or "syntactics" and "semantics." A "sign" I will take to mean a physical marking—a scratch on a piece of paper, a unit of magnetic flux in a computer's memory disk. Simple signs are the 0 and 1 in the binary code. A sign doesn't mean anything as such. But a set of different signs can be manipulated (they are physical objects) according to preassigned rules. These rules are the "syntax," the grammar, of the signs. Signs are understood from the "bottom up"—the syntactical rules tell us everything we can ever know about a sign; they *define* the sign.

Sometimes one gets a feeling that a sign "means something" by the way it gets manipulated; but that is just our projection of meaning onto a sign. For example, if the signs "2" and "3" are manipulated the way we manipulate the numbers two and three then it becomes easy to assign the signs their corresponding meaning. But that assignment is our doing.

"Symbols," by contrast, have meaning assigned to them by us— they have "semantic" content. They are, like signs, represented physically but their meaning is not (at least it is not immediately clear how to physically represent meaning; presumably our brain does this somehow). Symbols are context dependent, their meaning depends on the situations in which the symbol appears. There are symbols, like a sign such as "2" to which we assign an elementary meaning, and complex symbols, like a national flag. But the different kinds of symbols need not concern us here. What is important is that symbols are recognized from the "top down"; first we grasp the total context of a symbol and then see its "parts."

Symbols are what Hilary Putnam, following Wittgenstein, called "cluster concepts." The image for a cluster concept is that of rope, which although it is a unity, actually consists of many fibers none of which runs the full length of the rope. Likewise symbols, designating the meaning they symbolize, are composite unities and open to many interpretations. For example, the letter "A" is a symbol. It could refer to the first letter of the alphabet, the definitive article, an unknown quantity in an algebraic equation, or the sin of adultery in Hawthorne's *The Scarlet Letter*—a rich content of possible open-ended meanings. Because of that open-endedness, symbols are not easily defined—their definition is context dependent—and they are not subjected to a simple set of rules for manipulation. In his book *Metamagical Themas*, Douglas Hofstadter has an excellent and more detailed discussion about what he calls passive symbols (signs) and active symbols (symbols) that reinforces the brief discussion and distinction I have given here.

In spite of my attempt to make the distinction between signs and symbols as sharp as possible, it is not really clear if signs and symbols are really distinct. After all, *we* assign the meaning. We can, and often do, assign meaning to mere signs, and they become symbols. Similarly symbols may be simply very complex and wholistic representations of signs. Perhaps symbols *do* obey formal rules, but these rules are extraordinarily complicated, so complicated that we cannot easily state them. If we can somehow get symbols from signs, semantics from syntax, the distinction we have made would vanish. The problem of accomplishing this is called the problem of the representation of knowledge: how can we find a physical, rule-governed system of signs that incorporates content and meaning? Evidently our brain does this. On the neuronal level it is a network of signals. Yet on the behavioral level it responds to content and meaning. How it does this is unknown.

With the concepts of "top down" and "bottom up" and "signs" and "symbols" in place, it is not difficult to give a simplified overview of the cognitive sciences. Cognitive scientists study two main entities: either the brain/mind or computers.

Those who study the brain/mind can roughly be divided into two camps—the cognitive psychologists who study brain/mind function from a "top-down" perspective and neuroscientists who study the brain from the "bottom up." Generally the psychologists are interested in studying phenomena greater than about a millisecond and the neuroscientists less than a millisecond.

Those scientists who study computers can likewise be roughly divided into two camps—the computationalists whose motto might simply be "signs are symbols" and the connectionists whose motto might be "from signs to symbols." The computationalists view the computer program that manipulates signs as the essence of cognition. They point to machines that prove theorems in logic by manipulating signs—something that is difficult for humans to do and certainly a sign of intelligent behavior—as an example of artificial intelligence. The connectionist philosophy we outlined previously in "Connectionism/Neural Nets." Connectionists don't think that one can get "meaning" so easily out of sign manipulations in a computer. They think that the computationalists' idea of meaning is only their projection of meaning onto what are just signs. Connectionalists are inspired by the brain's complex network and seek, in part, to imitate it in a computer (or a set of parallel computers). The essence of cognition to them is the ability to respond to meaning—context-dependent information—and this has less to do with programs and computation than the way the machine itself is built—its network of connections.

This simplified overview of cognitive sciences is woefully inadequate if one considers the interdisciplinary nature of the science, the overlapping fields of interest. No one sits plainly in one field or another. Nonetheless I have found it useful. Historically, the computational camp of computer scientists and cognitive psychology grew up together in the 1950s and 1960s. The more recent development in the 1970s and 1980s is the connectionist camp and the new developments in the neurosciences. My own view is that many of the ideas of the computationalists and early cognitive psychologists did not work out—the initial intellectual program failed for the most part. Those noble failures, however, inspired the new approaches of the connectionists and the neuroscientists that are now progressing but have yet to fulfill their promise. They may fail, too. The history of cognitive science, let us hope, exemplifies the aphorism of Reinhold Niebuhr: "Sometimes truth comes riding into history on the back of error."

There are two main approaches to the study of the brain and its cognitive and behavioral manifestations—the "top-down" approach of the cognitive and behavioral psychologists and the "bottom-up" approach of neuroscientists.

In the "top-down" approach psychologists examine the systematics of human and animal cognition and behavior, relying on direct observation or reports by human subjects. These rigorous experiments are often ingenious, turning out definite and often surprising results, about learning, memory, visual and auditory perception, decision making, and language.

I am impressed by these results especially because they are surprising. As a student I volunteered for psychology experiments; it is always a learning experience. I remember once listening to a repetition tape—a loop of recording tape that played the same English word over and over again into my headphones. After a while I was supposed to no longer hear that word but distortions, other English words, in spite of the fact that the same word was being repeated. I told myself, Well that is not going to happen to me; I'm going to really concentrate. But concentration didn't make a bit of difference because the appearance of distortions has to do with how the brain handles repeated information. To my surprise and delight I soon heard other English words. The question of where *those* words came from intrigues me to this day.

Some of the most exciting experimental work done by cognitive psychologists is in the area of internal visual imagery. In the early 1970s Roger Shepard, a psychologist at Stanford University, and his colleagues showed subjects two geometrical figures displayed at different orientations and asked them to check as quickly as possible if the two figures were indeed the same. The response time was directly proportional to the angle through which the figures had been rotated. It was as if the subjects had formed a mental image of the objects in their mind and then rotated one to check the correspondence. Like real objects, the amount of time it took to do this was proportional to the angle of rotation.

Stephen Kosslyn carried this work into new directions. In a typical experiment he showed his subjects a scene of familiar objects and asked them to remember the picture. He then directed his subjects to recall the picture in their minds and move an imagined black spot from one object on the imagined picture to another. The time it took for them to do this was again proportional to the actual distance between the objects in the real picture—as if they were scanning the picture in their minds. Kosslyn went on to make computer models of this process.

In spite of the fact that most people have little difficulty forming mental images, a fact supported by experiments such as these, some people do not share the interpretation that these images are "pictures in the mind." They say this because computers don't use images. Although the work of Shepard and Kosslyn supports the cognitivists' notion of an internal representation of knowledge (the image) that can be studied independently of the brain, some cognitive fundamentalists think they have gone too far. These strict cognitivists, such as Zenon Pylyshyn, think that the imagery is just a by-product of a program—a set of rules incorporating desires and beliefs. They are looking for a *single* computational representation for cognition that is irreducible. As atoms are the building blocks of matter, this single representation would be the building block for all mental events. The notion that the mind has a plurality of distinct mental representations, such as linguistic propositions, visual imagery, or acoustic memories, is received by them with the same enthusiasm that a monotheist reserves for paganism.

My own view is that it would be remarkable if evolution (figuratively speaking), having taken the trouble to develop the visual system, would not have put it to other uses such as representing internal images. The brain has different parts used for different functions, and these can certainly represent information in different ways. To say that there is a single representational system (other than the neuronal network itself) goes beyond the current evidence.

Cognitive psychologists have done thousands of different experiments that reveal aspects of mental function. What I am critical of, because I think it is extremely premature, is the attempt to extrapolate that experimental insight into constructing a program for brain function—an invariant map of the mind. Someday this may be accomplished; but that accomplishment will be based like all the other maps in the natural sciences on a material order—in this case the material order of the brain interacting with the world.

If one wants to understand cognitive function in human beings, then I would bet on the neuroscientists with their "bottom-up" approach having a better chance at long-term success in figuring out how the brain produces the biological phenomena of a mind —replete with its capacity for consciousness, beliefs, and emotions. It's too bad that more neuroscientists don't take an interest in the mind and mental representations, but perhaps that's because they feel that "fools rush in where angels fear to tread." Many think that the "mind" is a rather fuzzy concept and avoid all discussions of it. Neuroscientists are aware, more than most people, of their vast ignorance of how the *brain* works. In 1978 neurobiologist David Hubel wrote, "Our knowledge of the brain is in a very primitive state. While for some regions we have developed some kind of functional concept, there are others, the size of one's fist, of which it can almost be said that we are in the same state of knowledge as we were with regard to the heart before we realized it pumped blood."

If I am correct about the existence of coherent, universal, and vulnerable maps and that there must be a material territory corresponding to the map, then the only hope for finding such a theory of the human mind is by examining the mind as supported by a brain that interacts with the material world. It is not clear that this can even be done, but attempts to find such theoretical maps not based on neuroscience and the material order of the external world must surely fail. In this effort to find a scientific theory of the mind, the experimental work of cognitive psychologists will be essential. Like two tunnel digging crews breaking through and joining in the middle of a mountain, I hope that cognitive psychologists with their "top-down" approach would go halfway to meeting neuroscientists with their "bottom-up" approach, the two joining forces on a middle ground. There already have been a few small breakthroughs mostly in the area of sensory perception.

One example, from another science, of the "top-down" and "bottom-up" approach joining on a middle ground is genetics, a case we already referred to. Classical genetics has had, like cognitive psychology, a "top-down" approach. The observation of regularities of discrete characteristics in living organisms over a succession of generations suggested an order beyond appearance —genes expressed in the organism. Here the "top" is the observed characteristics of plants and animals, the "down" the postulated genes and their laws of combination. Molecular biologists developed a "bottom-up" approach after the material basis for genetics was established. Genes were bits of DNA or messenger RNA that coded for protein synthesis. The previously discovered genetic laws could now be put on the firm basis of molecular interaction. The discovery of DNA thus confirmed what others suspected— the genetic regularities had a material basis, and molecular biologists worked out the code. The "bottom-up" molecular approach and the "top-down" classical genetics approach joined at the level of the gene. The gene could have been a Platonic concept, a mathematical artifact; but it was not. It had a material basis.

The "top-down" and the "bottom-up" approach supplemented each other in this example because there is a "causal decoupling" between the laws of chemistry and how proteins are synthesized— once one understands how the manufacture of proteins is coded in the RNA, you can forget the laws of chemistry on which that coding is based. There often is a convenient conceptual break in the causal reductionist chain from the microscopic to the macroscopic level. This break, or "causal decoupling," presupposes the reductionalist view of nature—the whole is equal to the sum of its parts. The decoupling simply reflects the fact that we often do not need all the details of the microscopic world in order to correctly use the rules that apply to a larger world. To understand the rules of protein synthesis you have to understand the details of chemistry; but you can forget the chemistry when you apply the rules.

This "causal decoupling" illustrates an important feature of scientific maps—the phenomenon is sometimes observed from the "top down" but ultimately understood from the "bottom up."

Without the aid of a microscope, Mendel could correctly deduce the genetic laws. But understanding why these laws, and not others, apply requires an understanding based on the microscopic level—the RNA, DNA level.

Is there a lesson in this example for cognitive psychology? Like classical geneticists, workers in cognitive psychology postulate an order, like the genetic order, that lies beyond appearance. Usually this postulated order is in the form of a model—like the many models for how human memory is stored in the body. While these models are not inconsistent with the general notion that there is a material basis for human memory, no one has yet demonstrated precisely how the memory is represented in the brain. The way computer memory storage works—local storage—is certainly not the way the brain does it. Holographic memory models—the notion that memory is stored globally rather than locally—also have problems. Each model is inadequate (although there are some interesting developments on collective properties of neuronal nets and an expanding knowledge of the neuroanatomy of the hippocampus, a part of the brain that plays a key role in memory). So how does the brain with its one hundred billion neurons do it? No one knows the answer for sure, even for simpler organisms with far fewer neurons than our brains. Cognitive psychologists, in spite of the massive data on memory, vision, cognition, hearing, learning, and so on have not constructed a scientific map that accounts for that data. There could be several reasons for this.

The first reason is that no such theory of the mind exists, short of the neuronal network itself—there is no intermediate state and no "causal decoupling." If this is true, it would be disappointing and imply that a deep theory of cognition is impossible. A second possibility is that a simple theory exists but has not yet been found. While certainly the most desirable possibility, it would be surprising if this were true in view of all the efforts to find a simple theory. Most likely an intermediate theory is extraordinarily complicated —different theories, for different kinds of memory and objects and relations remembered. If theories of memory exist (short of the brain network), it is probably because there is, in fact, a "causal decoupling" of memory from details of the neurocortex, just like the "causal decoupling" of protein synthesis from the laws of chemistry. My own guess is that if an intermediate stage exists, its discovery will come out of cooperative insights from both neuroscience and psychology—not from either alone.

Cognitive science has been inspired, rightly or wrongly, by the electronic computer. Unlike the brain, which was built by the Demiurge and is largely unknown, computers are built by engineers and are completely known. But some cognitive scientists are not especially interested in computer hardware, architecture, and design; they are interested in what one can *do* with computers. What one can do with a computer, not just in theory but in practice, is determined first by its actual design and second by the program—its instructions. And what one can do with standard digital computers is to compute, nothing more, nothing less.

Traditionally, some cognitivists have paid attention only to the program, not the actual machine, and its capabilities. They adopted the orientation of the formalist school in mathematics rather than that of the intuitionist. The computers they imagined, if they thought about them at all, were "gedanken" computers—mathematically specified but fictitious machines. Anything that was formally computable (essentially by definition) could be computed on a particularly simple gedanken computer, the universal Turing machine.

Usually we think of Turing machines as doing mathematical calculations, proving theorems, and manipulating signs. They mechanized mathematics and gave a clear simple definition of "computable"—a problem that could be calculated on a Turing machine. In principle, however, one can imagine a Turing machine processing the signs we use in ordinary language—the alphabet. The alphabet can be translated into a binary code, and this can be put into a Turing machine. According to the cognitivists, any arbitrary but coherent input information—such as the sentence "How are you today?"—could, by the operation of a set of rules (the program), be transformed by such a computer into an output such as "I am well. How are you?" The program, in short, could simulate intelligence; at least that is what we would call it if it appeared on a human being. But it would just be this little Turing machine cranking out its instructions.

I do not, at this point, want to engage in the debate of whether or not such a formal set of rules—the program—for manipulating signs can, in principle, simulate a "human" conversation so that we would attribute intelligence to the programmed computer. But it is clear that this simulation is, in practice, impossible on any existing computer because of hardware and software limitations.

The intuitionist viewpoint in mathematics, in contrast with the formalist viewpoint, requires that you actually construct the program. A still stronger viewpoint—what I have called the "constructivist viewpoint"—requires that you build or at least design in detail the computer as well. This has not been done. There are a few practical obstacles. First, the conversational exchange, described above, should take place within the lifetime of the universe; even if we knew how to program them, the fastest computers today cannot simulate a "human" conversation for very long. Second, real computers are subject to random errors in their operation; while errors can be minimized by increasing the redundancy in the computer's components, the number of components grows so large that to run a formal program of the kind envisioned without error could require a computer whose mass exceeds that of the universe. These are, of course, speculative limitations, but they serve to emphasize that if cognitive scientists and workers in artificial intelligence are to employ the computer as a conceptual paradigm, they ought to be talking about real programs and real computers, not "gedanken" computers. Fortunately many of them do, and those that do are better aware than most people of the enormous problems that stand in the way of achieving true artificial intelligence.

People like to make the brain-computer comparison, sometimes for fun and sometimes seriously. Such comparisons are a replay of the comparisons between mechanics and the operation of the human body that were so influential in France following Descartes's work. Cartesian medicine held that the body is a kind of automaton, with the bones as girders, muscles as elastic springs, tendons as cables. Julien Offroy de La Mettrie, a Cartesian physician, wrote in his book *L'Homme Machine*, "The human body is a machine that winds up its own springs." Of course the body does have a mechanics, and parts of it are very well described by the principles of mechanical engineering. But this approach misses the important details discovered later—the cellular and molecular organization of bones, muscles, and organs—the bioengineering of the human body. And, as always, God is in the details.

Many responsible scientists shy away from the brain-computer comparison. Herbert Simon, whose book *The Sciences of the Artificial* did much to promote the computational viewpoint and the development of artificial intelligence (AI), remarked, "I don't think neurophysiology has made a great contribution to AI, and I don't think AI has made a great contribution to neurophysiology." On the other side of the fence, Vernon Mountcastle, a distinguished neurophysiologist, concurred, "No fundamental discovery about the brain is going to come from the computer. Stimulating ideas and testable hypotheses may come, but you can't discover anything." The younger generation, however, is more interdisciplinary and moves freely from studying the brain to studying computers.

When the time came in the nineteenth century for dramatic improvements assisting human locomotion, people did not build vehicles with mechanical legs on them (these are being built only now—and the problems are considerable), they built trains with wheels, later automobiles, and then aircraft. These artificial means of transportation transformed human life. Likewise the improvement of computers will advance the construction of actual artificial intelligences. But these will not resemble human intelligence any more than wheels resemble human legs. I think that is an interesting advantage. Artificial intelligence, for example, will not be restricted by evolution to process spatial information in only three dimensions, they will be able to do it in any number of dimensions. And they will not get tired.

The connectionist viewpoint in computers rose, in part, as a reaction to the strict computational outlook and, in part as a response to the advent of new computer hardware, dedicated, special-purpose computers that are hand-built from microchips. This new hardware enables connectionists to experiment with their own network designs rather than using mainframe computers. The connectionists get a lot of inspiration from neuroscientists and from the architecture of the brain, which they often seek to emulate in their computer designs. Their ambition is to build neural nets that "see," "hear," "read," and "learn" with comprehension. They are committed to the idea that the network of electronic connections is more important for simulating intelligence than an internal program. Of course, in principle, a complex program can always simulate an electronic network, but in practical terms it does it far too slowly. Whether connectionist ideas suffice for building such machines is not yet clear. Time will tell.

My view is that the internal programs that the cognitivists are seeking in the mind simply do not exist unless they can be directly shown to be materially supported by a definite neurofunction.

Some kind of "causal decoupling" between the representations of knowledge and its material support must be true if a deep theory of cognition is to survive; but that "causal decoupling" must be demonstrated, not just postulated. In this sense, then, the possibility of a cognitive science will depend critically on what is discovered by the neurosciences. Ultimately both the surviving components of cognitive science and the neurosciences will become part of the emergent sciences of complexity—the new frontier of the natural sciences and the integrative vision of the cosmos they imply.

Even if there is some kind of internal program that describes the mind as cognitive scientists hope, the deep theory of that program will have to be based on neuroscience just as chemistry is based on quantum theory. The complexity of this undertaking is immense and lies in the future. People who argue against this reductionist view point to the fact that we hold beliefs, that we have a mind and possess consciousness—categories of psychological life that for them are irreducible to biological functions. Yet I would say against such views that the terms "consciousness" and "mind" as we loosely use them probably do not refer to anything we can scientifically study. I believe that in the future, as the cognitive and neurosciences advance, such terms will be replaced by other more precise categories of thought describing our mental experience, categories that may also find their way into popular language. Until that time we will have to make do with these vague but important concepts. Our intellectual progeny will excuse us.

It is worth reminding ourselves in this context that many eminent scientists in the nineteenth century thought that life depended on a "vital force" and without that force organisms would be dead matter. For such vitalists it was unthinkable that life could exist without a vital force. If such vitalists could be shown the discoveries of modern biochemistry, their reaction would probably be, "But how does that account for the life force?" Likewise, some philosophers, if they could be confronted with a future neuroscience, might respond by asking, "But how does that account for consciousness?" The point is that certain philosophical problems are not solved. Rather, the categorical framework of thinking about the problems is so radically altered by science that the questions no longer make sense.

Sometimes I gaze in open wonder at the house that science has built. It was not built all at once. Parts of it lie in ruin. Many errors have been made, and that may seem a shame; but it is not. As long as the sciences, including cognitive science, remain vulnerable to error and ruin, they may prove true and stand for a long, long time.

A great science proceeds like the Old or the New biblical Testament. First there is the succession of prophets, Isaiah, Jeremiah, Ezekiel, and Hosea. These prophets alerted the people of Israel; they are the mouthpieces of God. But these prophets are limited, and they have only part of the truth. Further, there are false prophets and true prophets, and at the time it is always hard to tell them apart. When Isaiah foretold defeat to an arrogant nation, he was serving notice on the Israelites that they were in a bad way. They certainly didn't think they were in a bad way, made fun of him, and thought they would win the impending war. No doubt the false prophets of the time told the Israelites what they wanted to hear. What defines the "true" prophet is that the turn of events proves him right. The false prophets are forgotten, and the true prophets make it into the Bible. The prophetic system, like evolution, is a selective system—what is "right," and accords with the environment, survives.

We do not yet know whether the prophets of the "cognitive revolution" are true or false prophets. We cannot yet determine whether the maps they believe describe the mind are really there. Only time will tell.

Sometimes the true prophets speak of a coming messiah—a divinely inspired individual who has a direct access to the Godhead and reveals the whole truth, not just part of it. In the natural sciences—physics and biology—we have seen the succession of prophets and been privileged to see a few messiahs as well—an Isaac Newton, Albert Einstein, or Charles Darwin—the giants who set forth an agenda for research into the next several centuries.

I can still remember those people waiting for the arrival of the extraterrestrials on the south coast of Big Sur. They were waiting for a revelation—perhaps a messiah who had not yet come. Likewise, the psychological and social sciences are awaiting the arrival of their messiah. They may still have to wait a long time. And the waiting is always aggravated by the realization that like the prophets, messiahs can also be false.

Chapter 10

The Man Who
Mistook His Brain for His Mind

"We shall certainly try hard to do as you say," he replied, "but how shall we bury you?"

"However you please," said Socrates, "if you can catch me and I do not get away from you."

—PLATO,
Phaedo

I am truly distinct from my body, and . . . I can exist without it.

—RENÉ DESCARTES,
Sixth Meditation

In the summers I often start my day with a run in the Henry Cowell State Redwood Park in Santa Cruz County, a cool forest of second-growth California redwoods. The giant trees are among the few large trees that can flourish in the strongly acidic soil (which they produce themselves), and here they have made their final stand. The ground is covered with shrubs and ferns; occasionally I see large yellow banana slugs moving slowly along in the damp, a slime trail in their wake. Much of the original redwood growth was timbered after the San Francisco earthquake and was used to rebuild the ruined city. Charred and decaying six- and eight-foot-diameter stumps mark the former presence of these giants. It is a pleasant run through the tall trees and clear air on a footpath next to a stream that flows into the San Lorenzo River and then down into the Pacific Ocean some six miles away.

When I finish my run I often spot "Cowboy Bill," my neighbor, when he comes out to feed his purebred Arabian stallion in a corral next to his house. He knows a lot about horses. Bill, in his nineties now, was born in California and worked in the region around the Livermore valley. He is not as steady or as mindful as he was a few years ago, an old mind in an old body. But he is a living time machine who can recollect an age that has vanished. He remembers the great earthquake of 1906; he was a child in a San Francisco hospital, and his father, walking through the ruins, carried him out to safety.

I had been reading some local California history and thought I'd like to try it out on Bill. There is a stream not far from here called Love Creek, and I was curious about the name. It turned out it was named after a real character, lawman Harry Love, "the Black Knight of the Zayante," who had lived nearby in the last century. Love died in a shoot-out in 1868 with a man he thought was paying too much attention to Mrs. Love. He was already famous for having fought with Abraham Lincoln in the Black Hawk war, serving as a Texas Ranger, and for killing Joaquin Murieta. Murieta, a notorious bandit of Spanish ancestry, started as a rancher, but a group of gringos raped and murdered his young wife. Murieta then became a bandit, looting, robbing, and murdering many people. He was a leader of a gang—a folk hero to some, but to others a desperate killer. In 1853 the California State Legislature made Love a captain and authorized him and a company of Rangers to rid the state of bandits. Captain Love and his Rangers decided to get Murieta. There was a gun battle in Tulare County, and when the dust settled Love brought Murieta's head along with the hand of his henchman, Three-Fingered Jack, to the governor and collected five thousand dollars. The head, preserved in a bottle of alcohol, was put on public display.

Old Bill listened to my learned historical recitation without emotion. When I finished he said, "As a boy, my dad knew Joaquin Murieta. Used to rent horses to him and his gang. He's seen that head, and it ain't the head of Joaquin Murieta." Then he stared at me, his experience confronting my mere learning, and said, "So much for *that* story!"

Defensively, I put Bill's responses off as an old cowboy tale and in my mind dismissed it. Then, six months after our conversation, a new book by historian Frank Latta, *Early California Bandits*, was published. Latta had interviewed Murieta's progeny in the 1930s. According to Latta, Cowboy Bill was right: Love never got him. Murieta was mortally wounded in a gun battle with a rival gang, made it back to his house on Niles Canyon Road, and died there. He was quietly buried by his family at his home. (A 1986 attempt to find his body, however, failed.)

Once I get into good physical condition my morning run through the redwoods becomes almost effortless. I turn my body over to one of my silent partners, and, liberated from the sense of major exertion (and I don't push myself), I am left free to think. My body and my mind, moving together in tandem through the world, form a strange but necessary partnership. What I have been thinking about is that partnership and the problem it portends, the mind-body problem—how can a nonmaterial mind be connected to a material body?

This is an old philosophical problem, and I will say from the start that I do not have a simple solution to it. But I do believe that I know how it can be solved and how it cannot. What follows, then, are my reflections on this puzzle—a "run" through of the mind-body problem. It won't be as smooth as a run through the California redwoods; it is easy to stumble, and one tires quickly. Yet I feel that every reflective person must, at some time, come to terms with the mind-body puzzle; it is a litmus test of one's philosophical, even metaphysical, dispositions. The fact that it is such a demanding test may be the reason so few people are willing to take it.

I vividly recall when as a child I first acquired the sense of the independence of my own mind from the world and the minds of others. It came with the realization that I could conceal information from my parents and others. My mind was a private world to which I alone possessed access (later I would discover that that access was limited), and it was my choice if others were to share my mental territory. This discovery, even while it implied separation and possible loneliness, stimulated my growing autonomy.

I became impressed by the power and facility of language, how by simply speaking I could directly enter another person's mind or another could enter mine. So although my mind was private, it was linked by visible and invisible symbols to a community of other minds, which stretched into the distant past as well as into the future. There was a freedom in the activity of my mind—I could imagine far more than I could see or do, fantasies having little to do with this world. My body, by contrast, was subject to the laws of biology and physics—the material laws of this world. The image I acquired for myself was that of a magnificent molecular robot with "a ghost in the machine." The culturally supported dualism between the free world of my subjective experience on one hand, and the objective character of a world that I did not control on the other hand, had a dramatic impact on my thinking, especially in adolescence.

Adolescence is often viewed as the period of life coincident with the sexual awakening of the organism and the familial and societal rearrangements this entails. But it is more than that. For when the organism comes to its sexual maturity it also realizes, on a deep level, that its death is also part of the biological process. Sex and death are part of the same biological package. Further, as human beings subject to the processes of life on this earth, we have no real choice in this matter, a circumstance that aggravates the distinction between our limited body and our apparently unlimited and autonomous mind. Out of the tension produced by the realization of one's biological being emerges the notion of an immortal soul. It comes as no surprise, then, that for many young people adolescence terminates with the confrontation with their deeper self and an urgent need to position themselves metaphysically. The outcome of this confrontation can alter the course of a person's life.

Traditionally there are a variety of responses to the apparent distinction between the world of the mind and the material world including one's body. Both religion and the law, either explicitly or implicitly, take a stand on this issue, for indeed, human and cultural values are profoundly influenced by one's stand on it. Some cultures see the world of matter and mind as distinct and that the world of matter is completely determined, a world from which the individual cannot be liberated except by enlightenment. Even one's mental life is seen as determined by an endless causal chain of events. By contrast, in our Western culture we believe we are mentally free. We value our freedom to think and do as we please and thus are responsible for our thoughts and actions. But if the human mind is really not independent of the body and the biological processes that regulate it, what then remains of that freedom?

While the responses to the mind-body distinction are varied, there are two main trends—monism, which maintains that the distinction between the mind and matter is only apparent, and dualism, which maintains that the distinction is real and essential. I will discuss these two responses in turn. But first I want to point out the difference between the "first-person perspective" and the "third-person perspective," a distinction I think is invaluable and will help clarify the subsequent discussion.

The first-person perspective is the view that I, as a thinking and feeling person, have of the world. My own background, beliefs, opinions, and emotions influence this perspective that, in all of its complexity, is peculiar to me. This is the perspective of my consciousness as I alone can see it; the voice within each of us that cries out to the universe, "Why me?" This is the perspective celebrated by existential philosophers such as Kierkegaard, who saw faith as the highest passion of human subjectivity, or Martin Heidegger, who saw the essence of human subjectivity as Dasein— being-in-the-world. Heidegger's philosophy of Dasein, his model of the ego, reminds me of descriptions I have read of the ancient temple of Jerusalem. The outside of the temple was very ornamental, but as one moved to the inside the trappings fell away until at last, in the innermost chamber, the holy of holies, the room was completely empty. The essence of Dasein, similarly, is nothingness, a fact that it tries to hide by the trappings of existence.

The first-person perspective is the starting point for many major philosophers; it is where I find myself when I think. And I cannot deny that I think because the very act of denial affirms that I think. This development, logically extended, leads to transcendental philosophy—a pure science of the ego examined introspectively, a philosophical outlook brought to its highest formulation by Edmund Husserl. This transcendental outlook contrasts dramatically with the extrospective orientation of the natural sciences.

The position of my consciousness when I adopt this "first-person perspective" is that my thoughts and propositions be true for me. The logical signal of the first-person perspective is that propositions can be preceded by "I think or feel that . . ." I do not wish to suggest that the first-person perspective is capricious, arbitrary, or "merely subjective." It need not be. All of mathematics, the logical structure of judgments, can be seen as an example of a first-person perspective. You and I may thus agree upon many things. But our experience of that agreement is necessarily distinct.

The fact that people can agree about the world leads to the possibility of another perspective—the third-person perspective. No one, of course, can actually have the consciousness of all people or even a group (except in fantasies) because of the singular and private nature of our consciousness. Yet it is possible for my consciousness to take the position that its propositions be true not just for me, but for everyone. This third-person perspective is what is adopted, not only in ordinary life but with greater rigor in the natural sciences. Third-person propositions can be verified by any competent person irrespective of their social, religious, or political views; they are by design intended to be true for anyone. The logical signal of the third-person perspective is that propositions can be preceded by "We think that . . ."

We are all born with the first-person perspective. The third-person perspective is an attainment. It explicitly acknowledges the independence of the material and mathematical world from the accidents and peculiarities of the individual consciousness that happens to know that world. The third-person perspective is an imperfect but public perspective; unlike the first-person perspective, its propositions can be falsified. Yet the fact that it is possible at all implies that science is also possible.

Mind-monists believe that the distinction between the mind and the world is an illusion, the consequence of the failure to reflect deeply about reality. They reason that all I can ever know necessarily appears as the contents of my mind; even the external world is part of that content. What one is seeing "out there"—the material world—*is* the mind.

There is a story of three Zen monks that illustrates this view. The three monks see a temple banner waving. The first monk says, "The banner is moving." The second monk says, "No, the wind is moving." The third monk says, "It is the mind that is moving."

We see from this perspective that there isn't any "inside" or "outside"; everything is part of consciousness, even the material world. Monists have achieved a kind of oneness with existence; the entire universe becomes a rich and complex fabric of mental representations. The material world is but one, and a peculiar one at that, of many such mental representations. I will give an elementary, albeit bizarre, illustration that also gets the idea of mind-monism across.

Once a couple of engineers wanted to make a computer model of a physical process involving some aerodynamic design problem. They decided to build a simple computer that was especially designed to computationally model these physical processes. While they were working out the design of the computer a friend came by. He announced that they were wasting their time. Instead of building a small special-purpose computer, he said, they should model their special-purpose computer on a more powerful super-computer that was available. Then they could run their original computer "inside" the supercomputer. This was done. What is interesting is that what was originally a hardware device became software within the larger computer. Maybe (and I think mind-monists would concur) all the hardware we see around us—the material world—is like the little computer inside the supercomputer, really just software, a representation of information. Everything is mind. One could, of course, say with equal satisfaction (as materialist-monists would) that everything is really matter, even consciousness.

Most natural scientists tend to be materialist-monists rather than mind-monists. They believe that everything can be accounted for by a materialist description, and that nothing else is needed. In the previous example of the engineers with their computers, materialist-monists would emphasize that everything is really hardware, including the little computer "inside" the big one. The little computer, which is really just a software program, they would point out, has a material representation inside the big computer—the storage of information in tapes and magnetic memories and so on. What you think is software processing actually corresponds identically to material processes occurring in the hardware.

When it comes to the mind-body problem materialist-monists are called "identity theorists"—they believe that the states of the mind are identical with states of the brain. Put simply, the mind is identical with the brain and its functions. The difficulty with the identity theory is not so much the question of whether it is right or wrong, but rather what does it mean? The mind is a rather "fuzzy" concept and "state of the brain" is equally fuzzy especially if one attempts to define it operationally—say, how the state of the brain is actually going to be determined. If one examines the position of some identity theorists closely, it turns out that the state of the mind and the state of the brain are *defined* to be identical. That is not helpful.

Some philosophers and scientists put forth the identity theory with a dogmatic insistence that it is the only reasonable view and develop a materialist fantasy to support their claim. This is a materialist-monism that becomes true by definition. As a natural scientist I agree that the identity theory—with its claim that consciousness is a biological phenomenon and can be studied as such—is *in principle* correct. But I disagree with those who assert that the identity theory is a fact or a fact to be established by foreseeable future research. I think that the mind-body problem *in practice* is more challenging than that, as I will describe in the sequel.

The monist position (at least in some versions) is unassailable. It is not possible to defeat the viewpoint by philosophical argumentation or empirical demonstration, and one can argue endlessly whether it is true or not without resolution.

I think that the monist position, when it is unassailable, is a dead-end street. When an idea about the nature of reality doesn't "move" or deepen over time, it suggests that it is a terminal idea— a dead end. There is no research program here. Like endless numbers of animal species, who, in spite of their magnificence become extinct when the environment changes, philosophical positions also become extinct if they can't change. Monism, by collapsing the material and mental worlds into one world, has deprived itself of an internal challenge that might have given it greater philosophical life. Dualism, by contrast, maintains a tension between the material and mental and hence has a motive for transformation and change.

A failure of radical monism is that it does not recognize the logical distinction between the first- and third-person perspective and collapses this distinction into either one category or the other. The totality of existence becomes either a representation in my mind (or a universal mind), or it becomes all a material process, including *consciousness*. While this can be done, it is regressive; the ability to establish distinctions is an accomplishment not to be forsaken for a quest for the unity and wholeness of existence. The unity of existence simply is *there*; it will take care of itself. Our role as thinking and feeling beings is to understand how that unity is accomplished, and to do that requires making categorical distinctions supported by experience. And dualism makes such a distinction.

René Descartes, the seventeenth-century French philosopher, is the modern founder of dualism. In 1637 he published his *Discourse on Method*, and shortly later, sitting in a Bavarian farmhouse, he wrote his *Meditations* (published in 1641), works that for their simplicity and conceptual power shifted the philosophical perspective of the West, profoundly influencing the future course of philosophy. Writing in the first person, he admitted to his reasoning only "clear and distinct ideas." Mathematical concepts like the objects of Euclid's geometry—points, lines, triangles—were a paradigm of such "clear and distinct ideas." Using his method of systematically doubting the existence of everything in the mental and physical world, he concluded with certainty that the only thing he could not doubt the existence of was the fact that he was thinking. Descartes, in the highest tradition of rationalism, placed the essence of being in thinking.

Applying his philosophical method of systematic doubt, Descartes divided existence into the material world of extended objects that could be examined by the natural sciences and the conceptual world of mental objects—thoughts, feelings, beliefs. The categorical distinction between matter and mind became a fixture of Western philosophy ever since. No one I know feels completely comfortable with this distinction because the universe is necessarily one being and not two. Yet there it is nonetheless.

Descartes viewed the body as a complex automaton, a machine, and the mind as an independent nonmaterial entity with rules of its own. He was aware of the difficulty of finding a solution to the mind-body problem—how can the nonmaterial mind interact with the material body? He made some suggestions, in his last book, *Passions of the Soul*, but none of them was very successful. His approach to the mind-body problem was interdisciplinary and drew on his polymathic knowledge of medicine, optics, geometry, and language. But he never solved it.

In spite of these difficulties, Descartes's view of existence (Cartesianism) deeply influenced the conduct of inquiry in his time and philosophically supported the emergent scientific revolution begun by his contemporaries Johannes Kepler and Galileo. More than the particular scientific discoveries Descartes made, especially the relation of algebra to geometry, it was his style of thinking, the worldview of reality he expressed in his philosophical writings, that so powerfully informed his age and made him a central figure. Central to that worldview was Descartes's image of the universe and the body as a giant complex machine.

The rapid progress of the natural sciences in the decades following Descartes's death swept the previous scholasticism and humanism aside. The demand for "clear and distinct ideas" was satisfied by the sciences and mathematics and diminished the previous respected role of the humanities—literature, law, history, art—for which "clear and distinct ideas" seemed lacking. With the successes of Newton's mechanics in elucidating the dynamics of the solar system, the mechanical worldview promoted by Descartes's followers seemed to triumph. But the reaction to Cartesianism was soon in coming.

The most cogent reaction came from Giambattista Vico, a Neopolitan philosopher and historian, a few decades after Descartes's death. He defended the integrity of the humanist tradition. Vico, even while accepting the Cartesian dualism, insisted that the Cartesians had it all backward. It was not the natural world that the human mind could intimately understand; the natural world, after all, was created by the inscrutable will of God. Rather it was the creations of the human mind itself—literature, law, history, art, the very subjects of humanistic study—that we could hope to understand completely and clearly precisely because they were made by us. In a famous and telling passage, Vico explained:

> In the night of thick darkness enveloping the earliest antiquity, so remote from ourselves, there shines the eternal and never failing light of a truth beyond all question: that the world of civil society has certainly been made by men, and that its principles are therefore to be found within the modifications of our own human mind. Whoever reflects on this cannot but marvel that the philosophers should have bent all their energies to the study of the world of nature, which, since God made it, He alone knows; and that they should have neglected the study of the world of nations or civil world, which, since men had made it, men could come to know.

The sciences were thus put in their place by Vico—they are the study of the material world of extension, a world alien to our humanity. The humanities, by contrast, examine the complex fabric of civil society, a world we know because we know ourselves; this is the realm of the mind in which our thoughts, feelings, loves, opinions, hopes, and terrors are the substance of existence. What we can truly know are the acts of our mind, the minds of other people, and the social word, not the natural world.

The rift between the "two cultures"—the humanities and the sciences—is a product of the Cartesian dualism of more than three centuries ago. It is a rift that has never been breached, because it is a rift in the structure of human existence itself.

Accepting the categorical dualism between mind and matter as an inherent division of existence creates a fundamental problem —the mind-body problem—as was recognized by Descartes. Although the nonmaterial mind and the material world are distinct, they are not independent of one another; each clearly interacts and influences the other. How is it possible for a nonmaterial entity—the mind—to influence the material world?

To emphasize this puzzle, imagine cutting up a human body— it is part of the world of extended objects—to find out where the nonmaterial mind has its point of influence. Clearly limbs, trunk, and internal organs other than the brain can be eliminated. (Interestingly, Egyptian embalmers disagreed: they carefully preserved the heart, liver, and lungs but discarded the brain as a piece of trash. It was the Roman physician Galen, in the second century, who first showed that the seat of the mind was the brain.) Then the question arises: Where in the brain do "I" reside? Parts of the brain can be further eliminated. (Descartes thought the soul was in the pineal gland at the base of the brain.) Eventually one gets down to language centers, parts of the cerebral cortex, as candidates for where "I" am. It is imaginable that if one were to attempt to localize any further, some wholistic property of the brain would be lost—along with the ego. Still, the question arises—how does this piece of gray matter produce the sense of self-consciousness and awareness, and how is it that lacking this piece, we are just complex automatons? Descartes, in view of the fact that animals could not speak a language, thought that they lacked the crucial piece—they *were* automatons and did not have immortal souls.

The idea of dissecting the body and brain to get at the mind seems bizarre, even silly. How can one, even in principle, arrive at the structure of intentionality and pure consciousness by studying the structure of an extended, material object—the brain?

Philosophers and scientists have taken several different positions, all within the framework of dualism, towards this puzzle—what I will call the positions of "categorical dualism," "substance dualism," "property dualism," and "epistemic dualism." That's quite a bundle of dualisms. But these distinctions will help us disentangle the various views of the mind-body problem. My own evaluation of these views is biased by my desire to see the mind-body problem as a researchable problem on the agenda of empirical science.

The position of categorical dualism is very simple. The mind and the body refer to entities that are categorically distinct; they are different logical types. Comparing the mind to the body is like comparing justice to meat. One entity is in the realm of concepts, the other in the realm of material objects. The mind-body problem thus arises simply because of a confusion of logical types.

This position is defensible (in the sense that it can be maintained consistently) and unresearchable. If the mind and body belong to different logical types, there can be no empirical investigation into their relation. Some people, dissatisfied by the "logical trick" of categorical dualism, insist that we view the mind and body as belonging to the same logical type. Since the brain is a material entity and if the mind is of the same logical type, then it must also have some kind of substantial existence. This approach then leads to the position of "substance dualism."

Let us explore the view of substance dualism—that the mind exists independently of, but interacts with, the body. A number of philosophers, including Karl Popper, as well as neuroscientists, including John C. Eccles, hold this view. Their position, somewhat oversimplified, is that the mind exists in a mental space, outside of space and time, and the brain is just a complex organ that acts as a "radio receiver" for the mind, translating its thoughts into the corporeal movements of the body. Of course if the receiver is meddled with, as could occur in a brain accident or during neurosurgery, the transmissions can be altered. But one should no more conclude from this alteration that the mind is produced by the brain than one would conclude that the music of a symphony orchestra is produced by a radio if an electronic part is removed from the radio and the music stops. So much in our ordinary mental experience—dreams, daydreams, imaginings—appears to be without any material support that it seems the mind can exist without the brain. This conclusion is shared by other substance dualists, including Descartes.

Yet, if we examine the idea of a "substantial" mind without material support from the standpoint of modern science, we see that it cannot be maintained. If a mind is anything, it represents organized information and implies a memory exists. The fact that information is transformed by my mind is self-evident every time I try to remember my birthday or a friend's face. According to physics, any information transmission or signaling requires a change in energy. Further, there is no way to provoke a change in energy or matter except by a change in kind—an endless causal chain of material events. This circumstance remains as true in quantum mechanics as it did in the earlier classical physics—no information can be transmitted without a transmission of energy. Any feature of our mental life that implies information is being processed must have material support.

Allen Newell and Herbert Simon, two of the founding fathers of cognitive science, think that this idea—that anything that transforms information or manipulates signs has to be supported by a material entity—is so important that they gave it a name—"the physical symbol system hypothesis." (It should really be called the "physical *sign* system hypothesis" in accord with the distinction between signs and symbols made in a previous chapter.) Newell and Simon see this hypothesis as playing the same role in the cognitive sciences as the hypothesis that atoms or cells exist played in the physical or life sciences. There is no way that symbols can be manipulated without a coincident physical process. But the notions that atoms or cells exist, while they once were hypotheses, are now facts—atoms or cells can be seen and manipulated. So what is so "hypothetical" about the physical symbol hypothesis?

Newell and Simon are more cautious than I would be when they call the notion of a physical symbol system "an hypothesis." The laws of physics as we understand them today allow no option. I would take the stronger position, as did Newton when he said *"hypothesis non fingo"*—I make no hypothesis. If having a mind implies that the mind can transform information—which thinking certainly entails—then such a mind cannot exist without material support. Substance dualism is in conflict with the laws of physics, at least as we know those laws today.

Since substance dualism does not work, dualists have taken yet another, more subtle approach—property dualism. The philosopher Patricia Smith Churchland describes it in her recent review (and refutation) of property dualism: "In contrast to the substance dualists, the property dualists do not believe there is a non-physical substance in which experiences inhere. Rather, they claim that subjective experiences are produced by the brain and can in their turn affect the brain, but they are not themselves identifiable with any physical properties of the brain. On this view, we cannot say, for example, that feeling sad is a neuronal configuration in such and such a neuronal ensemble." How is it at all possible for our subjective experiences not to be "identifiable with any physical properties of the brain"? That is the cornerstone of the property dualist's argument.

Property dualists maintain that the mind and our experiences are an "emergent" property of the material brain. According to this view, material elements when put together in a special way can acquire new "emergent" properties that cannot be explained in terms of those individual material elements. The whole is greater than the sum of its parts. For example, by assembling nucleotides together in the form of a DNA molecule, we find that the DNA has a new emergent property that no other molecule has —it can replicate itself. Furthermore, that property of DNA cannot be identifiable with any physical properties of the nucleotides, the elements of which it is made. Likewise the mind is an emergent property of the brain and cannot be reduced to it.

This argument is completely false. Let us see why. An emergent property is either of the same logical type as the elements from which it emerges or it is not. If it is not of the same logical type, then we are back in the position of categorical dualism: the "emergent" mind is categorically distinct from the brain. If, on the other hand, the emergent property is of the same logical type as the elements out of which it emerges, then there are two possibilities. Either the theory of the emergent property can be reduced to the theory of the elements out of which it emerges (reductionalism), or it cannot. If the theory cannot be reduced, then we are back in the position of substance dualism—the emergent property of mind had some new *substantial* property that cannot be explained in terms of its elements in the brain, the view that goes beyond the laws of nature as we now understand them. Alternatively, if the theory of the emergent property is in principle completely reducible to the theory of the elements out of which it emerges, then we have the standard reductionism of modern science, and the position of the identity theory that asserts that mental states and brain states are identical. In this view, which is held by most natural scientists, an emergent property *presupposes* reduction in theoretical explanation. The whole is equal to the sum of its parts.

We conclude that a consistent property dualist is forced into either the identity theory (which was what was to be avoided), categorical dualism (which is unresearchable), or substance dualism (which conflicts with the known laws of physics). The position of these dualists is thus not a very happy one. Why then does dualism have such an appeal? People might be more inclined to accept the notion of the mind as a function of the brain if it did not conflict so dramatically with their own experience of their consciousness. When I think I am unaware of any physical processes taking place. My mind, to me, seems independent of the physical world. To emphasize this, dualists, who maintain that the gap between mind and body is an issue of principle, point to the puzzle of free will and determinism to support their claim. What is the puzzle?

From my first-person perspective I am, in most ways, free to act as I please—I can choose the position of my body and where it goes; I choose what I say. Nothing seems more evident to me than that I am free in my actions, and I attribute this freedom to others as well. On the basis of this freedom I and others become moral agents—we have responsibility for our actions.

Our sense of free will is intimately associated with our ability to perceive the future course of our actions. Unlike animals (to the best of my knowledge), we can imagine the distant future, and we can make choices that affect the future. We thus are held morally responsible for some aspects of our condition, but animals are not. Some people might argue that behavioral reinforcement, both positive and negative, plays a role in our choices, and no doubt that is true. This would appear to make us less free. Yet the moment we become aware of that controlling reinforcement, as we often are and can be, then human orneriness will assert itself and the course of our future action is again unpredictable. I am impressed by the ability of individuals who exhibit compulsive behavior, such as an addiction to alcohol or drugs, to alter the course of their self-destructive behavior either through the strength of their free will or the appeal to a transcendent power to help support that will. No animal can do that. The dignity of our humanity rests on the evidence that our will is free.

Yet in spite of our immediate experience that our will is free, from the third-person perspective of science what I do appears very different. My body and brain are just a very complex electro-chemical system. The electrons and chemicals in my brain move in accordance with the laws of physics—they go where they are required to go. Perhaps there is some intrinsic randomness in their motion as required by quantum theory. But that is unimportant for this argument because my mind cannot influence how the electrons or chemicals distribute themselves (if it could, this would be a kind of self-telekinesis—mind acting on its own brain matter). From this third-person perspective I am just a quantum-mechanical automaton determined by the laws of quantum theory. There seems to be no room for my free will to act on this automaton without violating the laws of physics.

Maybe, then, our apparent free will is just an illusion. But how can that be when it is so clear that we can choose to do this or to do that at any moment? This, then, is the puzzle of free will and determinism: How do we reconcile our evident freedom to do as we please with the scientific view that we are complex quantum-mechanical automatons? Categorical dualists would assert that our free will is *not* an illusion. The mind is free. But then there must be something in the laws of physics and biology that is either wrong or incomplete. The freewill determinism puzzle, like the mind-body problem to which it is so intimately related, is a litmus test of one's metaphysical position.

This puzzle has been around for a long time. Before the rise of modern science, religious people believing in an omniscient God who could see past the future laid out like a motion picture had to confront the problem that all their future good and bad acts were already known to God. The course of their lives, in the eyes of God, was predetermined.

As a child the English poet Lord Byron had a governess who was a Christian determinist—a Calvinist. She urged him to devote himself to saving his soul. Byron accepted Calvinist determinism but drew the opposite conclusion: since his life was completely determined anyway, he could do (and did) anything he pleased without being responsible. The position one takes—free will or determinism—can have moral consequences. Some people may try to exonerate themselves of their crimes on the ground that they were not acting freely—they are insane, completely determined by the will of God, victims of their environment, compulsive, under the influence of drugs, and other imagined determinants of actions.

The fact that a moral and ethical dimension has entered our discussion of the mind-body problem should not be a surprise. In our everyday practical life we assume that people are free moral agents, and our society and laws recognize this. In order to reconcile human freedom with the determinism required by reductionalist science, Kant proposed another dualism—epistemic dualism—which I believe describes the circumstances of our existence correctly as well as being supported by scientific reason.

Kant recognized that we employ at least two different kinds of reason in coming to grips with reality, the "theoretical reason" of the scientist and the "practical reason" of the lawyer, businessman, or just about anyone else. The theoretical reasoning of the scientist sees the world according to natural theories. In *principle*, according to theoretical reason, the world is one, and its explication can be reduced to the properties of primary elements of material existence. This is also the standpoint of the identity theorist —the mind and consciousness are a biological-material process explicable in terms of natural laws. The states of the mind are in *principle* reducible to the states of the brain.

In *practice*, as any scientist will be the first to admit, such a reduction is, in detail, impossible to achieve. Hence the necessity for practical reason, which sees the mind as autonomous and the person as a free moral agent, an agent that for most practical purposes is independent of the brain. This is the reasoning most people use in dealing with the problems of life. If a person misbehaves, we say that they have done wrong rather than that their brain is malfunctioning.

Theoretical reason, the way of science, sees the mind-body problem from the third-person perspective; practical reason sees this problem from a first-person perspective. Kant's epistemic dualism explicitly acknowledges that we see the mind-body problem differently depending on whether we view it in terms of what in *principle* must be true or in terms of what in *practice* we can achieve. And that, I believe, is how it is.

Epistemic dualism gives its due to both the reductionalist approach of science and the ethical dimensions of human life. Unlike the previous dualisms, it is a dualism of method or of intention, not a logical or material dualism. Furthermore, it promotes a research program because the boundary between what "in principle must be true" and what "in practice we can achieve" is subject to scientific investigation. We may come to understand many features of our mental experience through advances in the neurosciences. But I doubt that the radical ambition of the identity theorists—a precise mapping of our experience onto neurofunction—will ever be practically realized. Let us examine some of the considerations that may establish how the boundary between "in principle" and "in practice" gets drawn.

In order to simplify this, let us first consider how this boundary is drawn in a few physical systems already examined by the natural sciences, and which, unlike the brain, are reasonably well understood. It is important to bear in mind that it is *theories* that may or may not be reducible to one another, not the material structures of the world (although we will often loosely speak as if they are). Two key notions that help support epistemic dualism and are exemplified by physical systems are: first, the notion that there is a "causal decoupling" between material levels that makes radical physical reductionalism and the identity theory practically unrealizable; and second, the notion of "the barrier of complexity" that allows the mind its practical freedom in spite of the fact that its material support, the brain, is completely governed by biological and chemical laws. I will discuss these two ideas in turn.

I have already described the notion of "causal decoupling" between levels of the reductionist chain from macrocosm to microcosm in terms of the gene. Although genetics is supported by a material structure—DNA—and ultimately governed by the laws of chemistry, once we know the rules of genetic combination we can "forget" the detailed laws of chemistry. Genetics becomes "causally decoupled" from the laws of chemistry.

Likewise, on a more microscopic level, the laws of chemistry depend on the existence and properties of the atomic nucleus sitting at the center of atoms. But the detailed laws of nuclear physics—the laws of quarks and gluons that bind the nucleus together—are not needed in order to understand the laws of physical chemistry. This "causal decoupling" between the levels of the world implies that to *understand* the material basis of certain rules

I must go to the next level down; but the rules can be *applied* with confidence without any reference to the more basic level. Interestingly, the division of natural sciences reflects this causal decoupling. Nuclear physics, atomic physics, chemistry, molecular biology, biochemistry, and genetics are each independent disciplines valid in their own right, a consequence of the causal decoupling between them.

Another feature that causal decoupling implies as we move up the material chain of being from the small to the large is the emergence of new qualitative properties of matter. Physicists are familiar with how new properties emerge from coherent physical phenomena. There is a whole branch of physics that studies "collective phenomena"—the emergence of qualitatively new collective features of an ensemble of individual molecules, atoms, or electrons. Perhaps the simplest example of a collective phenomenon is a water wave. Each molecule of water executes a simple up-and-down motion. Yet when large numbers of water molecules do that collectively and with the right timing, the result is a giant water wave. The wave moves across the water and can transfer energy across huge distances, but the water itself is relatively immobile. Some of the largest waves are the "greybeards," one-hundred-foot-high monsters that circle around the continent of Antarctica for months, building up their energy from the wind. Electrons in metals, ordered lattices of atoms, and many other physical systems can exhibit complex collective phenomena. The characteristic of these collective properties is that they are always understood on the basis of microphysical laws so that the whole remains the sum of its parts. Although the properties of the whole system follow from the properties of the parts, the whole system has features that its individual parts do not have—an emergence of new qualitative features from collective coherence.

Likewise one sees evidence for the emergence of new qualitative features in biology as well. DNA is a remarkable molecule. Unlike any other molecule, it can reproduce itself—make an exact copy of itself from other building-block molecules in its environment. By combining other molecules to make a DNA molecule, a new material feature has been created—molecular reproduction. This qualitative feature then becomes the material basis for genetics. Molecular biologists, rather than talking about molecular bonding and chemical interactions, start talking about a new language of information transfer, replication, coding, and protein synthesis, a language that reflects that new qualities exist that are not present in its individual parts.

It is interesting to observe that at certain junctions, representing "causal decouplings," natural scientists will change the way they talk about the things they are studying. A dramatic example is the junction between the material and nonmaterial worlds. Instead of talking about matter and its interactions—proteins, the nervous system, and so on—scientists will start talking about signals and information transfer. The change is subtle but important. In one step they cross over the line dividing matter and its interactions from the nonmaterial world of organized information. There is nothing mysterious in this important step, for we see that in talking about information scientists have simply extracted the interesting and essential component of what are in fact complex material interactions. But they are now talking about "nonmaterial" information and not matter.

For example, as we move further up the reductionalist chain to the biological level of cells, the nervous system, and the brain, scientists begin to speak of signals, information transfer, and processing. While the actual material structure—the brain and its axons, dendrites, synaptic junctions, and all these linkages—determines the detailed rules (as yet unknown) of how information is transferred and processed in the brain, we can, if we know the rules, begin to speak of signals rather than material processes. While today this can be done for simple organisms or parts of the brain, if we are to examine the more realistic situation corresponding to human experience, then, because of our ignorance of our brain's operations, we leave the realm of knowledge and glide off into speculation.

The information in our brain is processed and perhaps "packaged"—collected together in relevant bundles. Perhaps there are collective effects in the realm of the brain's information processing the lead to yet further "causal decouplings." There could be subsystems within supersystems—a hierarchy of information and command, resembling nothing quite so much as human society itself. In this image the neuron in the brain is like an individual in society. What we experience as consciousness is the "social consciousness" of our neuronal network.

This idea has been developed in detail by the neuroscientist

Michael Gazzaniga in his book *The Social Brain*. Gazzaniga sees the brain as organized modularly with the different modules engaged in a competitive struggle for dominance, like those silent partners I mentioned earlier, struggling for attention. My colleagues at Rockefeller University, the neuroscientist Jonathan Winson, takes a somewhat different view in his book *Brain and Psyche*. He sees the components of the brain not as competing, but as cooperating under the aegis of an executive authority—the ego. But it is fair to say that no one yet knows how the brain is controlled. As Francis Crick observed, "If a breakthrough in the study of the brain does come, it is perhaps likely to be at the level of the overall control of the system. If the system were as chaotic as it sometimes appears to be, it would not enable us to perform even the simplest tasks satisfactorily."

Finally, we may find that speaking in terms of information is ineffective in describing higher brain function and resort to speaking about mental representations, concepts, and so on. Such a series of "causal decouplings" may be extraordinarily complex, intricate beyond our current imaginings. Yet finally what we may arrive at is a theory of the mind and consciousness—a mind so decoupled from its material support systems that it seems to be independent of them—and "forgot" how we got to it. According to the theoretical reason, the biological phenomenon of a self-reflective consciousness is simply the last of a long and complex series of "causal decouplings" from the world of matter.

The notion that consciousness is "causally decoupled" from the brain is, of course, a conjecture—it is not proven. As a conjecture it remains a fantasy, the kind of fantasy that I am critical of when philosophers and others have them. One should actually provide detailed designs or acutally construct the device, organ, or material system that implements one's conjecture and not merely speculate. However, this conjecture does provide a research agenda, which will occupy scientists far into the future.

Besides "causal decoupling," a second feature that helps support epistemic dualism is the existence of a "complexity barrier." The brain is the most complex piece of matter in the known universe. And its complexity is probably an essential feature of its operation. We do not yet have a good idea of the complexity of the brain's neural network, but it exceeds anything we have ever seen before. Some modest sense of this complexity can be grasped if we realize that the brain must reflect, in part, the complexity of the world around us, including the natural, linguistic, and social environment, the store of our knowledge and memory, and a vast repertoire of motor and sensory skills.

Although we can speak loosely about complexity, it is also possible to be more precise. Mathematicians have a new field of study called "complexity theory," which I described in a previous chapter, "Order, Complexity, and Chaos." There are at least two different kinds of material complexity, called "simulatable" and "unsimulatable" complexity. To illustrate the difference between these two kinds of physical complexity, imagine two physical systems, the solar system and the weather.

First consider the solar system and the motions of all the planets in the night sky. Viewed from the earth, the motions of the planets seem rather complicated; some even exhibit retrograde motions—they stop, move backward, and then start up again. However, from the heliocentric viewpoint the motions of the planets are simple ellipses with the sun at one of the foci. Using Newton's laws, we can make a mathematical model of the planetary motions. According to this model, if we know the positions of the planets at one time—what is called the "initial data"—we can predict their positions for millennia in the future. Planetary motion is an example of "simulatable" complexity. Because I can make a mathematical model based on known physical laws and, importantly, can solve the equations, either by hand or more rapidly on a computer, I can find an effective mathematical simulation of the planetary motions and determine the future of the system.

The next physical system to consider is the weather on our planet, an example of "unsimulatable" complexity. The weather is extremely complicated and capricious—cold fronts, storms, dry periods, monsoons, and ice ages, to name a few features. Yet, as was recognized from ancient times, the weather exhibits some regular patterns. From our modern viewpoint we know the physical laws that govern the weather, just as we know the physical laws that govern the planets. So why can't we predict the weather as precisely as we can predict the motions of the planets?

In order to predict the weather it is necessary to have a knowledge of the temperature, pressure, and other physical quantities at every point in the atmosphere and surface of the earth at one time—the initial data. Of course we cannot do this precisely, but we can get approximate information in our computer simulations of the weather to try to predict its future course. But there is a crucial difference between the equations that describe the weather and those that describe the motion of the planets. If the initial data for the planetary motions contains some small inaccuracy, then according to the equations that govern planetary motion that inaccuracy will result in a relatively small inaccuracy in our knowledge of the future motions of the planets. Not so for the weather equations, as was discovered by Edward Lorenz (see the chapter "Life Can Be So Nonlinear"). A small difference in the initial data, according to these equations, can cause wildly different weather patterns. A sea gull flapping its wing on a Cape Cod beach can generate a pressure fluctuation that grows into a violent storm halfway around the world a month later. For this reason weathermen can predict the weather only probabilistically. As their detailed knowledge of the weather at one time improves, so will their ability to predict it more accurately, days and even a week into the future. But because the weather is an example of unsimulatable complexity, we cannot hope to mathematically model its detailed behavior very far into the future.

There is, of course, one computer that can simulate the weather exactly—the weather system of the earth is a *perfect* analogue computer of its own development. If we could somehow speed it up, we would have *exact* weather predictions. This rather trivial example (anything is its own analogue computer) illustrates an important point of principle—unsimulatable systems cannot be effectively mathematically modeled by a system any less complex than they are themselves.

John von Neumann, the mathematical genius, remarked in the 1940s that two outstanding problems confronting the sciences were weather prediction and the brain's operation. Today we have a much better grasp on the complexity of weather—we understand the main equations and know that it is an unsimulatable system. The brain, however, remains an enigma. Scientists have attempted to find a reliably accurate mathematical set of equations that describe the essential features of the neuronal connections and their operation. But my guess is that even if such equations are found, the brain's complexity will turn out to be another example of unsimulatable complexity. If this is so, then in spite of the fact that at some future time the biophysical laws for the brain may be known precisely, the simplest system that simulates a brain's operation is that brain itself. If these ideas are right, then there is a "complexity barrier" that lies between our instantaneous knowledge of the state of the neuronal network and our knowledge of its future development. The brain, and hence the mind, is another example of an unsimulatable system.

This "complexity barrier" does not imply that we cannot predict the future states of the brain at all, only that we cannot do so very far into the future. Ben Libet, a neuroscientist at the University of California at San Francisco who has collaborated with John Eccles, has devised an ingenious experiment that shows that the brain is activated to perform an act about one-half second prior to the person becoming aware that they have decided to do so. The "doing" precedes the "awareness." Interestingly, we know what the person is going to decide slightly before they do themselves because in the experiment we see that the motor cortex has been activated. This suggests that short-range predictability may be possible. But for all practical purposes long-term detailed predictability is unachievable.

I speculate that there may be a complexity barrier of yet another kind involved in describing the brain. Usually scientists assume that once they specify the microstate of a physical system at a certain time, they know everything they could possibly know about the system at that time. For example, if scientists know (as in fact they cannot) the microstate of the weather in some large volume of the atmosphere—know the position and velocity of every atom—they could analyze that data, averaging it over certain regions, and conclude what the macrostate of the weather is like—it's raining, or the sky is clear, and so forth. In principle, it is a relatively easy task to use the information about the microstate to deduce what is going on in the macrostate. Significantly, for the weather and other physical systems, small errors in the specification of the microstate translate into small errors in the specification of the macrostate. After all, what can a mistake about the position of an atom or two make in the description of the weather?

However, it is imaginable that even if one knew the microstate of the brain—the state of every neuron, every synaptic vesicle—it would be impossible to ascertain the state of consciousness; for example, to conclude that this person is having a dream. The reason is that a small error in the specification of the microstate could result in a large error in the determination of the macro-state.

Von Neumann, who thought a lot about how brains might work, hinted at this kind of complexity barrier when he remarked that the simplest model of a neuron may be the neuron itself. Any attempt to simplify the neuron and ignore the details of its micro-state would fail to take into account some important feature of its role in producing consciousness. I certainly hope this isn't true; it would mean that the kind of "causal decoupling" I described pre-viously would not work. One would have to know every detail of the brain—the complete, precise microstate—to know its macro-state. If this is so, then the kind of invariant maps of the mind some cognitive scientists are seeking do not exist.

My motive in describing "causal decoupling" and "the complex-ity barrier" was to provide some background support for the thesis of "epistemic dualism"—the idea that while in principle the mind is only a function of the brain, in practice this reduction is impos-sible. "Causal decoupling" indicates that consciousness, in spite of the fact that it seems to be independent of matter, is entirely supported by material processes. "The complexity barrier" indi-cates why consciousness will be undetermined in its future devel-opment (in spite of the fact it is governed entirely by natural laws). I do not wish to claim that I have proven that such a "causal decoupling" and the "complexity barrier" actually apply to the brain, only that I regard them as very plausible. Proof, such as there is in this problem, will have to await a deeper understanding of how the brain works.

Many people are uncomfortable with these ideas and wonder if it is possible to actually build an artificial brain, producing a con-scious mind. How can one do this using just organized matter? These people want (and deserve to have) a demonstration, an actual construction, of a material embodiment of mind. Many of the current discussions about the embodiments of mind invoke what I will call "analytic" and "intentional engines" and the rela-tion between these two engines.

The "analytical engine" was the lifetime project of Charles Bab-bage, an English scientist-inventor whose productive career spanned the early part of the nineteenth century. The analytic engine was a machine with gears and wheels that could compute, do arithmetic and other calculations—a mechanical version of the modern electronic computer. Babbage built a simple analytical engine, started up a second version, and before completing it conceived of a much more ambitious (and very expensive) version that was never built. Babbage even used punch cards for information inputs (an idea he got from automatic looms) and envisioned the use of programs. Unfortunately his imagination outstripped the mechanical technology of his time; his ideas had to await the advent of electronic technology. But Babbage definitely anticipated the modern computer. His engines, like modern computers, embody a set of definite rules that manipulate information. They might also be called syntactic engines because of the fact that all they do is obey formal rules—the meaning, the semantic content of the information, plays no role. The analytical engine was just a machine—it could do what it was instructed to do, no more, no less. Given an input, output would be identical every single time. Modern computers, in spite of their speed and sophistication, far beyond Babbage's imaginings, essentially do no more.

The "intentional engine" is the human brain interacting with the world. Intentional engines have the singular property that they possess intentionality—they hold beliefs, have emotions, exercise free will. In short, they are conscious and can represent meaning —they are semantic engines.

Are these two kinds of engines distinct? As I have described them they certainly seem to be distinct. But are we certain that by building a sufficiently complex analytical engine—lots of these assembled together—we cannot build an intentional engine? Further, can we take an intentional engine apart and find out that it is in fact built up out of lots of analytical engines? I do not know the answer to these questions; they are heatedly debated by philosophers and cognitive scientists. Some insist that it is impossible— that one can never obtain intentionality out of a rule-governed physical symbol system. Supporting this view, some argue that semantics can never be gotten from syntactics.

I do not understand all those arguments. But this much I do know. There already exists a rather continuous series of engines— from simple analytic engines up to the most complex intentional engines—which, if we understood them, would answer our questions and resolve the debate. The problem is that these engines were built by the Demiurge and not by us, and we do not know how he did it. The series of engines that I have in mind is the hierarchy of life on earth from the simplest phages—which act like microscopic robots whose parts are known to us—to human beings, the true intentional engines whose workings are mostly unknown. The simplest phages are governed by the rules of molecular biology and chemistry. For more complex organisms with elementary nervous systems, we can see that information is processed according to rules that are "causally decoupled" from chemistry. While one may argue whether there is any computation or sign manipulation going on or not, or if a program, like a computer program, is being executed, we know that information is definitely being processed and the rules of neurobiology are followed. And so on up the tree of life. If we knew how the Demiurge did it (alas, evolution is far cleverer than we are), we would probably not be asking questions about free will and determinism or be puzzled about the mind-body problem. For example, as we look at the sequence of organisms from the simplest phages to human beings, at what point do we attribute consciousness and intentionality to an organism? Are gorillas, dogs, and chipmunks conscious? Lizards and turtles? Insects? Does the mosquito *want* to bite me the way I *want* to eat? Categorical dualists usually answer these questions by saying only human beings are truly conscious. Epistemic dualists, on the other hand, have a researchable problem.

The same problem arises for artificial intelligences. At what point do we attribute intentionality to a computer (as distinct from its designer)? To help answer this I'd like to recount a little story.

In 1986 I sent a chess-playing computer to my friends Peter and Anna McClinton, who live in their compound on the banks of the Blue Nile ten miles south of Juba in the South Sudan. They have been working for more than a decade to set up a number of national parks, some larger than the Serengeti, to save the last large concentrations of megafauna. Besides the incredible logistical difficulties involved in maintaining their equipment, their work is hampered by a regional civil war. I was waiting for the news of the impact that the arrival of the first artificial intelligence in the South Sudan would have, and the other day I was rewarded by a letter from Anna. She wrote:

It is a beautiful, grey Saturday morning; temperatures are near enough 100, humidity not far behind, the generator hums, the refrigerators hiss, the dogs snore, birds chirp, flies buzz, and in the comfortably far distance we hear some mortar interspersed with bursts of machine gun fire. In other words God is in Heaven (not that I expected him to be anywhere else) and all is as peaceful as it can be under the present circumstances. Peter has gone to Juba to listen to the latest rumours, which gives me a chance to write to you.

Before I go any further I want to thank you for the wonderful chess computer which arrived safely on the last charter from the UK. We have named him Kasimir, and he immediately became a valued if controversial member of the family. How did we know it was a male computer? Why, he couldn't have been anything else, with those geometrically perfect squares and the silver-black-red (for the lights) colour scheme. Female computers, as everybody knows, have round squares and are pink and white.

Kasimir is our first computer of substance. The only other one we ever had experience with was one of those little pocket calculators. It took us a little while to understand him. In fact, during the first 24 hours of Kasimir's residence there were some heated arguments in this family. . . . Very soon I fell in love with Kasimir. I started doing crazy things like opening KRP-R4 or similar. I would sacrifice my queen, the rooks, the knights, the bishops and not even be aware of doing it. Kasimir won every single game, and I felt very good about it. Now will you please tell me one thing: why can't I be that happy to lose when my opponent is a human being? If that isn't love, I don't know what love is.

Then, one day, Peter outfoxed Kasimir. He sacrificed a piece to get a pawn through, converted it into a queen and had a mate in 3 moves. And he gloated. This made me mad. So, while Peter was not looking I changed the level to the most advanced one. Let's just see if he can beat that. He hasn't yet.

As the letter indicates it is easy, perhaps even appropriate, to attribute intentionality to a computer. Who cares how the computer does it—probably by a rapid, selective electronic search program for the best move. We can always take what the philosopher Dan Dennett calls an "intentional stance" and make our moves as if the computer were a rational, motivated being. We would do the same for people or animals.

I find the notion of an "intentional stance" a valuable concept because it describes something in my own experience. As an example of different intentional stances, consider the differences between the way a devoted cat lover views his pet cat and the way a behavioral psychologist or biologist studies a cat. The cat lover attributes consciousness, motives, beliefs, almost with spiritual overtones, to their pet feline, while the scientist sees only a Cartesian automaton, an organic robot. It will be the same with intelligent computers when they come. If you want to study the computer, you will adopt the intentional stance of a computer scientist. But if you want the computer to do something for you, it might be best to treat it as if it were an intelligent being with its own strategies and motives—one of God's creatures. Once again, the distinction between the stance of theoretical reason and practical reason is apparent in how we approach either cats or computers.

I do not know the final answer to the mind-body problem. I do know that if one adopts the position of epistemic dualism, or one close to it, the answer is researchable. We may already have rough pieces of the answer. Furthermore, this position is not only scientifically plausible, it is ethically responsible as well.

Much of this discussion of the mind-body problem was from the third-person perspective—the view of theoretical reason. Now with this background, I would like to return to the puzzle of free will and determinism. And to illustrate that puzzle I will allow the first-person perspective to directly confront the third-person perspective. I will do this within the context of a philosophical fantasy —the man who mistook his brain for his mind.

I like to engage in this fantasy because it both fulfills a wish and supports a prejudice. The wish is that I could see the operations of my own brain the way I can see the mechanical operations of my own hand. The prejudice is that if we could but see the material operation of our brain, even when we engage in silent thinking and meditation, then the delusion of the mind-body distinction would fall away. Unlike the movements of our hand, which we can see, we cannot see the movements of our brain, although we are aware of them as our mind. If there was a technological breakthrough (such as is described in the fantasy below) that enabled us to see the detailed operation of our brain even as we think our thoughts, then this new perception would radically alter our perspective on the mind-body problem.

The time is in the future, and medical engineers have invented the MBS—the magnetic brain scan, an advanced version of the

CAT scanner and MRI (magnetic resonance imagining) devices of the previous century. The subject wears a special "hat" that can detect electrical activity throughout his brain by measuring tiny magnetic fields. Its resolution is so refined that it can detect when individual neurons are fired. In front of the subject is a large transparent model of a brain, about one hundred times the diameter of the brain itself. This model consists of one hundred billion tiny color-coded lights, one for each neuron in the subject's brain. Whenever a neuron is fired in the subject's brain a corresponding light flashes in the model. Different neural pathways have different colors—it's set up for maximum clarity and display potential. The medical researchers usually use the MBS to study brain damage or how well a brain transplanted tissue has taken. However, this time a philosopher, who recently got a large grant enabling him to spend several hundred hours using the MBS, is going to try out the brain scanner on himself. The medical engineers warn him that this can be dangerous. For example, if the subject is watching the visual cortex on the brain model, he may see waves of light periodically flashing. What is happening is that a feedback loop has been set up, similar to the feedback loop that can occur between a microphone and a loudspeaker in an auditorium and which produces a loud whining sound. In order to avoid a visual cortex burnout, the engineers warn, just close your eyes quickly; that breaks the feedback loop.

In the days that follow the philosopher begins to familiarize himself with the pattern of lights he sees in the brain—his brain—before him. Most of the brain, he is amazed to discover, is dark, only a small part or parts are actually lit up; about 10 percent. All parts of the brain, however, are brought into action at one time or another. He explores his motor cortex by wiggling his different fingers and toes, smacking his lips, and so on. He activates his hippocampus every time he tries to remember something or someone from a few months ago. But memories earlier than about three years ago—childhood memories—are stored in a complex fashion in the neocortex and not the hippocampus. Soon he becomes familiar with various parts of his brain. Later he begins the exploration of "silent thinking"—he does calculations in his head, imagines unicorns, and has erotic fantasies—and finds out the active sites in his brain correspond to these. Sometimes the thoughts are not represented by any local activity of the lights but are a pattern that is spread out over the whole brain. He also notices that although he can activate a specific pattern by thinking certain thoughts—such as holding the notion of the number nine before his mind—there is lots more going on in the model brain. There are patterns he does not recognize and which presumably correspond to processes far below the level of awareness, the unconscious.

One feature on the MBS that is especially instructive is the "slow-motion replay." Most of the brain patterns come and go too fast for the philosopher to see in real time. But he can replay them as slowly as he likes. The slow-motion brain patterns reveal a whole new structure of detailed complexity that happens too fast in real time to be noticed. One thing the philosopher notices from the slow-motion replay is that as far as he can see most neurons fire deterministically—if a certain neuron fires, then five other specific neurons also fire shortly thereafter. These, in turn, imply that other specific neurons always fire or are inhibited. Viewed on this microtime scale, the brain seems to be a vast deterministic machine.

The philosopher is extremely impressed by this device and soon develops a reasonable mastery over it. In real time he learns how to generate specific patterns just by thinking certain thoughts. In contrast with the determinism he saw at microtimes, his feeling is now one of complete freedom: just by thinking he can make lots of those lights do just what he wants. In fact, he fancies himself a kind of "concept artist," creating especially beautiful moving patterns of lights by just going through a sequence of thoughts. He is puzzling about why the brain is so deterministic on the scale of microtime yet in real time seems subject to his free will. He concludes that if there is a "complexity barrier" between the scale of microtime where everything is determined and real time where everything is free, then this would resolve the old free will-determinism problem.

One day a friend, a biologist, visits him, and he demonstrates his skills on him. The biologist is unimpressed by his resolution of the free will-determinism problem and tells him that he thinks it is still an open question. He suggests to the philosopher that they first set up some electronic timing devices to check out the mind-body problem. "After all," he says, "using this machine, the problem can be settled experimentally. If the thoughts come first and then the neurons fire, it is because your mind is something different from your brain—your brain just does what it is told to do by your mind. On the other hand, if the neuronal patterns appear first and only then do you become aware of the corresponding thought, your brain is just functioning, and you, led by your brain, are necessarily following along. We have got to do this experiment carefully because the delay time in either case is probably very short."

To the philosopher's horror, and in complete conflict with the feeling of freedom he had in creating brain patterns, the results of the experiment show that the patterns and regions of the brain are activated about one-half second prior to his awareness of them. His consciousness, even the awareness of his freedom, is a consequence of the activity of the brain, not vice versa.

The philosopher is not about to accept this without a fight. He tries to think faster than the model's response; he changes his mind often and quickly. But like trying to outmaneuver your image in a mirror, his efforts are in vain. With every attempt to "outthink" the brain model, the model beats him to it. He is just following the patterns, a total slave to the preexistent neuronal signals in his brain. He falls into a slump of despair (also anticipated by the model brain by about half a second) as he realizes that his free will is an illusion; all that is happening is a bunch of activating and inhibiting neuronal events.

"Cheer up," says his biologist friend. "What difference does it make if your brain is activated before 'you' become aware of the thought? The only way that your brain will do anything is if *you* want it to. Maybe that 'you' is just another complex pattern in the brain, and so what if it does not respond to information coming from other parts of the brain before they show up in the model? But those decisions won't even be executed unless *you* decide." As he listens to his friend, the philosopher sees the model brain begin to react to this new information; something is stirring in the philosopher's brain.

"I get it," says the philosopher. "I've not been identifying with that big model brain out there, but really it's me, or rather a faithful representation of my mind, like my image in a mirror faithfully reflects my body. Maybe it's a better expression of the real me, than, say, my face, hands, or body. Still, I feel that this discovery—that the model brain "anticipates" my thinking—is like finding out that the image on the other side of the mirror is the 'real' me and not just an image. But you're right; it doesn't make any difference. Hannah Arendt, the philosopher, once remarked that the trouble with behaviorism is not so much that it is true but that it might become so. Many cultures have fallen into that rut.

"Over the last few weeks I have been playing with this brain scanner which gives me access to a part of my body I cannot otherwise see—my working brain. Finally I can *see* my thinking like I can see my hand move when I want it to. What my brain does is as unpredictable as the weather—in fact, even more so because it is capable of far more complex patterns than the weather. Lots of possible patterns and choices arise in an organ that complex and what 'I' am is a complex pattern that represents the execution of conscious decisions. All those choices and the execution of decisions are completely consistent with natural law. That is clear from the slow instant replay—the microview. But knowing these natural laws is of no help in determining what choice 'I' will in fact make, what patterns will arise—the brain is unsimulatable. And because of that I can accept the reality of my mental freedom. I now know what primitive people must have felt like when they first saw their faces in a photograph and thought their souls had been stolen. But, of course, they were not stolen."

The biologist, however, is not about to let his friend conclude so easily and asks, "Do you know why you had such resistance to seeing your mind as the brain scan—identifying with the model? I suspect that deep down you did not want to see your mind entirely supported by the body. For if your mind is entirely supported by your body, you must die with that body. The belief in an immortal soul is not so easy to give up!"

"You are wrong," says the philosopher. "I accept my personal mortality. But those incredible patterns in my brain representing the ideas of numbers, languages, music, deep feelings, and God, those patterns can appear in other brains, in other bodies, natural or artificial. Karl Popper said there were three worlds—the material world of matter, the mental world of one's thoughts, feelings, and emotions, and a third world consisting of the eternal concepts shared by all minds such as the transcendental concepts of pure mathematics. Popper's third world was just the notion of the 'absolute mind' of nineteenth-century idealistic philosophy in twentieth-century clothing. These transcendental concepts are represented as a complex network of neuronal patterns. And the coherence, depth, and beauty of those patterns is immortal, an eternal possibility that is coexistent with our universe. I could not ask for more. What *I am*, essentially, *is* already eternal. The rest dies with my body.

"My mind is part of nature, the eternal order of the universe, and it is a mistake to think otherwise. Some may wish to say that this is just backward—nature is simply an idea that my mind has. But in fact, as I now realize, there is no inconsistency between these ideas."

"I still think you are kidding yourself," says the biologist, smiling.

A sense of peace and understanding prevails, and neither the biologist nor the philosopher speak. The great model brain is quiescent, an occasional flicker of lights and a few periodic movements is all it reveals.

In summary: Monism, while it may offer a spiritual sense of connectedness or materialist simplicity, does not solve the mind-body problem; it ignores it. By ignoring a distinction, an opportunity for learning is lost. Furthermore, monism can lose the ethical dimension of human life. Dualism (the view of Descartes) characterizes the position we, as thinking and feeling beings, find ourselves. But several forms of dualism—categorical, substance, and property dualism—are either dead ends or wrong. Epistemic dualism (the view of Kant) is a dualism not of the mind and body, but within the reasoning processes we use to examine the world—a split between theoretical reason, which sees what in principle must be true and practical reason, which sees what in practice can be accomplished. I have advocated this position not only because it conforms with our experience, but because it puts the boundary between what is in principle and in practice possible to know about the mind-body problem firmly on the research agenda of the new sciences of complexity. And that is where I think it belongs.

Before ending this chapter, I would like to tell one more story.

In 1984 Tenzin Gyatso, the fourteenth Dalai Lama of Tibet, was visiting the United States. As executive director of the New York Academy of Sciences, I received a letter from the New York office of Tibet saying the Dalai Lama was interested in having a discussion with Western scientists about modern physics and cosmology, psychology, and biology—a cross-cultural exchange. I arranged for some of my colleagues at the N. Y. Academy and Rockefeller

University and others from Harvard and Yale, a limit of a dozen eminent scientists, to meet with him one afternoon.

I was slightly concerned that the Dalai Lama, who might rest on the formal dignity of his high office, and my fellow scientists, who were used to the informal exchange of ideas, would not effectively communicate. But my concerns came to naught shortly after he arrived—he had a rich sense of life, a warm, open, and humorous personality; he was an engaging and passionate man.

The discussion that took place in the Tudor-style library of the N. Y. Academy revolved around the mind-body problem. The Dalai Lama, grounded in the ancient tradition of his people as well as his own experience, maintained that the essential mind was an independent reality, although accidental aspects of it such as personality, tastes, and values were linked to the body, the physical world, and historical circumstances. Like many Eastern religious people, Tibetans maintain a belief in reincarnation—the view that one's essential being upon physical death survives and then becomes reincorporated in a new body at birth.

The Dalai Lama was quite knowledgeable about Western science (certainly more knowledgeable than the scientists about Tibetan religion, philosophy, and psychology) and quite interested in learning more. He impressed us with his openness. It was clear to me that the learning of Tibetan scholars, their research into the human mind and wealth of psychological insights, had insights to offer the West, although the translation into a common conceptual basis might prove difficult. Indeed, one of the reasons, I suspect, for his visit was to indicate to Westerners, and scientists in particular, the complexity and depth of Tibetan studies. The Chinese Communists, who devastated the Tibetan religious culture after their conquest of Tibet, admired the West for its science and technology. Perhaps if Chinese Communist leaders realized that Tibetan culture was valued by materialist Westerners, they might begin to share that value also.

There was not much of a meeting of minds on the mind-body problem. The scientists, although I suspect none shared the Dalai Lama's view, disagreed among themselves. It was a lively meeting with good exchange. Since I was moderating the discussion, it was improper for me to actively participate, but near the end of it I could not resist asking a question about the Dalai Lama's view of reincarnation.

I told him that one of the greatest ambitions of Western science

and philosophy was the construction of an artificial intelligence—
a device, fabricated entirely out of electronic parts, that would
exhibit intelligent behavior. It could talk as if it were a person. The
Dalai Lama indicated he knew about the program of artificial intelligence.

I then said that this device would be so constructed (or instructed) that he could have a profound discussion with it, as if he
were talking to another high lama about Tibetan philosophy. For
example, they could meaningfully discuss the various stages of
Bardo-Thol (The Tibetan Book of the Dead) or aspects of deep
meditation. Then I asked my question: "Would you, Your Holi-
ness, say that this artificial intelligence was a reincarnate being?"

When he had seen that I had tried to trick him, he threw back
his head and laughed at the joke. Then, changing his attitude to
one of seriousness and with a sense of the material present that
characterized his discussion throughout, he pointed to the space
in front of his chair (which was empty) and said, "There, there!
When you have such a machine and put it *there* before me, then
we will have this discussion again!" In other words, put up or shut
up. I was secretly pleased, however, that he shared my view of
strict constructivism—you have got to design and build, not just
talk about your philosophical fantasies. And on that note of good
humor the meeting was over.

Chapter 11

The Body Never Lies

What but the wolf's tooth whittled so fine
The fleet limbs of the antelope?
What but fear winged the birds, and hunger
Jeweled with such eyes the great goshawk's head?
Violence has been the sire of all the world's values.
                                                    —ROBINSON JEFFERS,
                                                    The Bloody Sire

A physics colleague of mine was complaining about his difficulty teaching the elementary concepts of quantum mechanics to non-science major undergraduates at a leading university. The students, he said, were bright but apathetic; they just didn't get excited by the remarkable concepts of quantum physics. I couldn't understand why he was having this difficulty and tried to make a few suggestions: "Tell them how electrons can tunnel right through a barrier—like stepping through a wall. That's almost magical and has no correspondence in the world of our everyday experience. Or tell them about the quantum field concept—how everything in the universe is represented by fields pervading space and moving in time and which specify the probability for finding quantum particles. That is certainly a strange, yet correct, way of viewing our universe."

But my friend went on to say that he had tried all that and to no avail. The reason for his failure to excite the students was that they didn't see anything especially wonderful about the quantum theory. Brought up on the fare of popular television, scientifically irresponsible books and magazines, the students believed in ESP, flying saucers, mental voyages to other worlds, and all kinds of psychic phenomena. Quantum mechanics seems tame, even old-fashioned, by comparison. According to some pollsters, about 70 percent of all U.S. college undergraduates believe in some kind of psychic or supernatural forces lying outside the findings of natural science. Unfortunately there is no way for empirical science to compete with the excitement offered by occult science. If there is ever a contest between reason and emotion, emotion always wins, at least in the short run.

I like to browse in occult bookshops if for no other reason than to refresh my commitment to science. It is a humorless literature. But what an incredible imagination the writers have! While their spontaneous imagination and feelings cannot lie, their interpretation of them can be profoundly self-deceiving and self-serving. As a result, the factual contents of the books are almost entirely fraudulent. However, what is not fraudulent about occult books is the depth of the human need for spiritual connection to the forces of existence they reveal. With that sense of connection comes a feeling of power and worth for those people who usually have none. Here people can find acceptance that is not based on their social worth.

The occult literature speaks to the need for individual freedom and liberation from the mundane, material world. Yet everywhere in the occult literature I read of hierarchies—the higher and the lower spiritual powers, levels of attainment and consciousness, greater and lesser beings, the enlightened and unenlightened, masters and beginners, and so on, hierarchies that mirror the real ones we live in. And the people who become obsessed with these things are usually trying to position themselves in such a spiritual hierarchy, aspiring to attain a higher awareness often by submitting to an authoritarian figure or a discipline. The result can be a form of mental enslavement, a terminal form of conscious development promoted as "enlightenment." No moral good can ultimately come from that which is untrue. A good antidote to the occult literature is the magazine *The Skeptical Inquirer*, which reports and critically examines paranormal phenomena.

Although the findings of quantum theory seem tame compared to the "discoveries" of occultists, they have the feature of being true irrespective of whether you believe in them or not. Quantum theory, arriving in the late 1920s, completely transformed the way physicists thought about the physical world. The deterministic and causal ideas of Newtonian physics that had held sway for centuries were dramatically modified when it came to devising a mathematical description of the quantum atom. A visualizable, mechanical picture of the atomic world, the kind of picture Newtonian physicists were accustomed to, could not be maintained. Physicists, against their own intellectually conservative instincts, were forced by the quantum theory into drawing radically new conclusions about the nature of reality, conclusions that transformed the world in which we live.

Empirical science, such as the quantum theory, works, and it develops and matures. Scientists often discover a new territory of reality and practical-minded people turn these discoveries into new processes, products, and sometimes major achievements—vaccines that eradicate diseases, medicines and operations that alleviate suffering and prolong useful life, electronic communications systems spanning the planet, voyages to the moon and other planets—awesome and wondrous accomplishments that have made possible modern civilization. No one seriously doubts that science works. But why does it work? What is it that scientists do that makes their enterprise so extraordinarily successful? In this chapter I will endeavor to answer these questions. The answer is often thought to lie in what is popularly called "the scientific method."

There is an enormous philosophical literature on the scientific method—attempts to answer the question of why science works and what scientists do. Most of it is entirely worthless. Often it is written by philosophers who have never examined the conduct inquiry as scientists are actually carrying it out and who have never done scientific research themselves. The method of science then becomes not what it is but what it ought to be. It takes on obscure proportions, becomes detached from practice, and is hardly recognizable, especially by scientists.

Of course scientists also write about the methods of science (particularly as they get older) and have the advantage of "hands-on" experience. So they do not make the mistakes of the philosophers. But they, in turn, are often insensitive to the philosophical problems of method—they know *what* "works" but not *why* a method leads to rigorous knowledge that can distinguish science from psuedoscience. My own sympathy (not surprisingly) lies more with the practicing scientists, people like the biologist Claude Bernard, the physicist Albert Einstein, or the physiologist Peter Medawar, who have written about scientific method.

The methods of scientists have been described as anything ranging from a logical, precise procedure to a complete anarchy of method. I will be describing some of the main ideas below. But before doing so, I will outline my own view so that the reader can anticipate where I am headed.

I think that describing the conduct of scientific research as a "method," a recipe that prescribes a set of rules, is wrong. A formal "scientific method" simply does not exist because scientific discovery is too complex, a complexity that mirrors the complexity of the material world itself. Because of that complexity, nonrational and intuitive elements are necessarily part of the discovery process.

Scientists are not educated or trained to follow any scientific method, nor do they, in fact, follow explicit rules any more than, say, does a businessman or lawyer. There is no "expert system" for scientific research, although some simple skills can be formalized. Scientists, as they go about their work, possess a "tacit knowledge" —an intuitive knowledge like that of riding a bicycle, which can be experienced and if experienced also described, but which cannot be strictly formalized as a set of useful rules. Textbook scientific method (such as there is) teaches one as much about how to do science as a book on bike riding teaches you how to actually ride a bike. Nonetheless it is possible in rough outline to describe what scientists do; I think the "hypothetico-deductive system" comes close enough. Basically the "hypothetico-deductive system" consists of making an educated guess, a scientific hypothesis, followed by rigorous tests and criticisms of that hypothesis. This is not the only method scientists employ, but it gets the main idea across—scientific method is an appropriate mixture of inspiration and rigor. Finding that "appropriate mixture" is the mark of a great scientist.

It is one thing to *describe* scientific inquiry, but it is another thing to say *why* it works. The reason science works is because it studies an ordered world that can be known by an ordered mind. Why the world is ordered is unknown. But that it is ordered seems undeniable. To be sure *what* we know of that ordered world and how we view it is determined in part by our culture and history. We are restricted by the limitations imposed by our instruments, techniques, and cognitive limitations reflected in the theories we invent. Yet in spite of these influential external factors, the reason for the possibility of scientific knowledge lies ultimately in the nature of the world—the existence of a cosmic code—a reason that cannot be dismissed without also dismissing more than a millennium of scientific investigation and discovery.

Atoms, galaxies, bacteria, cells, and viruses all were once unknown but have now become part of the repertoire of reality. Science explores reality and does so effectively. Why? I think that science is effective because it is a "selective system," like the process of evolution or the competitive business economy. What a selective system does is to discriminate and select specific members from a set—a repertoire of objects or well-defined concepts—on the basis of some feature or property. In the case of scientific research, what is being selected for are definite hypotheses, informed guesses that are the basis of a theory. The competitive pressure, the selection mechanism, are provided by an environment of strong critical feedback, review, and experimentation, and this selects a small number, usually one, of the hypotheses out of a repertoire.

But scientific theories that incorporate such hypotheses are not true simply because they survive the competition any more than a species is "true" because it survives. A scientific theory cannot be absolutely true the way a mathematical theorem is true. A theory could be false and still have true consequences. But the fact that there is no absolute certainty for a scientific theory also implies that unlike a mathematical theorem, it is open and vulnerable to change. And because of that capacity for change, theories can evolve. Sometimes a scientific discovery endures a long time in an environment of testing and criticism. Then, like the cockroaches, which have also endured a long time, it acquires the sense of "permanent" existence. To be certain, sometime in the future cockroaches may get edged out by another species. Likewise scientific ideas can become extinct. Yet if they endure, like the cockroaches, then, like atoms, DNA, even quarks, they become part of our repertoire of reality simply because they exist and have done so successfully for so very long. Empirical science is a selective system for finding the building code of the Demiurge.

That summarizes my own view. Now I would like to return to

some of the ideas about scientific method people advanced in the past.

Scientists and philosophers of science describe the conduct of inquiry in two main ways—"the inductive method" and "the hypothetico-deductive system." For a well-written contemporary review I heartily recommend Peter Medawar's two essays "Induction and Intuition in Scientific Thought" and "Hypothesis and Imagination." Although Medawar for the most part ignores the continental philosophers and scientists, the essays are excellent.

Generally induction means to argue from the particular to the general circumstance; deduction means to argue from the general circumstance to the particular. While it may seem superficially that induction and deduction are equally valid and rigorous because "they go up and down the same staircase," they are not. Only deductive reasoning can be made rigorous. (The mathematicians have a form of proof called "inductive proof," but this is a special use of induction and does not apply to the discussion we will give here.) Almost nobody today believes that the inductive method is rigorous or describes scientific method. Yet scientists, when they write articles or give lectures, often act as if they subscribe to it. According to the inductive scenario, first come the facts, and then, as would a master detective working with clues, the scientists compose a grand theory. Like a church congregation that has ceased to believe, some members of the community of scientists continue to act out the inductive method like an empty religious ceremony with the hope of instilling a sense of scientific piety. What about deduction?

The only examples of rigorous deductive proof are to be found in mathematics and logic. One begins with a set of general axioms and definitions, such as Euclid's axioms of plane geometry. Using nothing but those axioms and the rules of logic—which can also be axiomatized—mathematicians deduce theorems. These are statements about the mathematical object, such as the statement that two interior angles of an isosceles triangle are equal. Mathematical proof is so rigorous that it can be reduced to a mechanical procedure—computers can grind out proofs of theorems. But the lesson learned from such deductive systems is that you *never* get out more than you put in to begin with—the general axioms and definitions. While the results may be surprising, even awesome, they all follow just the axioms and judiciously chosen definitions.

Empirical scientists, however, do not observe in the laboratory anything resembling a general axiom. Instead they observe and uncover new facts about nature. How do they ever come to formulating general principles of nature from just lots of facts about nature?

One possible answer for contemporary science goes back to Francis Bacon, the Oxford University dropout who, in the early seventeenth century, popularized the notion that to gain the secrets of nature it was not sufficient to passively observe, one had to do experiments. He also espoused the inductive method of logical moving from the particular to the general.

We apply the inductive method in everyday life. For example, a person drinks a glass of milk on Tuesday and Thursday and upon reflection remembers that he had an upset stomach on just those days. On Saturday this same person conducts an experiment by drinking a glass of milk, and indeed his stomach becomes upset. From this series of specific instances he then draws the general conclusion that milk always upsets his stomach. Likewise an experimental physicist may set up a delicate apparatus to measure the initial and final energy of a complex quantum particle collision process. Every time the process takes place the initial energy is equal to the final energy within experimental error. He checks it in other examples and then goes on to formulate the general law of energy conservation—again an argument from the specific to the general. This is what scientists do, isn't it—gather the facts and then draw general conclusions?

The answer to this question is emphatically no—no in practice and no in principle. Scientists, when they undertake an experiment, already have something in mind, a framework of thought, a set of anticipated options for the outcome. Just like the person who decided one day to test his reaction to milk, scientists already have formulated a hypothesis before they gathered data. So much for practice of the inductive method; what about the principle of scientific induction?

John Stuart Mill, the nineteenth-century English political and social philosopher, was the primary proponent of the inductive method in science in his books A *System of Logic*, *Problems of Life and Mind*, and *Philosophy of Scientific Method*. Mill's social philosophy held sway as long as the interests of the rising merchant classes and the workers were seen as congruent, but his views lost influence later in the century. He ignored many of the scientific developments of his time, such as the theory of evolution and statistical mechanics and, even more important for his own program, the invention of formal logic by Augustus De Morgan and George Boole. Ernest Nagel, the philosopher of science at Columbia University, remarked about Mill: "His hatred of obscurantism, his love of clarity, and his passionate devotion to carefully reasoned analysis have won him admirers and emulators even among those who reject many of his specific assumptions and conclusions." His strength was his clarity of thought and his commitment to justice.

Mill's ambition was to make the inductive method logically rigorous. He described it thus: "Induction is a process of inference; it proceeds from the known to the unknown; and any operation involving no inference, any process in which what seems the conclusion is no wider than the premises from which it is drawn, does not fall within the meaning of the term." Very well and good. But Mill goes on to say, "The business of inductive logic is to provide rules and models (such as syllogism and its rules are for ratiocination) to which, if inductive arguments conform, those arguments are conclusive, and not otherwise." The problem with this reasoning is that induction is never conclusive.

Mill, however, thought that induction works and can be made rigorous because nature is inherently uniform (he raised this assumption of uniformity to the level of a "fundamental principle or general axiom"). There is a simple image that I find clearly illustrates the difference between induction and deduction and the trouble with Mill's principle of the uniformity of nature.

Imagine two points on a geometrical plane. These points are a metaphor for scientific data gathered in the laboratory. The problem is to construct a line, a metaphor for a theory, that includes these points. If, following Mill, we appeal to the principle of uniformity of nature, we might suppose that a straight line going through the two points is the most "uniform." This is how Mill thought one could deduce a theory (the line) from a few pieces of data (the points). But the same two points can also be joined by a circle, also a "uniform" line or, in fact, an infinite number of other "uniform" curves. Even if there are more than two points, there are still an infinite number of lines that can join them. It is impossible to construct a unique theory from just a finite number of observations. Induction is not rigorous.

This image also serves to underscore the difference between deduction and induction. With deduction one *begins* with the theory or general axiom, represented as a specific line on the geometrical plane. Then, simply by looking, one can deduce which points lie on the line—what the observations must be according to the theory. But, as we showed above, one cannot go the other way—from specific data to a unique theory—as required by induction.

Mill had hoped that by making induction rigorous, the same method that was used with such great effect in natural sciences could also be applied to help society by advancing the recent social sciences. In this ambition Mill was profoundly mistaken. First because the success of the natural sciences had less to do with any method they employed; it had to do with the fact that the material order of nature admits of regulative laws. Second (as was emphasized by Mill's main critics, the philosophers C. S. Peirce and John Venn) there is no rigorous inductive method—it is impossible to prove a general law from specific instances; you cannot get more out of a logical system than you put in and still expect to be rigorous. Only deduction is rigorous.

In spite of these major failings Mill's prestige and expository skills were such that his writings gave voice to the methodological outlook of many, if not most, scientists of his time (although I doubt that he influenced them directly). Most scientists, especially in the English-speaking world, if they were at all methodologically reflective, identified themselves as Baconians—believers in the inductive method. In an autobiographical sketch, Charles Darwin, a legend in his time, said that he "worked on true Baconian principles, and without any theory collected facts on a wholesale scale." However, he was more candid in his letters to friends and colleagues, where he stated that he saw no point in collecting facts unless they supported a theory. It is clear that he had the kernel of the idea of evolution even before he read about Malthus's law —that populations would always increase beyond the capacity of the food supply to support them. He knew, intuitively, where he was headed. But to this day scientists, like Darwin, pay lip service to Baconian induction even while they practice something entirely different. Philosophers as well have been taken in by induction. Hans Reichenbach wrote: "The principle of induction is unreservedly accepted by the whole of science and that no man can seriously doubt the principle in everyday life either."

Mill's articulate defense of inductive thinking did not arise gratuitously. For Mill saw clearly that if inductive thinking, in the wider sense in which he employed it, was *not* rigorous, then what would remain of scientific knowledge? Its secure foundation would be lost, and the grand theories of science would be no more than inspired guesses. Mill wanted proof, not unsupported hypothesis. He distrusted human intuition and imagination, a vestige of his utilitarian upbringing by his father.

Mill's philosophical antagonist, as far as debate on scientific method was concerned, was William Whewell, master of Trinity College, Cambridge, a don with a wide-ranging knowledge of the sciences who in the 1840s published his book *The Philosophy of the Inductive Sciences*. Whewell is remarkably modern in his outlook. He is surely one of the intellectual fathers of the hypothetico-deductive system. No doubt his experience as a scientist (he introduced the term into English) served him well in distinguishing what scientists did from the myths that surround their work. He wrote extensively on many subjects and, most significantly for us here, recognized that scientists superimpose an imaginative element of their own mind in gathering data. In thoughts echoing the philosopher Kant, he wrote, "There is a mask of theory over the whole face of nature."

Whewell grasped, as Mill did not, that scientists begin by imaginatively putting forth a hypothesis, an informed guess. "A facility," said Whewell, "in devising hypothesis, therefore, is so far from being a fault in the intellectual character of a discoverer, that it is, in truth, a faculty indispensable to his task. To form hypotheses, and then to employ much labor and skill in refuting it, if they do not succeed in establishing them is a part of the usual process of inventive minds. . . . Since the discoverer has thus constantly to work his way onwards by means of hypotheses, false and true, it is highly important for him to possess talents and means for rapidly *testing* each supposition as it offers itself." This description of discovery is not that of the innocent investigator picking up facts like pebbles on the beach for later scrutiny. But it does, in fact, describe the procedure real scientists often use: first the hypothesis is made, and then the critical and rigorous apparatus of experiment and logic is brought into play.

Whewell anticipated by more than a century the hypothetico-deductive system, which was given its strongest formulation by the philosopher Karl Popper. Whewell even recognized the importance of falsification—that such hypotheses can never be proven to be true; they can only be shown to be false. His contemporary on the other side of the English Channel, the great biologist Claude Bernard, would concur: "A hypothesis is . . . the obligatory starting point of all experimental reasoning. Without it no investigation would be possible, and one would learn nothing: one could only pile up barren observations. To experiment without a preconceived idea is to wander aimlessly. . . . Those who have condemned the use of hypothesis and preconceived ideas in the experimental method have made the mistake of confusing the contriving of the experiment with the verification of its result." For people like Whewell and Bernard, the act of discovery and proof were completely distinct. Discovery partook of the nonrational, the intuitive processes of the mind, while proof was a rigorous, even mechanical, logical procedure.

Sometimes discoveries are completely accidental, such as Sydney Ringer's discovery of the influence of calcium on muscle contraction. Around 1900 Ringer was studying frogs' hearts perfused with a saline solution of doubly distilled tap water. One day the technician who prepared the water was ill, and Ringer prepared the solution himself and got completely different results from those obtained previously. Upon questioning the technician later, Ringer found out that he had not distilled the water (thus removing the calcium) because he thought London tap water was pure enough. Ringer took this clue and went on to elucidate the role of calcium in muscle contraction. Many stories like this show that major discoveries come from chance. But once the chance discovery is made, the investigator makes a guess, a hypothesis that supports the chance discovery, and proceeds to rigorously test it.

Whewell's thinking greatly disturbed Mill, who had to see the light of reason in all that was highest in the best of human accomplishment. In Whewell's view the origin of scientific hypotheses was not explained—they sprang out of the darkness into the light of reason propelled by nothing more than the imagination of the scientist or perhaps a chance discovery. They were mere guesses. Mill's work on the logic of induction in which he tried to make it rigorous, was, in part, a reaction to Whewell's book (who then later responded to Mill in another book, *The Philosophy of Discovery*, 1860). He criticized Whewell as attacking the logic of the syllogism (which he did not). Mill was rigorous but irrelevant. Most scientists today would side with the spirit, if not the details, of Whewell's arguments, while Mill's logic is a Victorian museum piece.

The debate between Mill and Whewell (there are others, but these are the main figures in Britain) is at root a difference between those who want to establish certainty in the theories of empirical sciences, a certainty like that prevailing in the theorems of logic and mathematics, and those who realize that this is impossible. Those who realize this certainty is unattainable in empirical science do not renounce logical rigor; instead they apply it only where it is appropriate—in logically *deducing* the testable consequences of a general hypothesis and in establishing the logical completeness of experiments and observations. But the method of discovery involves imagination, luck, randomness, guesswork, and likewise, the hypothesis that supports discovery is put forth as an intelligent guess, an imaginative leap into the unknown. Taking that imaginative leap is what distinguishes great scientists from others.

The same dialectic between those who sought certainty in empirical sciences and those who knew it was not obtainable also characterized the discussions about scientific method on the continent of Europe. Kant, who set the philosophy of science on its modern course and in so doing created the schism between science and the philosophy of science, had a rather modern view of the nature of scientific hypothesis—he understood their provisional status. In his lecture notes compiled by a student and published as *An Introduction to Logic* he remarked that it must *certainly* be true of every hypothesis that it could *possibly* be true. Kant viewed hypotheses as concepts we might believe as if they are certain but in the back of our minds we know that they are "suppositions . . . the full certainty of which we can never attain."

The controversy about the nature of scientific hypothesis came to a head at the end of the nineteenth century when a major debate broke out about the existence of atoms. It is instructive to examine this debate from our viewpoint of understanding scientific methods. From the scientific conferences of that time, one can see that physicists and chemists were about evenly divided over the question of whether or not atoms actually existed or were merely a convenient "hypothesis." Since no direct evidence for the existence of atoms was available at that time (it did not come

until Einstein's 1905 paper on Brownian motion and Perrin's subsequent measurements based on Einstein's theory), the controversy caused people to choose sides about the nature of
hypothesis. What were some of the issues involved?

The atomic theory—the notion that matter was divisible down
to discrete particles and no further—goes back to ancient times,
but the modern version came from the chemical laws discovered
by John Dalton in 1808 and others in the early nineteenth century.
In 1809 Joseph Louis Gay-Lussac announced his results showing
that gases combined in integer proportions, results that supported
Dalton's ideas. The most remarkable atomic hypothesis was put
forth in 1811 by Amedeo Avogadro, who asserted that equal volumes of two different gases at the same temperature and pressure
had the same number of molecules. Later in the century attempts
were made to calculate Avogadro's number for a fixed volume of
gas. William Prout, a physician and amateur chemist (he discovered hydrochloric acid in the stomach), formulated a law in 1815
that the atomic weights of elements were integer multiples of the
weight of hydrogen, a law that, while not perfectly true, lent credence to the atomic hypothesis. Curiously, Prout himself did not
see it as evidence supporting the existence of atoms. The upshot
of these and other developments was that scientists realized that
chemical substances combined as if they were made of discrete
atoms. There was a lot of indirect evidence for the existence of
atoms from chemistry, but as yet no direct evidence. No one had
seen an atom or a molecule.

Independent, but still indirect, evidence for the existence of
atoms came from physicists when they came to examine gases.
They found that by assuming gases, like the air around us, consist
of enormous numbers of atoms and molecules moving in every
direction until they bounce off another atom or molecule or some
object, they could account for the already known laws of gas thermodynamics. Various thermodynamic properties of gas such as
pressure and temperature could easily be accounted for by the
motion of molecules, what came to be called the kinetic theory of
gases. In the 1860s and 1870s physicists were estimating the diam-
eters of air molecules. In spite of the success of the kinetic theory
of gases, the idea that gases, and indeed all matter, consist of
atoms was still simply a hypothesis.

Ernst Mach, the physicist-philosopher, was one of the most influential scientists of his time, the end of the nineteenth century. Mach did not believe in the existence of atoms. He made many significant contributions to physics (the Mach number, which denotes the velocity of an object in multiples of the speed of sound, is named after him), and he asked penetrating and deep questions about Newtonian mechanics. But Mach was also interested in the philosophy of science. Like Mill, Mach was suspicious of the use of the speculative imagination that ran beyond the experimental facts and hypotheses that were unwarranted by observation. Mach believed that physical theory—the mathematical description of nature—should stick close to the experimental observations. Equations containing quantities that could not be directly measured and did not refer to physical observables in the laboratory he thought were meaningless. With this outlook it is easy to see why Mach was doubtful about kinetic theory, a theory that hypothesized the existence of invisible atoms and whose mathematical equations made explicit reference to the motions of these atoms. Mach thought of atoms as a heuristic device. "It would not become physical science," he wrote, "to see in its self-created, changeable, economic tools, molecules and atoms, realities behind phenomena. . . . The atom must remain a tool . . . like the function of mathematics." In the end physical theory should refer only to *measurable* quantities, not to quantities referring to invisible and unknown entities.

Mach defended his position with great integrity. But he was wrong about the existence of atoms and the merits of the kinetic theory. The road to progress in physics went in a different direction. Atoms became part of the repertoire of reality. Furthermore, the equations describing the material world, as became evident with the advent of quantum theory in the 1920s, were very abstract and contained many variables that did not correspond to observable quantities. Yet these abstract equations were indeed the language of nature, and by applying them one could deduce the observable quantities measured in the laboratory.

Einstein in his early years subscribed to the general philosophy of Mach (although, unlike Mach, he believed in the existence of atoms; indeed, he showed how one could prove they exist). In his *Autobiographical Notes* he pays the following tribute to Mach: "I see Mach's greatness in his incorruptible skepticism and independence; in my younger years, however, Mach's epistemological position also influenced me very greatly, a position which today appears to me to be essentially untenable. For he did not place in the correct light the essentially constructive and speculative nature of thought and more especially of scientific thought; in consequence of which he condemned theory on precisely those points where its constructive-speculative character unconcealably comes to light, as for example in the kinetic atomic theory."

Einstein's early work on special relativity exemplified Mach's insistence that one stick to measurable quantities. For example, Einstein cut through the centuries of "metaphysical baggage" being carried by the concepts of space and time when he said that "space" was what was measured by a measuring rod and "time" was measured by a clock. What could be simpler? Yet when he turned to inventing the general theory of relativity, the crown of his achievements, he parted company with Mach. General relativity theory employed the mathematics of Riemannian curved four-dimensional space and abstract invariance principles. After inventing general relativity, Einstein described the method he used in obtaining it in a letter to his friend the philosopher Maurice Solovine. Remarkably, what he describes in this letter is essentially the hypothetico-deductive system.

According to Einstein's letter to Solovine, he began with the world of his experience and knowledge of physics and experiment. Then, on the basis of this knowledge, he made an inspired guess, "an intuitive leap" to make an "absolute postulate"—the hypothesis. There is no way that this postulate could have been deduced from experience alone; it went beyond experience, although it was consistent with it. The absolute postulate in Einstein's work was the idea that physical space was a curved Riemannian space with the curvature specified by his gravitational field equations. The absolute postulate could not be tested directly. But because the postulate was a logically precise concept, one could rigorously deduce empirical consequences from it. In Einstein's case these were the three famous tests for general relativity—a small shift in the orbit of the planet Mercury, the bending of light around the limb of the sun, and the slowing down of clocks in a gravitational field compared to a field-free region.

Should a test fail then, since the empirical results are logically linked to the absolute postulate it must fail too and require modification or rejection. Consequently the absolute postulate is falsifiable; it is a "scientific" hypothesis. Should the tests, however, succeed (as they did for general relativity), one cannot thereby conclude that the absolute postulate is verified. "False" theories can give correct results. Furthermore, other postulates might have given the same predictions—something that cannot be logically ruled out. One can never verify a scientific postulate with complete certainty. Nonetheless, as more and more tests conform to the postulate, the confidence in its applicability is enhanced. It is clear from this letter (and the fuller exposition of its implications by Gerald Holton) that Einstein fully grasped what has become known as the hypothetico-deductive system.

Even though working scientists like Einstein understood the role of the informed imagination in scientific work and realized that scientific knowledge was provisional, the quest for certainty among the philosophers of science went on. The Vienna Circle, led by the philosopher Rudolf Carnap, set out on a vast program of "logical-empiricism" or "logical-positivism," which attempted to separate scientific knowledge from the rest of knowledge, such as metaphysics, theology, literature, knowledge they often deemed "meaningless." Influenced by contemporary developments in formal logic and language philosophy, the logical-empiricists saw the role of philosophers of science as examining the logic of scientific laws, the set of statements about natural reality. Science, for them, was a system of logical statements. They saw their enterprise as analogous to the rigorous work of formal logicians, but instead of examining mathematical theorems and proofs for their logical content, it was the statements of empirical science that they examined. Much of their thinking hinged on the logical notion of "verifiability"—scientific statements, in contrast with nonscientific statements, were supposed to be verifiable and testable. The Vienna Circle philosophers aggressively set out to separate what was testable and meaningful from that which was meaningless nonsense. Philosophy, once the handmaiden of theology, had become the whore of science.

Logical-empiricism was in reality a radically idealistic program promoting perfectibility in scientific knowledge. And like all "perfect" things, it did not have the adaptability and flexibility required for survival. Inasmuch as it was true it was not relevant, and inasmuch as it was relevant it was often not true.

The chief difficulty of the logical-empiricist program lay in the notion of "verifiability." Carnap and his collaborators originally envisioned the criterion of verifiability as providing a sharp demarcation between "meaningful" and "meaningless" sentences. But upon close inspection their idea of verifiability could not be maintained. As I remarked before, physical laws could be false and yet have true consequences; they could be false and yet be "verifiable." This is not at all what Carnap had in mind. Later in his life, Carnap backed off from the strict verificationist program and instead used the weaker term "confirmation." He wrote, "If verification is understood as a complete and definite establishment of truth then a universal sentence, e.g., a so-called law of physics and biology, can never be verified, a fact which has often been remarked. . . . Thus instead of verification, we may speak here of gradually increasing *confirmation* of the law." But even the notion of degrees of confirmation was difficult to maintain.

Perhaps more than any other recent philosopher, Karl Popper has influenced thinking about science. He was associated with the Vienna Circle early in his life, and its ideas, especially its sense of the formality of the philosophy of science, influenced all of his later work. But it was Popper, thoroughly in tune with the spirit of Whewell, Einstein, and other anti-inductivists, who made a clear break with the verificationist philosophy of science and brought the hypothetico-deductive method to its highest formulation.

In his seminal volume *The Logic of Scientific Discovery*, he begins with a round of criticism of inductivism: "Now this principle of induction cannot be a purely logical truth like a tautology or an analytic statement. . . . " He goes on to criticize the verificationist criterion of truth and then raises the notion of falsifiability as the criterion, not of the truth of scientific propositions, but as a principle of demarcation between what is and is not a scientific method. He writes: "These considerations suggest that not the *verifiability* but the falsifiability of a system is to be taken as a criterion of demarcation. In other words: I shall not require of a scientific system that it shall be capable of being singled out, once and for all, in a positive sense; but I shall require that its logical form be that it can be singled out, by means of empirical tests, in a negative sense: *it must be possible for an empirical scientific system to be refuted by experience*."

Popper's work has been criticized by his fellow philosophers for his excessive formalism or the fact that he focuses on the theory rather than the practice of science. Others remarked that Popper's view only accounted for the rationality of science as seen retrospectively, not prospectively. But in the main he stated the hypothetico-deductive method clearly (although he was not the first) and thus brought the philosopher's quest for certainty in the theories of natural science to an end. Theories are all necessarily provisional, even "false" in some absolute sense. They can never be verified, only falsified. The idea that natural laws are etched on eternal tablets never to be changed came to an end.

An ironic consequence of Popper's work is that it opened the door to an altogether different kind of philosophy of science having little to do with his own commitment to logic and objectivity. If the absolute truth of scientific theory is an impossibility, then what are scientists doing that is so special, and what distinguishes their endeavor from any other cultural activity? In the 1960s and 1970s intellectual emphasis began to shift from formal and logical explanations to psychological and sociological accounts of scientific theory. Science was viewed as a cultural activity developing historically over time and subject to different "styles of reasoning." It was the *process* of science that mattered to these post-Popperian philosophers of science, not the *product*. For example, Imre Lakatos, a Hungarian philosopher of science who immigrated to England, saw modern science as a set of "research programs" stretching over the last several centuries, and these "research programs" represent the sense of scientific reality. As Ian Hacking, an English philosopher who helped promote Lakatos's ideas, noted, "Lakatos tried to make the growth of knowledge a surrogate for a representational theory of truth."

Yehuda Elkana, an Israeli philosopher of science, advanced the idea of an "anthropology of knowledge"—"that the quest for human universals outside a cultural context is meaningless." Consistent with this anthropological view, he compared the literary forms of tragic and epic theater to different forms of viewing scientific progress. The tragic form reflects the "solemnity of the remorseless working of things . . . the inevitableness of destiny," he wrote. In science the tragic form corresponds to the view "that the great truths of nature, had they not been discovered by a Newton or an Einstein, would sooner or later have been discovered by someone else. . . . " Scientific progress, as we see its historical development, is inevitable. By contrast, the epic theater

sees nothing as inevitable. In the words of the cultural critic Walter Benjamin (quoted by Elkana), "It can happen this way, but it
can also happen quite a different way." As Elkana and other social
thinkers saw it, the direction of scientific research depends on
historical and cultural factors, which are unpredictable. But most
practicing scientists would disagree with this view (including Einstein, although Elkana sees Einstein as a proponent of the epic
view). While cultural factors certainly play a role, the main factor
is the actual material order of the world. There is no "comparative
science" between cultures like a comparative literature because
the discoveries in science are regulated less by the culture than the
structure of the universe itself.

The most extreme position in this spectrum of thinkers is occupied by Paul Feyerabend, who in spite of his evident scholarship
can only be described as a punk philosopher. His book *Against
Method* (1974) attacks the entire enterprise of scientific methodol-
ogy as misconceived and impossible. Feyerabend is committed to
the idea that a radical restructuring of knowledge may be necessary. He sees no distinction between the conduct of scientific inquiry and voodoo. In his essay "How to Defend Society Against
Science" he observes: "My criticism of modern science is that it
inhibits freedom of thought. If the reason is that it has found the
truth and now follows it then I would say that there are better
things than first finding, and then following such a monster." Or
again in the same essay: "Three cheers to the fundamentalists in
California who succeeded in having a dogmatic formulation of the
theory of evolution removed from the textbooks and an account
of Genesis included (but I know that they would become as chau-
vinistic and totalitarian as scientists are today when given the
chance to run society all by themselves. Ideologies are marvelous
when used in the company of other ideologies. They become bor-
ing and doctrinaire as soon as their merits lead to the removal of
their opponents)." Such remarks drive the few scientists who have
read him right up the wall. He provokes the liberal intellectual
conscience of fellow philosophers by extrapolating some of their
views to their logical conclusions and thus going them one better.
By staking out his extremist position (he invites controversy) and
arguing forcefully against any claim to truth by modern science,
he has achieved the simple consistency of nihilism. I find him
refreshing. Probably some of Feyerabend's views of science are

correct if we could but see our science from the perspective of a thousand years hence; but we have no way of knowing which of his views, if any, will be sustained.

While it is not possible to examine all these recent philosophers here, it would be useful to have a look at Thomas Kuhn's ideas if for no other reason than that so many scientists have read his influential book *The Structure of Scientific Revolutions.*

When it was first published I read Kuhn's book. In Kuhn's view normal scientific inquiry is conducted within what he calls a "paradigm"—a way of doing science, a conceptual framework, a shared sense of natural reality. A scientific revolution comes when there is a "paradigm shift." After a long period of "normal science" the consensus among scientists begins to disintegrate, the revolution comes, and then science reforms around a new paradigm. An example is the shift from classical to quantum theory or the shift from special creation theory to evolutionary theory.

Kuhn's book illuminates the social and intellectual transformations within scientific revolutions. According to his account, the younger generation of scientists embraces the new paradigm when it comes. They work within its framework while the older generation, unable to change its ways, carries the previous paradigm to their graves. Thus, scientific change is accomplished. This succession of the generations, the sons burying their fathers, is movingly recounted in Russell McCommach's novel *Night Thoughts of a Classical Physicist.* This book is about the life of a German university professor, a classical physicist living in the first decades of this century who sees his world crumble before the advent of relativity and quantum theory. Unable, both intellectually and emotionally, to bear the changes in his worldview, he kills himself. That's strong "selective pressure." In this connection I also think of Captain Fitz-Roy, who commanded the *Beagle* during Darwin's voyage and was Darwin's dinnertime companion and conversationalist. Fitz-Roy, a devoted Christian and creationist, could never accept Darwin's new evolutionary ideas when they came and later, as an old man, used to harass lecturers promoting Darwin's ideas. Kuhn's book speaks powerfully about the social and intellectual transformations in the history of science. Still, I could not help thinking that he had not identified the root cause of scientific change, only its manifestation.

In the final chapter of Kuhn's book, entitled "Progress Through

Revolutions," he attempts to give an account of why scientific knowledge progresses and why other fields of human enterprise, such as literature or theology, do not have that quality of progress. Although he identifies characteristics of science, such as the ability of scientists to agree on a single paradigm during a period of normal science, that are not shared by other intellectual enterprises, he does not account for why science has these special characteristics and hence is "progressive."

In order to come to grips with why Kuhn's thesis fails to explain why science works the way it does, I decided to try an intellectual experiment, what I call the "method of content substitution." I imagined that Kuhn was *not* talking about science at all but high fashion as is seasonally promoted in New York and Paris for the purpose of selling a new line of clothes. There were periods of normal fashion changes and then major "paradigm shifts," brought about by a younger generation. Remarkably, a lot of what was said in Kuhn's book I could easily imagine describing the high fashion world as well as science. That troubles me. The reason this content substitution works so well is that if you ignore the fact that science discovers the invariant structure of nature, the building code of the Demiurge, then the social conduct of science and the promotion of its ideas can resemble the world of high fashion.

Although it often takes the form of a generational conflict between intellectual "children" and their "parents," the shift of a paradigm occurs and takes hold in the scientific community simply because it has greater conceptual and explanatory power, it is a better map of reality, and makes contact with the cosmic code—the order of the cosmos. A new set of scientific ideas does not take hold primarily because of social factors, except in perversely constrained social conditions, like Lysenkoism under Stalin (which denied the validity of modern genetics) or "Aryan" science under Hitler (which asserted that theoretical physics was a perversion of the Jews and only experimental physics was pure and valid), and these cases are recognized as such. (The reader is invited to try the "method of content substitution" on Kuhn's book using "Aryan" science—also a "paradigm shift"—if the example of the world of high fashion seemed too farfetched.) While social and psychological studies of the conduct of inquiry are very illuminating—the role of patronage, the formation of scientific elites, the student-teacher relation—they are background to the irradicable fact that natural science changes only in response to new experimental environment or a more embracing coherent map of reality that arises from within its own structure. In short, science changes when we discover a new truth about the world.

The primary metaphor that Kuhn appeals to is that of "scientific revolution." Many people have argued against this metaphor as distorting the nature of scientific change. Pierre Duhem, the French historian, in his ten-volume work *Le système du monde* (1913) argued that science was evolutionary, not revolutionary, and that seventeenth-century science was in fact less a revolution than the result of the gradual culmination of medieval science.

The word "revolution" has been much abused, appropriated from describing political events like national revolutions to describing changes in our thinking whether it is about science, technology, or a new commercial development. Historians of science and scientists share some of the blame for this misappropriation; they want to draw attention to the fact that there are major discontinuities in the development of science. But I think that the proper metaphor for scientific history (if one insists on metaphors) is not that of human social and political change, but that of the evolution of life on earth. The reason I prefer the natural to the social metaphor is that the social metaphor gives the impression that like national revolutions, scientific revolutions are an exercise of will and determination, while the natural metaphor implies that the change is wrought by the environment of human experience or the hidden order of nature itself, which lies outside human will and purpose. That is how it seems to me to be.

At this juncture, I want to explore the metaphor of scientific change as an example of a selective system, like evolution is a selective system. In part I want to contrast this metaphor with the one that is more often put forward—that of a social revolution, which emphasizes cultural, social, and psychological factors. The evolutionary metaphor emphasizes the importance of material and environmental factors such as new instrumentation, methods, and ideas and the fact (seen retrospectively) that a new discovery was "out there" ready to be made. Ultimately, however, I do not believe that it is really possible to disentangle the social, cultural, and psychological factors from the "material" factors. They are part of the environment, too. It is clearly the interaction between these complex components—the human world with the order of nature

—that produces changes in our knowledge of the natural world. However, the "revolutionary" metaphor has been given such currency that many people, who ought to know better, develop and popularize the view that science is simply another social enterprise. This misconception, like occultism, deserves rebuke. I insist that scientific ideas, because of their special vulnerability to failure imposed by the actual order of nature, are subject to a unique, self-imposed selective pressure, a criterion for survival that is transcendent to the particular culture in which these scientific ideas originate.

I believe that the order of scientific change can be described, like evolutionary change, as a selective system. If the environment changes because of a revelation by a new instrumentation or a conceptual insight (which then becomes a cognitive "instrument"), so do the scientific theories. Theories are selected for and selected against, and they survive as long as the empirical and cognitive environment supports them. The arbitrator of this selection process is the invariant order of the natural world as revealed by observation.

Kuhn also develops the evolutionary analogy in the last chapter of his book, and this is revealing. He especially points out that the great resistance to Darwin's ideas was not the notion of evolution (which many naturalists had already accepted before Darwin), but his notion that evolution was blind, the forms of life were not heading for some final perfection. Kuhn also suggests, by analogy, that perhaps science has no final truth (a point emphasized by C. S. Peirce for similar reasons). However, what Kuhn misses in this analogy is that the primary selective pressure on scientific ideas is something that is *external* to science—the invariant order of nature. Kuhn's main focus throughout his book is the change in science due to developments *internal* to the scientific community. Without that crucial distinction, science becomes like any other human enterprise, like the fashion industry. Either by oversight or from a desire to emphasize social factors, Kuhn has overlooked the key to understanding scientific change.

Scientific change is usually gradual. But sometimes it changes suddenly. I liken these gradual and sudden changes to the kinds of changes we see in the evolutionary record. The gradual changes correspond to genes being passed on from generation to generation with little modification. The sudden discontinuities correspond to an extinction or rapid genetic reshuffling, often in response to a major environmental change.

For example, the fossil record often reveals a remarkable stability for some organisms over long periods of time, rather than what might be expected on the basis of a simple application of natural selection—continued, gradual change. The long periods of stability, however, are punctuated by short (by evolutionary standards) periods of dramatic change. This thesis of "punctuated equilibrium," put forward by the evolutionary biologists Stephen Jay Gould and Niles Eldridge, may also apply to changes in the sciences if we pursue the evolutionary metaphor. Indeed, as Kuhn has emphasized in his book *The Structure of Scientific Revolutions*, a science is characterized by long "normal" periods terminating in "revolutionary" periods. Biologists are not agreed about the precise causes for the rapid change (nor the relatively stable periods) in the fossil records, but in the case of science, with retrospective hindsight, we can see what caused the period of rapid change. It is invariably the consequence of the application of a previously unavailable instrumental or methodological technique. Examples are Galileo's use of the telescope that opened the heavens, Anton van Leeuwenhoek's invention of the microscope that enabled him to see bacteria. The introduction of such instruments before a prepared mind dramatically changes the "environment," and the scientific outlook changes accordingly.

The notion that science proceeds much like evolution is not new. I already mentioned Duhem's work that minimizes the notion of scientific "revolutions." There is also the "evolutionary epistemology" of the philosopher Charles Peirce, who saw scientific truth as subject to an evolutionary process. Karl Popper also did not miss the significance of the analogy between hypothetico-deductive method and natural selection. He devoted part of his Herbert Spencer Lecture in 1973 to a comparison between genetic adaptation, adaptive behavior, and scientific discovery, concluding that, in spite of the differences between these three systems, "the mechanism of adaptation is fundamentally the same." According to Popper, in each of these three systems the instruction for change comes from within the system. Similarly, selection comes, in part, from without and is established by "the method of trial and the elimination of error"—a negative feedback loop. Popper noted: "I have suggested that progress in science, or scientific discovery, depends on *instruction* and *selection*: on a conservative or traditional or historical element, and on a revolutionary use of trial and the elimination of error by criticism, which included severe empirical examination and tests; that is attempts to probe into the possible weakness of theories, attempts to refute them."

Popper also mentioned an analogy between the theories of scientific progress and the theories of antibody formation put forth by Niels Jerne and Sir Macfarlane Burnet (1955). The basic idea of Jerne was that the ability of the body to recognize an invading antigen was part of the inborn genetic structure of the body, although possibly subject to random variations in the recognition system. The antibodies are rough negative templates of the invading antigens and are thus able to counteract and destroy them. Like evolution, the immune response is also a selective system in which the system is instructed from within—the genetic instruction plus random variation—but the selection depends on the external environment—the specific invading antigens. I find the analogy quite compelling.

Why do scientific ideas survive (Newton's mechanics, Darwin's evolution theory)? Why do some not survive (Phlogiston theory, Lamarkian biology)? To answer these questions it is interesting to note the existence of scientific fashions—ideas that come and go —which fail to survive. No scientist, with a career spanning a few decades, has not seen the rise and fall of a scientific fashion; in fact, he or she may have participated in one. Intellectual fashions have the signal feature that they are founded on either no evidence or faulty or incomplete evidence, and they only appear as such retrospectively, when their proponents are already fighting a rearguard action. There is no way to avoid participating in them, because they are generally honest in their initiation. So what if the evidence is incomplete? No one waits until the data is complete; by that time someone else already has boldly developed a theory or undertaken further experiments. But the fact that there is an honest "fashion industry" in science research is crucial to the selective process.

Such trial and error, random variation and search is necessary for a selective system, be it science or evolution, to work. Not only is there trial and error in the work of an individual investigator, but this trial and error approach can characterize the research of an entire profession—a "fashion industry." And appropriately so.

Science rarely progresses because it has a direct goal in mind. It is, like the evolutionary system, blind as to where it is headed. There is a kind of randomness in its progress, a randomness severely constrained by previous experience. But when an idea works, the individual and the profession lock into it—the random searching stops, and research becomes more goal-oriented. The ideas that work are selected, in the end, not so much by human beings as by the Demiurge—the order of nature itself. And therein lies the unique peculiarity of science: its truth is not regulated exclusively by us.

There is a story entitled "Francis Crick Goes to Heaven," which I first heard from molecular biologist Sydney Brenner. It illustrates a feature of natural selection, that it is a sloppy, cumbersome process but one that works—much in the way I like to think that the scientific process works. It is a story about the pragmatic wisdom of nature (as if nature could have such wisdom).

Crick, the codiscoverer of the molecular structure of DNA, dies and goes to heaven. He is met by Saint Peter, who asks if he has any special requests. "Yes," says Crick, "I want to meet the Man himself and ask him a few questions." Peter says that there are not many requests of *that* kind, but it can be arranged, and he tells Crick to follow him. After passing through the Elysian fields, with their cool springs and lakes around which beautiful people are at play, their every desire fulfilled, Peter and Crick come to the mountains and enter a dark valley. The way is strewn with wrecked machines, electronic parts, broken glass and test tubes, organic garbage, old computers—a junkyard. At the end of the valley is a shack, which they enter, and inside is an old man, his coveralls stained in grease, blood, and chemicals. He is bending over a lab table filled with more junk, hard at work. "Francis, meet God; God, meet Francis," says Saint Peter. "Pleased to meet you," says Crick, "but I want to know how you made the muscle system for the fly's wing. It's so ingenious." "Well," says God, "I did it a long time ago, and it's really very simple. Let's see now if I remember. You just take a bit of tissue and then it's . . . well, twisted . . . and then, somehow . . . and then you rearrange . . . slap together these protein chains . . . and . . . Well, I don't remember *all* the details. But who cares? It works, doesn't it?"

The point of the story is that evolution is not systematic or precise. It does not have to fulfill someone's intellectual expectations of perfection. It is not a "rigorous method." A sloppy fit that works will do. Likewise with the conduct of inquiry and the progress of science—who cares about *all* the details; if an idea is right, it will survive. Survival, of course, is not the same as truth. But the possibility of truth will do. Survival is also *not* the criterion of a good scientific idea (occult science "survives"). But it is survival *and* the capacity for change and evolution—vulnerability—that distinguish scientific theory.

I have argued that the change in scientific ideas is a selective process and emphasized that the selection is ultimately not made by us. As Werner Heisenberg, one of the founders of the quantum theory, said, "I also learned something perhaps even more important, namely that in science a decision can always be reached as to what is right and wrong. It is not a question of belief, or Weltanschaung, or hypothesis; but a certain statement could be simply right and another statement wrong. Neither origin nor race decides this question: It is decided by nature, or if you prefer, by God, in any case not by man."

My view, that the evolution of sciences is like the evolution of life, autonomous and mostly independent of human will and purpose—an "organic" development—is not very popular these days. Some philosophical and social thinkers emphasize that scientists promote certain values and interests (they do!), that science is subject to social and political forces (it is!), and that the supportive culture establishes the worldview that makes scientific inquiry at all possible (it does!). Others, supporting this position, would agree, and argue that natural science is "a world" standing alongside other worlds—music, art, literature, law—and that its claim to access an aboriginal reality is just a construct in the mind of scientists. However, when the claim is made that the natural sciences are *nothing but* a social enterprise alongside others, and which promote and articulate a view with no special claim to truth, then I draw the line. While our view of natural reality may be a construct, it is a construct that is like no other because it was not determined exclusively by us.

To illustrate this contrast between purely constructed worlds and natural science, I have a story. A history graduate student at his oral exam at Harvard was asked by a professor what he thought historians did—a good, basic question. The student responded that the activity of historians researching the past was like a person entering a dark house and then turning on the lights and seeing the rooms and furniture. "Ah," the professor responded, "but who built the house?" The professor was reminding his student that history was a construct. Unlike history, however, the natural world is not constructed by us, although its representation, the maps of reality, most certainly are.

The conduct of scientific inquiry is extraordinarily complex, not as complex as the evolution of countless organisms over the aeons, but still very complex. Yet we are beginning to learn how to handle that kind of complexity, and real progress might be possible in understanding the details of how science grows. I do not believe that in the future the task of understanding the development of science will be left to the philosophers or the conventional historians of science. I believe that it will become a new enterprise in its own right. The reason for this belief is that the instrumentation for the study of the methods and progress of science is changing.

For example, some scientists are now promoting a major project —putting the entire corpus of scientific knowledge for the last three hundred years into a computer system. It is a giant project and correspondingly expensive. But if such a project is implemented, new approaches that utilize the rapid access to massive scientific information can and will be taken in understanding the historical structure of science as a selective system. This approach will not answer all of our questions but will certainly go some of the way. Already people who study the growth of new fields of science, such as is done at the Institute for Scientific Information in Philadelphia, can use cluster analysis of the citations involving key words that identify an emergent topic. They can visually display the growing clusters and see newly emergent areas of research influence one another. Such studies do not probe the deeper questions of scientific change, but with more information and more sophisticated computers even that may be possible someday. Understanding the development of science is a problem in the understanding of the complexity of selective systems. The instrument that manages that complexity is the computer, and with a sufficient data base we may be able to see, for the first time, the patterns of growth of science. And the success of this future enterprise can be judged by how little traditional philosophers will be interested in it as they move on to other, less tractable, problems.

The image I would choose for the intellectual framework of modern science is that of the most beautiful and complex unity I know—the human body. Before the accomplishment of the human body (if it may be viewed as an accomplishment) all philosophy and epistemology, all interpretation and criticism shrink to insignificance. Our bodies, their versatility, plasticity, endurance, and survivability are the result of two billion years of evolutionary process we do not yet comprehend. But, irrespective of whether or not we understand it, we are witnesses to the magnificent human body, singular, definite, and vulnerable to change. And it works, "sloppy fits" and all. If in our intellectual pursuits, such as science, we could but imitate the selective processes that brought it into being, even if we fail to understand those complex processes in detail, then we would be assured of the survivability and flexibility of our knowledge.

Then science, like the body, could never lie.

Chapter 12

Warriors of
the Infinite

*No one shall expel us from the paradise which Cantor created
for us.*

—DAVID HILBERT, 1926

I always loved mathematical puzzles. As a teenager in the 1950s
I struggled to solve the four-color-map problem—how to color a
map consisting of countries so that one *had* to use more than four
colors to distinguish boundaries between countries or, alternatively, show that the most one needed for any map was four colors.
This problem had not yet been solved in spite of the fact that it
could be simply stated and grasped. I spent the better part of
several weekends trying to find a map that needed five colors. The
maps had to be rather elaborate because mathematicians already
knew that any map with forty or fewer regions only needed four
colors. At one point in my struggles I realized that if I curled up
the sheet of paper I was using into a cylinder and joined the ends
to make the doughnut-shaped figure of a torus, then I could find
maps that did need at least five colors. I was pleased with this
result. But later I found out that mathematicians had already
proved that a maximum of seven colors (instead of four) was
needed for the torus. The topology of the surface mattered.

I never found a map on the plane that needed five colors because this is impossible. The mathematical proof of this result came twenty years later in 1976 by the mathematicians Wolfgang Haken and Kenneth Appel. They reasoned that if a map needing five colors existed, then there had to be a smallest such map—a "minimal" five-color map. Their strategy was then to show that if such a minimal map exists, it could always be further reduced, so that it wasn't really minimal. Then the only logical possibility is that no such five-color map exists at all, thus proving the four-color theorem. They succeeded in showing this only by using a computer to check the reducibility—it was *that* complicated. A teenager didn't stand a chance.

What I remember of my struggle with this and other mathematical puzzles is my confrontation with logical necessity. If I agreed to play a "mathematical game" like the four-color-map game according to certain logical rules, then some things were simply impossible. They were not just impossible at that time but for all time; and this impossibility was not just a matter of opinion or a feature of human psychology but was inherent in the rules themselves.

This ironclad sense of necessity can seem like a prison. Yet like many disciplines in which there are rules, the logical rules of mathematics open a vast and complex realm of existence rich enough to challenge the deepest resources of the human imagination.

What is mathematics? Almost from the time humanity first learned to count, people puzzled about the nature of mathematical objects like numbers or points, lines and triangles, beginning a discussion that continues to the present day. This discussion, while it has deepened our understanding, is still unresolved. Fundamental questions remain. In what way do mathematical objects exist? Do they exist at all? If they do not exist, then to what do the theorems of mathematics refer; what are we talking about?

Some modern philosophers of mathematics do not think that the theorems of mathematics require any kind of mathematical objects to exist, they are simply logical statements, a formal prescription without a necessary content. For example, the theorems of Euclid's geometry can be viewed as purely logical statements that do not require our visualizing lines and triangles to fulfill those logical statements. Ernest Nagel, the Columbia University philosopher, supported this view when he observed: "The interpretation of logical principles [as, for example, mathematical theorems] as ontological invariants [as, for example, points, lines, geometrical figures] seems . . . to be an extraneous ornamentation." Bertrand Russell, the logician (at least early in his career), and Jules Henri Poincaré, the mathematician, in spite of their philosophical differences, concurred on this point—mathematical axioms are simply logical definitions, and there need not exist any entities that satisfy the axioms. Mathematical truths are simply the truths of logic—they are true by definition.

Others, following a tradition stretching from Plato to Kurt Gödel, the twentieth-century logician, think that mathematical axioms are more than mere definitions and mathematical objects more than "extraneous ornamentation," but that instead the coherence of a system of axioms appeals to a deeper intuition about an order of reality—an order transcendent to the order of formal mathematical logic. They feel that mathematical truths are something more—truths about entities. Form is insufficient; content matters. If this is not the case, they would argue, how then can mathematical intuitions occur in the human mind? Where do they come from? They would argue that there must exist an order of being, transcendent to our experience, which renders that experience intelligible and from which our intuitions come. But there are still other views of mathematics, one of which is empiricism, a philosophy often associated with David Hume, the eighteenth-century English thinker.

Mathematics and logic are surely a product of the human mind and culture. Yet their products are universal and objective and go beyond the particular mind or culture that created them. The nature of logic—its necessity—is that it is inherent in our very thinking and in the structure of the world. One cannot shake away from it. Even when mathematicians and logicians invent new mathematical and logical systems that apparently have nothing to do with the natural world or the way we happen to think logically, their requirement—that the system be consistent, true, and interesting—appeals to their experience of the ordinary world of being and thinking. Sometimes the tie between the ordinary natural world and mathematics seems so close that some mathematical philosophers—the empiricists—want to establish the consistency of mathematics on the evident, yet mysterious, coherence of the natural order. In spite of the difficulty in maintaining such an empiricist view of mathematics (after all, empirical science appeals to mathematical logic for the coherence of its theories, not the other way around), some philosophers would concur with philosopher Lazlo Kalomar's remark, "Why do we not confess that mathematics, like other sciences, is ultimately based upon and has to be tested in practice?" Mathematical truth becomes dependent on our experience of natural order, in marked contrast with the transcendental view of Plato and Gödel or the formal-logical view of Russell.

The contrasts between these views of mathematics—the formal-logical view, the transcendental view, the empiricists' view, as well as others—will be examined in this chapter. Interestingly, many of the themes and contrasts of our previous chapters on the nature of science and the mind-body problem resurface here, especially the contrast between the transcendental view, which sees the mind as autonomous, and the naturalistic view, which sees the mind as part of nature and subject to its laws. I will argue, as I did in the previous chapters, that the categorical framework of our thinking about these problems and the philosophy of mathematics in particular is going to be altered and informed by the emergent sciences of complexity. Indeed, mathematics itself not only provides the language of the sciences of complexity, but is subject to that science, right at its logical foundations. If scientists in the future crack "the problem of cognition"—how to represent meaning and content in a formal, physically realizable system—then I believe we will discover that we have been asking the wrong questions, making false distinctions in discussing the philosophy of mathematics. In order to get a better conceptual grip on these issues, I want to give a sketch of the history of mathematics with an emphasis on the philosophical problems. That history will illuminate the present controversy and set the stage for our discussion.

Long ago ancient people, noticing the regularities in nature, began to think about them in a different, abstract way. Merchants and traders exchanging goods devised numerical accounting systems and elementary arithmetic. Although the regularities such as the simple counting of objects, the boundaries between farm fields, and the sound of vibrating strings may be part of the world of commerce and nature, we can abstract and universalize these regularities so that they become part of the realm of pure thought. If one adds three sheep to eight sheep, one gets eleven sheep, and adding three goats to eight goats, one gets eleven goats. From this example we see that the abstract notion of number arises once we recognize that the result of addition can be obtained without any reference to sheep and goats but only to the abstract notion of number.

It was the ancient Greeks who first self-consciously grasped the concept of an abstract science of the ordered universe, an abstraction that seemed to appeal to a transcendent reality of universal objects. They perfected a realm of mathematical thinking in the areas of whole numbers and geometry and the methods of logical deduction that set the Western mathematical tradition on its long journey to the present day. Although the Greeks built on the previous knowledge of the Babylonians and the Egyptians, their accomplishment is all the more awesome in that they broke with these powerful influences. Some Greek philosophers emphasized that mathematics lay at the foundations of reality. In his dialogue *Timaeus*, Plato described a vision of the cosmos as organized on the basis of geometrical principles—a vision, remarkably, being realized today in modern field physics. Interestingly, Aristotle rejected this emphasis on mathematics and stressed the role of logic at the foundations of our thinking about reality. This dialectic between mathematics and logic continues to our time. The Greeks, it can be said with only slight exaggeration, discovered the Western mind.

One of the highest achievements of the Greek mind was the application of logic to the principles of plane geometry, an achievement embodied in Euclid's ten axioms. Axioms are the fundamental propositions, the definitions, that are the starting points for any mathematical system. For example, one of Euclid's axioms states that between any two points only one straight line can be drawn. As obviously true as this proposition seems, it has to be clearly stated as an axiom. Using this axiom and the others, one can go on to define geometrical objects such as triangles and squares and, significantly, logically deduce theorems—statements about these objects that don't seem so obvious, for example, that the sum of the angles in any plane triangle adds up to exactly 180 degrees. Interestingly, the Greeks first pondered the objects of geometry and later grasped that their properties could be deduced from a set of axioms. Today we have turned this around—we view the axioms as fundamental, not the objects; in fact, many mathematicians don't care if there exist any objects that satisfy a set of axioms.

In a way it was the powerful spatial imagination of the Greeks that both led them into the beautiful ontic realm of geometrical objects and limited their imagination and intuition to what could be visualized. The fact that Euclidean geometry was but a special case of geometry could only be grasped millennia later when the logical independence of the famous "parallels postulate" was understood, an insight that gave rise to non-Euclidean geometry. In this case spatial intuition led them astray. (One wonders how we are led astray today.)

In Greek mathematics one had glimpses of a transcendental universal order of concepts, lying outside the mundane world, the very thoughts of the mind of God, inasmuch as our individual intellects could hope to grasp them. For the truths of mathematics are not just true for you and me, but for any mind able to grasp logical necessity. In this sense, then, the truths of mathematics are transcendent to the world—an order of necessity not subject to the evidence of the senses or the specificity of the world. And likewise the mind itself, like the realm of concepts, is of the natural world but not in it. So powerful is this insight—that there exists a transcendent order of reality as clearly exemplified by mathematical truth (and some would claim moral truth as well)—that it has dominated Western thinking and been embraced by our religions, even unto the present day. But is this so? Is the notion of a realm of transcendental concepts a self-serving intellectual hallucination? Perhaps one should be asking not only what is mathematics, but *where* is mathematics? In what sense does the logical space of concepts exist? Where does the Euclidean triangle—a perfect idea —exist? Again we return to the questions raised earlier in our discussions of cognitive science—the problem of the representation of knowledge in the mind.

During the Middle Ages there were major advances in logic by church schoolmen along the path set forth by Aristotle. Mathematics, which was inspirational for Plato's view, was relegated to a minor role in Aristotle's philosophy in which logic became the key to reality. Some scholars maintain that it was the reemergence of Platonism and its emphasis on geometry during the Renaissance that set the stage for the scientific revolution and the mathematical (rather than purely logical) description of nature.

It was not until the founding of the modern sciences of physics and astronomy by Copernicus, Kepler, Galileo, and Newton that great mathematical developments began. The analytic work of Descartes and Vieta in the seventeenth century applied algebra to geometry for the first time, thus replacing the deductive arguments of the Greeks with symbolic manipulations of algebraic quantities—a technique invented by the Arabs. Through Descartes's introduction of a coordinate system, a reference frame in space, geometric objects could now be studied algebraically—an immense simplification that gave the mind a symbolic analytic "handle" on geometry. It was through such an analytic device that a window was opened to view higher-dimensional objects. The mathematical mind could now manipulate geometrical objects in more than just two or three dimensions.

These analytical developments of the seventeenth century also promoted the mathematical notion of a function—one variable y could be a function of another variable x, written $y = f(x)$. The function f specified a precise, deterministic relation between the variables x and y—a logically causal relation that could, and did, become the basic form of all physical laws. In this way natural phenomena could be expressed in the language of mathematical equations instead of just words—an immense advance in comprehension and quantification.

Another major mathematical invention of the seventeenth century was the creation of the calculus by Newton and Leibnitz, a tool that was used to build Newton's edifice of classical mechanics. Dealing with the infinitesimally small and managing infinite processes was always a stumbling block for the Greeks. Now with the arrival of calculus and modern algebra, these obstacles were removed. The path lay clear for a mathematical description of nature.

The language of classical physics was differential equations, an outgrowth of the calculus. Of the two forms of human expression —language and mathematics—it now became clear that mathematics would become the means by which humans would describe nature. The older, linguistic description of the Greeks and medieval philosophers of nature seemed inadequate and cumbersome once the appropriate mathematical tools became available. But with mathematics firmly identified as the proper language of physics and astronomy, the question arose about the symbiotic relation of natural science to mathematics—why can nature be described mathematically? Kant once remarked, "In every special doctrine of nature only so much science proper can be found as there is mathematics in it," thus linking empirical science and mathematics.

That there is a link between empirical science and mathematics is incontestable. Natural science often uses previously developed mathematics. For example, the development of non-Euclidean geometry in the nineteenth century, culminating in the work of Bernard Riemann on the curvature of space, was used as the conceptual building block of general relativity by Einstein decades later. The notion of an infinite dimensional vector space and operators on a Hilbert space developed in the early twentieth century served as the mathematical underpinnings of the quantum theory of the late 1920s.

Although the flow of ideas from mathematics to natural science has been immense, it is not a one-way flow. Physicists often discover novel aspects of mathematics in their attempts to solve equations describing physical processes. For example, Newton invented the calculus to solve physical problems. Furthermore, new classes of mathematical solutions are found trying to solve physics problems. The realization that the spectrum—the set of possible values—of some mathematical operators could be both discrete (taking on only special values) and continuous (taking on all values) was discovered by mathematical physicists looking for the light spectrum emitted by the hydrogen atom. The recent advent of the computer—which not only solves problems but *is* a problem in complexity itself—has given rise to a host of new mathematical developments.

In principle mathematics could develop completely independently of the natural sciences. In fact it has not done so. Yet many eminent mathematicians view not only the logical structure of their discipline as completely independent of the material world, but flaunt the abstract and transcendental character of mathematics. These mathematicians are repelled by the notion of applied mathematics. Jean Dieudonné, a retired member of the Bourbaki group in France, was pleased to remark in his text of 1977 that algebraic geometry, his favorite subject, had no relation to physics at that time. By the 1982 edition of the text, however, the remarks were removed, a consequence of the fruitful application of algebraic geometry to the gauge field theories of quantum particles. Number theory, long an isolated realm of pure mathematics, has sprung to prominence in coding theory and computer science.

What puzzles me is why the development of the natural sciences and mathematics are so closely correlated. Why the nearly coincident deepening of both realms, one of pure thought, the other empirical? Why were the mathematical tools of Riemannian geometry and Hilbert space waiting to be used by physicists who were developing ideas about the natural world—ideas that could not have been anticipated by the mathematicians? While I do not have a satisfactory answer to this puzzle, I have some guesses.

Mathematics is extraordinarily general in its development; mathematicians *strive* for such generality and attempt to prove their results by logically exhausting all possibilities within a highly specific class of problems. Further there is the overall ambition to mathematize any logical structure that can exist and then study it to the limits of human ability. In short mathematicians have created *lots* of mathematics, and anything for which they could develop a mathematical description they did within the limits of their imagination, lifetimes, historical background, and resources. Perhaps we should not be so surprised when the mathematical tools we need to study some new development in the empirical sciences are ready and waiting.

A second reason for the symbiosis of math and science has to do with the limits of the human imagination. Mathematicians and scientists are born into the same world, the same intellectual culture. Each century has its style, its worldview, and the conduct of intellectual life is informed by this style. Social and cultural convention play their role too in establishing what is an acceptable problem to work on and what is viewed as bizarre and therefore less acceptable. Scientists and mathematicians often draw their inspiration from the natural order and the logical order that it reflects. Our culture limits our imagination at the same time that it nurtures it, and this happens uniformly for intellectual life. The correspondence between math and science in the Renaissance, the Enlightenment, the nineteenth and twentieth centuries, should not surprise us. Since the description of nature and its coherence is, as emphasized by Kant, a product of our cognitive faculty just like mathematics, perhaps their correlation is even necessary.

With the continued development of mathematics in the nineteenth century, a new fundamental problem arose. Mathematicians attempting to sum various infinite series of fractions found out that they got different answers depending on how they manipulated the sum. The response to this distressing situation, which suggested an inconsistency in mathematics, was the development of rigorous methods of proof. It became important—indeed crucial—to examine precisely the nature of mathematical operations. Through the work of Cauchy, Dirichlet, Fourier, Gauss, Bolzano, Weierstrass, and others, mathematical analysis was put on a much more rigorous foundation and the apparent inconsistencies eliminated. The notion of mathematical rigor became entrenched.

Nineteenth-century mathematicians vastly extended the initiatives previously begun in calculus and differential and algebraic equations, opening up huge new territories. The genius of Carl Friedrich Gauss and Augustin-Louis Cauchy developed new analytical methods extending calculus into new realms. Joseph Fourier discovered the mathematical series that bears his name. New kinds of numbers, the quaternions, were discovered and elucidated by William Hamilton. Pierre Simon de Laplace, taking up earlier work, developed probability theory into a mathematical discipline. Everiste Galois created group theory, which solved many of the classical problems associated with algebraic equations. New non-Euclidean geometries were understood and explored. The algebraic approach to geometry was profoundly deepened by Richard Dedekind and Leopold Kronecker. Other developments, too numerous to mention here, flowed from the rich imagination of European mathematicians—an eternal body of knowledge that soon became the legacy of all humanity and formed the language of much of twentieth-century science.

Nineteenth-century mathematics was characterized by a sense of the discovery of new mathematical objects—entities that lay "out there" in the realm of mathematical imagination. The notion of abstraction that, by contrast, characterizes the movement of twentieth-century mathematics, although it had already begun in the nineteenth century, had not yet taken hold. Abstraction came, in part, from new developments in logic, a discipline that in the nineteenth century was still viewed as quite distinct from mathematics. These nineteenth-century developments in logic ultimately came to play an important role in the philosophy of mathematics. Let us look at them.

Augustus De Morgan in 1847 published his *Formal Logic*, which put Aristotelian logic in quantitative form and initiated the study of logical relations. A major nineteenth-century development in logic was George Boole's *Law of Thought*, which appeared in 1854. Boole's motive was to replace the ordinary logic of language with an algebraic symbolism and formulae, and in this he succeeded, hastening the trend toward abstraction. Boole's work certainly influenced the famous *Begriffschrift* of Gottlob Frege, a booklet of eighty-eight pages that appeared in 1879 and possibly the most important single work in logic. Contrasting himself with Boole, Frege wrote, "My intention was not to represent an abstract logic in formulae, but to express a content through written signs in a more precise and clear manner than it is possible through words. In fact, what I intended to create was not a mere *calculus ratiocinator*, but a *lingua characterica* in the sense of Leibniz."

Frege started his career struggling to give a precise logical analysis of the idea of a sequence. To accomplish this he invented a formula language intended to construct logic as a language that did not need to be supplemented by any intuitive reasoning. He wrote in the introduction of his great work, "My initial step was to attempt to reduce the concept of ordering in a sequence to that of *logical* consequence, so as to proceed from there to the concept of number. To prevent anything intuitive from penetrating here unnoticed, I had to bend every effort to keep the chain of inferences free of gaps. In attempting to comply with this requirement in the strictest possible way I found the inadequacy of language to be an obstacle; no matter now unwieldy the expressions I was ready to accept, I was less and less able, as the relations became more complex, to attain the precision that my purpose required. This deficiency led me to the idea of the present ideography." Frege invented the truth propositional calculus, did the first analysis of propositions into function and arguments, rather than subject and predicate, and devised the theory of quantification in which derivations are carried out purely in terms of the explicit form of the expressions.

Frege and Boole set the theme for future developments in logic —a formal, almost mechanical approach to reasoning. Frege demanded that in thinking about mathematical reasoning we use explicit symbolism, explicit axioms and rules, and explicit proofs. Hence a mathematical proof, viewed as a sequence of logical statements, could itself be viewed as an object for mathematical examination (a point of departure for David Hilbert's "proof theory"). Later in his life Frege became interested in the philosophy of mathematics. In a review of an early work by the philosopher Edmund Husserl on the foundations of arithmetic, he convinced Husserl of his error of "psychologism"—that mathematical knowledge depends on human psychology rather than objective and certain judgments—thus leading Husserl to adopt an apodictic approach in his future work.

Frege's work set the stage for the golden age of modern logic in the late nineteenth and early twentieth century. His great power was that he rendered logical ideas explicit. Yet he expressed misgivings about one of the axioms of his system—axiom V—and indeed this troublesome axiom turned out to imply an inconsistency, as was pointed out by Bertrand Russell in 1901. What occurred next in the movement toward abstraction was creation of set theory.

Mathematicians in the nineteenth century became warriors of the infinite—they did conceptual battle with managing the infinitely large or the infinitely small. Most of the rigorous methods were invented because of the problem of manipulating such quantities. Yet throughout this development infinity meant one thing—the limit of a sequence like the sequence of integers $1, 2, 3 \cdots$. It was through the genius of Georg Cantor in the last three decades of the nineteenth century that the remarkable structure of infinity began to be revealed.

How can we possibly think about infinity? After all, our minds, even the best minds, are finite. No one can count to infinity. Yet even primitive people whose counting system does not go beyond ten (anything beyond ten is effectively "infinite" for them) can still compare two sets of objects each larger than ten and determine which is larger. They do it by matching objects in the two sets and seeing which set has objects left over—that is the larger set. Cantor, building on the earlier work of Bernhard Bolzano, basically did the same thing with infinite sets, such as the set of all the integers. After comparing different infinite sets of mathematical objects, he found that some of them still had something "left over"

—there were different "sizes" of infinity. How could he arrive at such a remarkable conclusion?

First let us suppose that there is a lowest infinite set—the set of all integers 1, 2, 3, 4, 5 · · · where the " · · · " means it goes on indefinitely. This is an infinite set. One might, at first, think that the set of all odd numbers is smaller than this set; after all, the even numbers comprise only half the numbers. But this way of thinking, while it applies to finite sets, does not apply to infinite sets—a part can be equal to the whole. This reason has to do with the fact that the set of all integers can be put into a one-to-one match with just the odd integers, according to

$$1 \ 2 \ 3 \ 4 \ 5 \ 6 \cdots$$
$$| \ | \ | \ | \ | \ |$$
$$1 \ 3 \ 5 \ 7 \ 9 \ 11 \cdots$$

so that the two sets are comparable—the set of odd numbers is of the same order of infinity as all the integers. Likewise, the squares of the integers, 1, 4, 9, 16, 25 · · · can be put into a one-to-one correspondence with the integers; they can be counted. Such sets are called "denumerable"—one can make a list of the objects in such sets and put them in a correspondence with the integers.

At first one might think that the reason the odd numbers or the squares of the integers could be put into a one-to-one correspondence with the integers is that there is a "gap" between successive members of these infinite sets. Can one also count objects that are densely close to one another? For example, the infinite set of all rational numbers is the set of all fractions, ratios of integers like $1/4$, $7/3$, or $126/901$. If we imagine these fractions designated by their corresponding points on an infinite line, then on any finite segment of that line, there are an infinite number of such rational numbers. They are densely packed. Can one count them?

Cantor showed how this was possible. Imagine the infinite array of all rational numbers

$$
\begin{array}{lllll}
1/1 \rightarrow 2/1 & 3/1 \rightarrow 4/1 & 5/1 \cdots \\
1/2 & 2/2 & 3/2 & 4/2 & 5/2 \cdots \\
1/3 & 2/3 & 3/3 & 4/3 & 5/3 \cdots \\
1/4 & 2/4 & 3/4 & 4/4 & 5/4 \cdots \\
1/5 & 2/5 & 3/5 & 4/5 & 5/5 \cdots
\end{array}
$$

where the numerators 1, 2, 3 $\cdots$ denote the column and the denominators 1, 2, 3 $\cdots$ denote the rows of the array. Clearly, every rational number appears at least once in this array; some rational numbers like $1 = \frac{1}{1} = \frac{2}{2} = \frac{3}{3} \cdots$ appear an infinite number of times. By working one's way through the array as indicated by the arrows, one can start to count the rational numbers—put them into a correspondence with the integers. For every rational number there is a corresponding integer. Hence the set of all rational numbers is denumerable.

When Cantor discovered this result, he exclaimed, "I see it, but I don't believe it!" But are there nondenumerable sets? Remarkably, the answer is yes, as Cantor showed.

Consider the set of all real numbers in the interval between 0 and 1. This includes rational numbers like $\frac{1}{4}$ and $\frac{37}{43}$, as well as irrational numbers like $1/\sqrt{2}$ or $1/\pi$. Suppose we assume that we can make a list of all these numbers expressed as a decimal expansion so that $\frac{1}{4} = 0.25$ and $1/\pi = 0.3183 \cdots$ Instead of writing out the numbers explicitly, let us denote these decimals symbolically so that the first decimal in our list is $0.a_1a_2a_3 \cdots$ and the second is $0.b_1b_2b_3 \cdots$ where the a's and b's are definite integers. Proceeding in this way we may imagine listing *all* the decimals between 0 and 1 and putting them into a correspondence with the integers

$$1 \longleftrightarrow 0.a_1a_2a_3 \cdots$$
$$2 \longleftrightarrow 0.b_1b_2b_3 \cdots$$
$$3 \longleftrightarrow 0.c_1c_2c_3 \cdots$$
.
.
.

One might think that one has therefore shown that all the real numbers between 0 and 1 can be counted. But by using "Cantor's diagonal method" it is possible to construct a number not on this infinite list. This method consists of examining the first digit of the first number on the list, a_1, and picking some other number, x_1. This number, x_1, will be the first digit of the new number. Next, go to the second digit of the second number on the list, b_2, and pick some other number, x_2, for the second digit of the new number. Proceeding in this way for all the numbers on the list we end up considering a new number $0.x_1x_2x_3\cdots$. This number cannot be on the list because it differs from every number on the list in at least one place; that is how it was constructed. Hence, the beginning assumption that we can list all the real numbers between 0 and 1 must be false—the continuum consisting of all real numbers cannot be counted! It is an example of a nondenumerable set. Like the primitive people who cannot count above ten, we find that the infinite set of all possible numbers—the continuum—cannot match the set of all integers. The infinity of all numbers, the continuum, is "larger" than the infinity of just the integers.

Cantor hypothesized that there were no sets of "size" intermediate between the set of integers and the set of real numbers between 0 and 1. Many people tried to prove this until, in 1963, it was shown by the logician Paul Cohen that it could not be proven from the familiar axioms of set theory—it was an independent axiom. Perhaps with other axioms it could be proven.

But Cantor already knew that the size of sets did not stop at the continuum—there was an "infinity of infinities." For example, the set of all curved lines in a plane cannot be put into a one-to-one correspondence with the continuum of points on a line—equivalent to the set of all numbers between 0 and 1. For we can imagine a set of curved lines each one of which intersects every point on a line in the plane. We need draw just one more curve and see that there are no more points left for it to intersect. Hence the set of curves lines is "bigger" than the set of points on a line—the continuum. Cantor showed that the hierarchy of infinite sets goes on forever.

In 1883 Cantor described his seminal work as follows:

> The description of my investigations in the theory of aggregates has reached a stage where their continuation has become dependent on a generalization of real positive integers beyond the present limits; a generalization which takes a direction in which, as far as I know, nobody has yet looked.
>
> I depend on this generalization of the number concept to such an extent that without it I could not freely take even small steps forward in the theory of sets. I hope that this situation justifies or, if necessary, excuses the introduction of seemingly strange ideas into my arguments. In fact the purpose is to generalize or extend the series of real integers beyond infinity. Daring as this may ap-

pear, I express not only the hope but also the firm conviction that in due course this generalization will be acknowledged as a quite simple, appropriate, and natural step. Still I am well aware that by adopting such a procedure I am putting myself in opposition to widespread views regarding infinity in mathematics and to current opinions on the nature of number.

Many mathematicians thought Cantor was crazy (he did have a nervous breakdown; he resumed work in 1887, but died in a mental institution in 1918) and that his infinite sets were monsters. He was particularly attacked by his former teacher Leopold Kronecker and by Henri Poincaré. Yet the proponents of set theory eventually won the day and showed that set theory provided a unifying framework for all of mathematics. In fact, today the view is that mathematics is identical to set theory. (The realm of logic, however, is greater than just set theory.) In 1926 David Hilbert expressed the feelings of most mathematicians when he said, "No one shall expel us from the paradise which Cantor created for us."

Some of Cantor's ideas about sets were seen to be too naive, and subsequent attempts were made to formalize and axiomatize his original ideas, especially by Ernst Zermelo and Abraham Fraenkel. However, with the new unifying tool of set theory at their disposal, mathematicians at the end of the nineteenth century began to dispute the very foundations of their discipline. A new field of research, the foundations of mathematics, came into being, which attracted some of the greatest mathematicians and logicians of our century. These mathematicians were sharply divided about the very nature of mathematical reasoning, divisions with a long history that were contrasted starkly in the light of the new set theory. We will examine three of these main doctrines: the logicism of Bertrand Russell, intuitionism of L.E.J. Brouwer, and formalism of David Hilbert. Many of these doctrines had to do with how mathematicians viewed sets, the role of logic, and what they thought a mathematical proof actually is. All shared an equal commitment to rigor; it was deep issues of principle that divided them.

A major reason for the examination of the foundations of mathematics was that set theory was extraordinarily powerful and applied to all of mathematics, yet it was fraught with outright paradoxes if one used it naively. To demonstrate this I'd like to tell a short "theological anecdote" about an experience that I think most young people have had who have reflected on the nature of God.

When I was in high school I remember critically reflecting on what kind of being God could possibly be—I was curious. God was clearly an all-knowing, all-powerful, compassionate Being, but one who helps only the other beings who do not help themselves. Does God help himself? If he does not help himself, he should then help himself. If he does help himself, then he should not help himself.

This kind of contradiction troubled me. I also remember asking that if God was all-powerful, could he do things like change the laws of logic? If he could change the laws of logic, then he was a kind of lawless Being incomprehensible to the human mind. On the other hand, if he couldn't change the laws of logic, he wasn't all-powerful. These alternatives left me dissatisfied. While I know that there are flaws in this "teenage theology" (it can, however, be given a rigorous formulation), it left me with the feeling that either God was not subject to the laws of logic, in which case there was no point in my thinking rationally about God, or he was subject to the laws of logic, in which case he was not a very impressive God. Such concerns do more than preoccupy teenagers. I know that Kurt Gödel developed a proof for the existence of God (I haven't seen it). He was certainly aware of the logical paradoxes associated with most logical notions of God.

A set is basically a collection of objects—the elements of the set —that may be infinite in number. One of the most elementary paradoxes of set theory occurs if we now consider the set of all sets, that is, a set that has all other sets as its elements. That seems simple enough to grasp until we ask, Does the set of all sets contain itself as a member? If it does not contain itself as a member, then, since it is a set itself, it cannot be the set of all sets. If, on the other hand, it does properly contain itself as a member, then it must be the element of a more inclusive set and cannot therefore be the set of all sets. A variety of paradoxes, usually involving a self-reference such as this one, occur in logic and set theory if one is not careful. The most famous is the Cretan liar paradox, which arises if we consider a sentence that states of itself "I am not true." It is important to eliminate all such paradoxes because they imply an inconsistency—a single statement that is *both* true and not true. Once a single inconsistency occurs in a logical system one can then go on to prove that any statement in its negation must both be true—in short, there is no truth.

Bertrand Russell was much taken by these logical paradoxes ever since he found one in the work of Gottlob Frege (the troublesome axiom V), rendering that important and seminal work inconsistent. Russell thought that the paradoxes arise by neglecting the distinction between different "types" of concepts. For example, a "set of sets" is a different "type" from a set itself, and it is improper to compare different logical types—like comparing "apples" with "fairness." The "set of all sets" is like a snake trying to swallow itself by beginning at the tail—it cannot be done. Yet a snake of one type—a large snake—can swallow a snake of another type—a small snake. By distinguishing different "logical types," one avoids the paradoxes. Logical types are of interest to more than logicians. The anthropologist Gregory Bateson has used this notion extensively in elucidating human behavior and biological organization.

Russell thought that mathematics was a branch of logic—a system of thought that deals with structures independent of their actual meaning. While this idea did not originate with Russell (many mathematicians and logicians, including G. Leibnitz, A. De Morgan, G. Boole, C. S. Pierce, E. Schröeder, G. Frege, and G. Peano, contributed to it), it reached its clearest formulation and execution by him. Simply stated, Russell's thesis is that mathematics is part of logic. Specifically, mathematics is identical to set theory, and set theory is part of logic.

In logic one can state various rules. For example, if A, B, and C are propositions (we don't care what they mean), and if A implies B and B implies C, then A implies C—a rule of logic, independent of the meanings of A, B, and C. Russell thought that mathematics —geometry,. number theory, analysis—was like that. In a sense triangles and numbers do not exist, only the logical propositions about them exist; or to say the same thing, such mathematical structures have no meaning outside of their logical definitions. Furthermore, the proper language for the expression of logical relations was not ordinary human language but symbolic logic. In 1910–1913 Russell and his collaborator Alfred North Whitehead published the massive three-volume *Principia Mathematica*, in which the theorems of analytic geometry, natural and real numbers, are described in terms of the laws of logic. John G. Kemeny, the contemporary mathematician, poking fun at the philosophers once remarked of the *Principia* that it is "a masterpiece that is discussed by practically every philosopher and read by practically none." If you have ever tried to read it, as I have, you will know why. It is filled with abstract symbols, and one does not get to the proof that $1 + 1 = 2$ until the second volume.

The *Principia* had a significant influence on how people thought about the relation of logic and mathematics—it was a watershed. Yet it was not satisfactory. The theory of types, which was introduced to avoid paradoxes, turned out to be unbelievably cumbersome—even different kinds of numbers (like real and rational numbers) belonged to different types. Also, Russell and Whitehead were compelled to introduce several "artificial" axioms that seemed contrived. As Herman Weyl, the mathematician, commented on the *Principia*, "Mathematics is no more based on logic than the utopia built by the logician." Mathematics, it seems to many people, was more than just logic. But what else was required for mathematics?

The intuitionists thought that mathematical objects and truths do exist, but only within our mental life and intuitive imagination. Led by the Dutch mathematician L.E.J. Brouwer, the intuitionists were critical of Russell's logicist program. Mathematics, they argued, was much more than logic; it was grounded in the capacity of our mind to describe mathematical entities and discern their properties. Objects that could not be so intuited did not have a valid existence. Brouwer got from Kant the notion that certain cognitions are built into the human mind—in particular mathematical cognitions—and that empty logical propositions such as those Russell advocated for the content of mathematics missed the essence of mathematics, its objective content. Brouwer demanded a clear and distinct idea of mathematical objects.

Brouwer was critical of the "law of the excluded middle," which asserted that either a property P of some mathematical object was true, or its negation was true. This seems to be a rather reasonable law. Why was Brouwer so critical? The reason for his criticism was that the law of the excluded middle permitted a typical kind of proof often used by mathematicians called *reductio ad adsurdium*, in which one proved a proposition P had to be true by proving its double negation: not, not P. According to the law of the excluded middle, the proposition P and not, not P are logically the same. Mathematicians often proved the existence of things without actually constructing them by simply showing that if they did not exist, one was led to a contradiction using the law of the excluded middle. Although one then would know the object existed, one would have no intuition of its details and structure, and to this Brouwer strongly objected. Brouwer thought that all proofs had to be *constructive*—either one proved the proposition P by actually proving P directly or alternatively showed directly that P was absurd. By disallowing the use of this method of proof, Brouwer removed one of the most powerful tools in the repertoire of mathematical proof.

Brouwer's criticism of mathematical proof was especially vented at the formalists, led by David Hilbert, a major figure of twentieth-century mathematics. Einstein, who evidently did not think much of these disputes, referred to the "frog and mouse battle" between Hilbert and Brouwer about the foundations of mathematics. (Einstein himself had a priority dispute with Hilbert about the mathematical theory of general relativity, a dispute that was settled amicably.)

Hilbert was a native of Königsberg, the hometown of the philosopher Kant. Königsberg was a center of mathematics, and here Hilbert formed a trio, the "Königsberg circle," with two other major mathematicians, Adolf Hurwitz and Hermann Minkowski (who discovered the four-dimensional implications of Einstein's special relativity). Unlike many major mathematicians, Hilbert did not reveal his great gifts until his twenties, yet when they were revealed they were overwhelming. Hilbert made major contributions to the theory of invariants, algebraic numbers, and geometry. His work, in some instances, was so general and far-reaching that he wiped out an entire field of investigation—there was nothing left to do. He would work exhaustively in one field of mathematics, such as algebraic number theory, would make major contributions, and then abruptly drop it and turn his genius loose on another, altogether different field. In some areas he set the foundations.

He soon was established in Göttingen, the center of German mathematics, as the leading mathematician in Germany, if not Europe. He often lectured directly on his research and then subsequently published on epoch-making paper. At one point he took up the challenge of constructing a completely abstract science of geometry—a model that fulfilled the axioms of geometry without using any reference to the actual objects of geometry. Once, full of excitement about this challenge, while waiting for a train in the railway station in Berlin with two colleagues, he remarked, "One must always be able to say 'tables, chairs, beer-mugs' instead of 'points, lines, planes.'" In other words, it did not matter what specific objects satisfied the abstract axioms. Hilbert was one of the great leaders in the movement toward abstraction, which has dominated twentieth-century thought.

In 1900, in a lecture to the Second International Congress of Mathematicians in Paris, Hilbert set forth twenty-three unsolved problems in mathematics, proposing that progress in mathematics be judged by progress in solving these problems. Just as the ancient Greeks had given us a number of problems, such as doubling the cube, Hilbert, in the same tradition, set forth his problems. He began his famous lecture by telling the audience: "Which one of us would not fondly wish he could lift the veil behind which the future is hidden, so that the forthcoming advancement in our science and the secret of its development in the future could be glanced at!" By 1950, midpoint of the century, about twelve of the problems were solved. Many of the solutions to Hilbert's problems went quite deep and opened new fields of mathematics.

Later in his life, after he felt his major creative powers wane, Hilbert reflected almost exclusively on the nature of mathematics, an interest he held throughout his life. He saw mathematics as a deductive system based on axioms. But to prove theorems starting from the axioms, it was necessary to use logic, elementary number theory, and set theory, and unless one was careful it was easy to run into trouble because of the paradoxes associated with set theory and logic. Hilbert thus set out, as a major program, to prove the consistency of mathematical deductive systems. For example, he proved the consistency of Euclidean geometry by assuming the consistency of number theory. His idea was to take an area of mathematics like Euclidean geometry and try to reduce it to another, simpler area like number theory that was on a firmer ground. Untimately one could prove the consistency of all areas of mathematics by putting it on firm ground forever.

To achieve that firmer ground Hilbert introduced the "finitary standpoint"—any formal system that would have finite operations and would allow only propositions that could be expressed in a finite number of symbols. Proofs, for example, that required an infinite number of steps were not allowed.

Hilbert's program gave birth to a new discipline in mathematics —proof theory in which mathematical proofs themselves became the objects of mathematical and logical inquiry, leading to a kind of self-reflection or self-reference within mathematics. The purpose of proof theory was to demonstrate the consistency of a set of axioms—a group of propositions expressed in the language of symbolic logic. Mathematics, henceforth, was to be seen as reduced to a set of symbols that perfectly expressed its logical constant, what is called a formal mathematical system. In this view the essence of mathematics is *completely* embodied in the physical symbols written, for example, on a piece of paper and the exact rules that tell you how they are to be manipulated. "The subject matter of mathematics," said Hilbert, "is . . . the symbols themselves whose structure is immediately clear and recognizable." The task of the proof theorist is to prove the consistency of such formal systems, that is, to demonstrate that if one manipulated the symbols according to the explicit rules, one would never arrive at a proposition along with its negation. As Hilbert put it, "The problem of consistency . . . reduces obviously to proving that from our axioms and according to the rules we set down we cannot get '1 $\neq$ 1' as the last formula of a proof." Furthermore, once one was assured of the consistency of a formal system of axioms one could confidently go on to prove theorems—the set of all true propositions (strings of symbols) that followed from the axioms. This was the formalist program, and in some sense it was identical to the program of mathematics itself. With the task of mathematics presented with such clarity and purpose, it seemed as if mathematics had been forever inoculated against infection by the twin diseases of paradox and inconsistency. So there seemed to be nothing to stand in the way of the mighty formalist program. Then came Gödel's proof, which showed that the formalist program of proving all theorems in a mathematical system, even proving their consistency, was an impossible dream.

Kurt Gödel was a product of the remarkable intellectual ferment of Vienna—a society that produced Ludwig Wittgenstein, Karl Kraus, Gustav Klimt, Ludwig Boltzmann, and Sigmund Freud, among others. Gödel's intellectual instinct led him to examine the very foundations of mathematics. In 1931 he published his famous theorem, which applied to the formal logical systems like the *Principia* and the Hilbert formalist program. Gödel's theorem simply stated that any formal logic system that contains at least the axioms of arithmetic must either be inconsistent (nobody wants *that*) or contain true propositions expressible within the formal system that are unprovable. This result was utterly remarkable and had no precedent in the history of logic and mathematics. What it meant was that some truths of mathematics could never be proven. Mathematics was in this sense incomplete. Interestingly, one of Gödel's theorems explicitly stated that finitary consistency proofs cannot be given. So Hilbert's dream of proving the consistency of all mathematics is impossible.

Gödel proved his famous theorem within the canons of formal logic, and his rigorous proof is not easy to follow. But in essence in boils down to this: Gödel, using some properties of simple arithmetic, succeeded in constructing a proposition within the system that states of itself, "I am not provable." This statement, if it is false—the statement *is* provable—implies an inconsistency within the system. The other Gödelean option is that the statement is true—it really *is* unprovable. But this means that the mathematical system is incomplete in the sense that there are true but unprovable statements within the system. This proposition, it is important to note, avoids the liar paradox of the statement that says of itself, "I am not true," because truth and provability are distinct properties of propositions. Significantly, he showed that the proposition that this system is consistent was one such unprovable statement.

How does Gödel's theorem apply to actual mathematics? Unfortunately his theorem does not always tell us which propositions are not provable. Some people think that Goldbach's conjecture —the proposition that every even number is the sum of just two primes ($12 = 5 + 7$ or $42 = 19 + 23$) is a true but unprovable proposition in the familiar formal system (it has been checked by computers for very large even numbers). But it's hard to tell; perhaps tomorrow someone will prove it or show that it is false. Some people once thought that the four-color-map problem eluded proof because of Gödel's theorem, but they were mistaken. Irrespective of the problem of determining which theorems cannot be proven, we know that such theorems exist. The formalist view of mathematics—that one could, in principle, grind out all the true theorems of mathematics—came to an end.

In spite of the fact that Gödel's theorem profoundly altered our view of mathematics, Gödel himself felt that mathematics, which is identical to set theory, was in good shape—one could avoid inconsistency at the price of completeness. The deep problems for Gödel were problems in logic that went beyond familiar set theory, problems that he continued to ponder for the remainder of his life.

Gödel spent his later years in the United States at the Institute for Advanced Study in Princeton. He and Einstein were good friends and use to walk each other home, discussing the foundational problems of existence and, on a more mundane level, politics. Once Einstein confided to a colleague, "Now Gödel has really gone mad. He voted for Eisenhower!"

Gödel was a retiring and shy person who avoided a public presence. I met him once when he came to Rockefeller University in June 1972 to receive an honorary degree. After the ceremony a colleague of mine asked Gödel what he was thinking about while seated on the podium between David Rockefeller, the financier and philanthropist, and Frederick Seitz, a distinguished physicist, then president of the university. Gödel, I recall, was silent for a long time as we walked across campus, and then, as if awakening from a trance, he responded, "Yes! I was also between them *spatially!*" I have no idea what he was thinking.

During his later years he continued to pursue foundational questions and his vision of philosopy as an exact science. He became engaged in the philosophy of Edmund Husserl, an outlook that maintained that there is a *first* philosophy that could be grasped by introspective intuition into the transcendental structure of consciousness—the very ground of being. He thought that it was meaningful to question the truth of axioms—that axioms were more than just a formal system but revealed a quality of logical existence that lay beyond them and provided their ultimate foundation. Commenting on the perception of mathematical objects, he said: "But despite their remoteness from sense experience, we do have something like a perception of the objects of set theory, as is seen from the fact that the axioms force themselves upon us as being true. I don't see any reason why we should have less confidence in this kind of perception, i.e., in mathematical intuition, than in sense perception. . . ." Gödel was an "epistemological Platonist" who, later in his life, as I remarked previously, even devised a mathematical proof of the existence of God. He died in 1978, essentially of malnutrition (he did not eat for fear that his food was poisoned) in Princeton, New Jersey. He was one of the deepest logical thinkers of all time, and his work will be remembered for millennia.

Gödel's work transformed the direction of thinking about the nature of mathematics. Even in pure thought there was a limitation to what could be proven. In the wake of Gödel's work logicians continued to deepen their understanding of formal systems. Today, modern logic is divided into set theory (originally developed by Cantor, Zermelo, and Fraenkel), model theory (modeling of axioms), proof theory (Hilbert and Gödel), intuitionism (Brouwer and his student Heyting, who revived it as constructive reasoning, eliminating the law of the excluded middle in the 1930s), and recursion theory, which owes its origin to making precise the notion of algorithm—a program for solving a mathematical or logical problem. Recursion theory, about which we have not yet spoken, owes its origin to the genius of Gödel, Allan Turing, and Alonzo Church and its contemporary interest to the rise of electronic computers.

Through the work of Frege, Russell, Hilbert, and others, it became clear that mathematical logic involved the manipulation of strings of symbols according to well-defined rules. Mathematical proofs are examples of such manipulations. Alan Turing, an English mathematician whose work was characterized by a singular originality and depth of purpose, realized that it was fruitful to view such logical manipulations as being done on a machine (later called a universal Turing machine). As previously explained, the machine, which is viewed as a conceptual machine, not a real one, consists of a tape with a set of symbols which according to its preassigned program it can either erase or print. The fact that a Turing machine is so simple and yet, as Turing showed, embraced the full notion of computability, is the basis of its conceptual power. The Turing machine mechanized logic, thus reducing it to its completely formal kernel.

With the concept of a Turing machine in hand, Turing applied it to the fundamental questions of mathematical logic. The questions turn on what can and cannot be done on such a machine in a finite amount of time (the vestige of Hilbert's finitism). For starters he showed that the most complex computer could always be reduced to such a universal machine. If something can be calculated at all, it can be calculated on a Turing machine. Or to turn this around, a Turing machine *defined* what was meant by "computable." He went on to define a new class of numbers—computable numbers that can be calculated on a universal machine with a finite program of instructions. For example, the number $\pi = 3.14159 \cdots$ with an infinite decimal expansion is a computable number because it is possible to write a rather short program that will compute the expansion of π. The program for π will grind on forever because π has an infinite number of digits in its expansion —yet the program itself is finite. For other numbers—noncomputable numbers—no such finite program exists. This distinction between computable and noncomputable numbers is closely related to the distinction we described earlier between simulatable and unsimulatable systems. For an unsimulatable system there exists no program that will model the system that is simpler than the system itself.

Gödel's theorem revealed itself in a new guise in terms of the Turing machine. We can imagine that the machine has been set up to prove theorems within some axiom system. Suppose it starts out to prove a "theorem" and never stops. How do we know if the machine, in the course of proving a theorem, will ever stop? This is the famous halting problem. Gödel showed that there exist undecidable propositions in axiomatic systems of sufficient richness, and hence we know that for such propositions the machine will not stop. But we cannot tell ahead of time which propositions they are—the halting problem is itself undecidable—the decidability of some propositions is itself not decidable.

Church's work, although he did not appeal to the machine concept, was logically equivalent to Turing's. He proved a fundamental theorem (now known as Church's theorem) about the *logical validity* of propositions expressed as logical formulas. A formula is said to be *logically valid* if it is true irrespective of what interpretation we give to its symbols, functions, and constants. Church's theorem states that no Turing machine can decide whether an arbitrary logical formula is logically valid. If we accept the idea that all intuitively computable formulas can be computed on a Turing machine (Church's thesis), then his theorem implies that no machine will ever tell us if an arbitrary formula is logically valid —it will take ingenuity, guesswork, and imagination to do that. This result seems to lend credence to Gödel's famous remark that perhaps there are things that a mind can do that a brain cannot.

Or it could simply mean that our brains are not reducible to a universal Turing machine—an alternative interpretation of Church's theorem.

As fascinating as these developments in logic and the foundations of mathematics were (and they are still ongoing), they are viewed askance by practicing mathematicians. The development of logic and the investigations of foundations of mathematics was a response to the paradoxes that crept in at the end of the nineteenth century with set theory. That seems to have been settled now. Logic today is seen as a kind of backwater—a fundamental backwater, to be sure—compared with the immense ocean of modern mathematics. André Weil, a major mathematician of this century, remarked of the connection between mathematics and logic: "If logic is the hygiene of the mathematician, it is not his source of food; the great problems furnish the daily bread on which he thrives." And again he says in the same vein, "We have learned to *trace* our entire science *back* to a single source, constituted by a few signs and by a few rules for their use; there is an unquestionable stronghold, *inside which we could hardly confine ourselves without risk of famine*, but to which we are always free to retire in case of uncertainty or of external danger." Mathematicians derive their sustenance from content, not from form. Russell's vision of mathematics as identical to logic may even be correct in principle, but it is sterile in practice. Saying mathematics is identical to set theory is like saying poetry is identical to organized sentences—it misses the point of content and meaning.

Although the focus of this chapter is the philosophy of mathematics (and hence the emphasis on logic and the foundations of mathematics rather than mathematics proper), it is important now to put things into perspective. The philosophy of mathematics is a swamp into which few practicing mathematicians care to wander. They prefer to work on the problems of mathematics. Yet practicing mathematicians hold philosophical views about their discipline, and some have contributed mightily to it (like Hilbert). So it is important to examine the views of a few mathematicians, even if they are antiphilosophers.

It is difficult for an outsider to grasp the immense development of mathematics in this century, the new fields that have been created and that have enriched our experience. There is a shift in the emphasis of mathematics of the twentieth century from what

went before. Roughly speaking, all mathematics can be characterized by the interplay between mathematical objects such as numbers or geometrical manifolds, on the one hand, and their
morphisms—the way they are transformed by mathematical maps
or functions—on the other. Objects and morphisms—that is the
central theme of all mathematics. Prior to this century, mathematicians focused primarily on the objects and their properties—
what was "out there" in the realm of mathematics. For example,
in the nineteenth century new kinds of numbers were discovered
—quaternions and complex numbers were studied in depth. New,
non-Euclidean geometries were found and their properties explored. In this century, however, it is not so much the objects of
mathematics that are of central interest, it is their morphisms. The
abstract *relation* between mathematical entities became the object
of study, and the entities themselves played a secondary role.
Mathematicians finally came to realize the power of abstraction—
in some sense the morphisms *defined* the objects. Some morphisms, for example, left the objects invariant like rotation of a circle
about its center and thus could be used to define the object "circle." It is how objects transform that defines what they are. The
powerful concepts of morphism and mapping have been greatly
exploited.

It is difficult to expose the entire landscape of modern mathematics. J. Fang, the historian of mathematics, likened mathematical development to the growth of a city. At the center is the old
traditional city—a preserved landmark, representing ancient
mathematics. The new city is growing all around it. We see the
nineteenth-century city with its solid, serviceable buildings surrounding the old city, and around this are the sprawling suburbs
of the twentieth century stretching out to the horizon and growing
rapidly—the new fields of mathematics. So vast are the suburbs
that they completely dwarf the inner city. Some suburbs have
become so large that they have become cities in their own right.
There is a communications problem between the suburbs—some
are hardly aware of the existence of others. The cozy realm of
mathematics has grown almost out of control, and any claim by a
logician that he can set order to this world is ridiculous; it is impossible to keep up with all the work.

Then along comes Nicolas Bourbaki, the great twentieth-
century French mathematician, the heir to Hilbert and Poincaré,

who arrives on the scene in the guise of a city planner to make order out of chaos. Bourbaki, with the self-confidence of a visionary, sets out to review and transform nothing less than the entire corpus of modern mathematics. Nothing mathematical is alien to him. Irrespective of how one views Bourbaki, his work, in the words of mathematician Paul Halmos, is such that "without [it] twentieth-century mathematics would be, for better or for worse, quite different from what it is." A stronger assessment of Bourbaki is given by Emil Artin: "Our time is witnessing the creation of a monumental work: an exposition of the whole of present day mathematics. Moreover this exposition is done in such a way that the common bond between the various branches of mathematics becomes clearly visible, that the framework which supports the whole structure is not apt to become obsolete in a very short time, and that it can easily absorb new ideas. Bourbaki achieves this aim by trying to present each concept in the greatest possible generality and abstraction."

Who is Nicolas Bourbaki? Bourbaki is the name of a group of the leading French mathematicians who, realizing that a single individual could no longer achieve the synoptic grasp of the whole of mathematics, formed a collective and wrote (initially, at least) under the pseudonym of Nicolas Bourbaki. Bourbaki was united by a common philosophy of mathematics (essentially abstraction and generality) and a common desire to have some fun. Already in the 1930s the productive Nicolas Bourbaki was turning out mathematics papers of incredible imagination and depth, astonishing the world of mathematics. A new genius had arrived. At first his identity was not known (except by his publishers, Hermann and Co.), but now we know the *membres fondateurs*—Henri Cartan, Claude Chevallier, Jean Delsarte, Jean Dieudonné, André Weil—the top French mathematicians of their generation. Bourbaki undertook the encyclopedic task of covering all of mathematics in his *Elements* (appropriately named after Euclid's book), the volumes of which are still being published. The original members have long since been replaced and added to—it is a great honor to be part of Bourbaki. They often meet in the French countryside during the summers and sometimes in Paris to do their collective work and plan future volumes. A great *esprit de corps* is evident during these sessions. Recalling these days, Cartan remarked, "It was necessary that each member had to forget his specialty for a while; he was forced to learn everything from scratch. Every problem had to be jointly discussed and, accordingly, the final version could come only out of the sequence of such discussions."

The name Bourbaki has an interesting origin. According to legend, two Greek, Cretan brothers, Emanuel and Nicolaus Skordylis, fought so heroically against the Turks during a seventeenth-century invasion, they were called "Vourbachi" or "slugger-leader" by the Turks. The brothers assumed the nickname given to them by their enemies and bequeathed it to their children, and Vorbachi became Bourbaki in Greek.

One hundred years later a great-grandson of Emanuel called Sauter Bourbaki, a seafarer, was sent by Napoleon's brother to Egypt with the message that Napoleon should return to France for the coup d'etat. After the successful seizure of power, Napoleon in gratitude guaranteed the French education of Sauter Bourbaki's three sons. One of the three sons became a French officer, and his son Charles was the father of a general in the French army. General Charles Bourbaki led his army in the Franco-Prussian war, was defeated, and went on to lead the remnant of his army to Switzerland. There Bourbaki attempted suicide but failed. After the war he tried to enter Parliament, at which he also failed, and he died in 1897 a disappointed man. His statue stands in Dijone, the hometown of Jean Dieudonné, one of the founders of Bourbaki.

When Nicolas Bourbaki first made his appearance, Cartan maintained that Charles Bourbaki had a sister who married a grandchild of Nicolas Vourbachi, and their offspring was Nicolas —a mathematician without peer who began writing mathematical papers in the 1930s. Any suggestions by other mathematicians that Nicolas Bourbaki did not really exist was met by vehement protests in the form of letters to whoever dared to make such accusations. One such person was the editor of the *Mathematical Reviews*, a Mr. Boas. Bourbaki even started a rumor that in fact it was Boas that never existed and that B.O.A.S. simply stood for a group of editors at the *Reviews*. By the end of World War II, however, the true identity of Bourbaki was well known.

Bourbaki developed a coherent philosophy of mathematics, a view far removed from Russell's view that mathematics is equivalent to logic. Directly critical of this outlook, Bourbaki wrote: "It is a meaningless truism to say that this deductive reasoning is a unifying principle for mathematics. So superficial a remark can certainly not account for the manifest complexity of different mathematical theories, not any more than one could, for example, unite physics and biology into a single science on the ground that both employ the experimental method. The method of reasoning by means of syllogistic chains is nothing but a transforming mechanism, applicable just as well to one set of premises as to another; it could not serve therefore to characterize these premises." Practicing mathematicians, like Bourbaki, have never made the mistake of confusing mathematics with logical formalism.

Bourbaki was devoted to the study of mathematical "stuctures" in their most abstract generality—set theory (taken as a foundation for all mathematics), algebra, general topology, functions of a real variable, topological vector spaces, and integration are the subjects of the first six volumes, the first part of the *Elements*. The central method of Bourbaki is abstraction—the process of ever-greater generalization to find the unifying principles of mathematics. The "structures" are founded on axioms, which are formally arbitrary but as every mathematician knows are, in fact, severely limited by the capacity of the mathematical imagination to give content to them. The role of axioms for Bourbaki, as it was for Hilbert, was not to provide rigor (Hilbert remarked that "any fool" can play at that), but to impose an organizational framework on mathematics.

Even the critics of Bourbaki are unified in their outlook that logic and mathematics are distinct. In a sense the whole concern with logic, axioms, and the foundations of mathematics initiated by Frege, Russell, and Gödel can now be seen as an immense detour—perhaps a necessary one—around the actual conduct of mathematics. Logicians might object to this characterization and insist on the central importance of their work for mathematics. How can mathematicians overlook something so fundamental as logic they might argue. How, for example, does mathematics avoid paradoxes and potential inconsistency? "Oh, quite, quite easily," says Sam Eilenberg (a member of Bourbaki). "It is usually done *by circumlocution*. In the abstract theory of categories, there is obviously no question of any foundational difficulties, because a category is defined as a mathematical structure, as a group, or anything else. There is no problem. The problem only comes up when you start to give examples of categories. Then, if you formulate examples in terms of *the* category for all groups, you are obviously in trouble. Now you obviously don't have to look at *the* category of all groups; you want to look at *a* category of groups, because in any particular question there will be only a certain family of groups that will occur, and they will generate for you a category; so if you are willing to accept this limitation, all you have to do is replace the word 'the' by the word 'a' and you are again in a perfectly legitimate situation. . . . There are any number of ways of getting around it."

Mathematics, as practiced, is less of a logical discipline and more of an intuitive science. The methods of thought of a practicing mathematician resemble those of empirical scientists—methods that are embodied in the hypothetical-deductive system. Using their intuition—what Hilbert called *Spürkraft*, hunch power—mathematicians make guesses about mathematical structures. Venturing out into a mathematical territory, they look for simple, unifying, nontrivial theorems. The results are admired by how far out the mathematician has gone, how difficult the territory, how magnificent the prize he has returned. When a great problem is solved it usually opens up new vistas on yet uncharted lands or closes the trail for further investigations. Mathematics, we see from its conduct of inquiry, remarkably resembles what we called the hypothetical-deductive method—a fruitful combination of imaginative and rigorous thought. As I have argued about ideas in the natural sciences, ideas in mathematics survive because they are fertile and can endure in the environment of concepts. Like all ideas, they participate in a selective system. The logician's approach to the philosophy of mathematics only covers a small fraction of the territory of modern mathematics—and a rather sterile one at that. In a sense there really is no contemporary philosophy of mathematics—an account of what mathematicians actually do and what are the binding concepts and themes of the conduct of their inquiry.

How do we characterize mathematics? Some of the great mathematicians themselves have provided answers, none of them completely satisfying. Descartes saw mathematics as a science of order and relations, as did the Greeks before him. Leibnitz developed the idea that mathematics explores the structure of all possible worlds (including, one hopes, ours). Poincaré and Weyl saw mathematics as the science of infinity. More recently we discovered new definitions of mathematics—the science of complex systems or the modeling of reality in symbolic forms or as games.

The thing that is peculiar about math (and all these definitions) is that there is no *there* there—no external reality. While mathematics may originate in reflection about the sensual world, its ultimate life is in the mind—the nexus of pure judgments about a logical order. Mathematics, in spite of its connection with empirical science, is autonomous and must be created for its own sake. The irony of mathematics is that although it is purely the product of the human mind, it takes on a life of its own, a structure seemingly transcendent to human experience and independent of it. In the case of empirical sciences, we also witness that sense of independence—but there we can attribute it to nature, which *is* independent of our minds. For mathematics there is no such excuse. How then is such independence of the realm of mathematics possible?

To answer this let us recall how a mathematical system gets started. One postulates some axioms and definitions, like Euclid's axioms and definitons. The axioms have to be mutually consistent, simple, clear, and general and, most important, must lead to something interesting. In the case of Euclid's axioms the entire structure of plane geometry follows. The axioms of number theory and arithmetic are equally fertile. The mark of these mathematical axiom systems is their surprising richness. Other consistent axiom systems could be sterile—they don't lead to anything interesting.

Mathematics itself seems to be an example of complexity—logical complexity. From a few elementary logical propositions—the axioms—that one takes as given flows a rich implicative structure. I believe that it is because of the possible complexity arising out of a simple logical system that mathematics acquires its quality of independence and autonomy from the mind. Although its starting point is simple enough—a set of axioms that can be easily grasped by the mind—the inquiry opens into a rich, complex realm of propositions that seem to take on a life of their own, a vast logical landscape over which the human imagination can wander but which cannot be grasped as a whole by the mind. The realm of mathematics is like an unsimulatable automata functioning on the basis of a few simple rules.

Michael Rabin, an Israeli mathematician, once characterized the realm of mathematics with the following wonderful image. Imagine the set of all true propositions about mathematics as occupying a vast space—the space of all true theorems. Some of these theorems have been proven, a rather small set of all the true theorems, and these we imagine as a thin illuminated line, a bright string with a few branches transversing this dark space. The dark part of the vast space consists of all true theorems that we have not proven and that probably never will be proven. The reason we cannot prove these true theorems is that the proofs require such a long time to calculate that even the largest supercomputer grinding away for the lifetime of the universe cannot accomplish the proof. They require such a large but finite computing time that we will never know if they are true. Other "true" theorems might require an infinite computing time—these are the theorems that are undecidable within a specific axiom system. The bright line shows us the true and provable theorems, the ones that don't require so much time, the ones that ingenious mathematicians can find using human skills.

The computation view of mathematics, to which Rabin's image appeals, is not new, but its emphasis has been rising in the last several decades. What is this computational view? I like to characterize it by the phrase "the mechanization of mathematics." According to this view, it does not make sense to talk about mathematical entities without saying how you can calculate them —grind out proofs on a mechanical calculator. The realm of mathematics is identical with the realm of the calculable. How can mathematics, which appeals to a transcendental realm of pure concepts, be reduced to machinery—a manipulation of symbols? Let us examine how this can be done, or if it cannot be done, why it cannot be done.

The question about how mathematics is possible is curiously similar to the question of how is language possible. Both language and mathematics are products of the human mind supported by the human brain. I do not believe that the question of how the human mind does it—thinks of infinite sets—and does it so rigorously will be grasped until we understand how the brain functions far better. Mathematics, for all of its transcendent character, is ultimately the consequence of a material organ, the brain. Perhaps mathematics, as we understand it as a universal science, is actually rather particular, a consequence of our particular brain structure and its particular evolution on our planet. Is it possible that we could build artificial minds that would view mathematics very differently and create a different universe of mathematical objects? Or are all minds, artificial or natural, constrained by the material laws of this universe to arrive at basically the same mathematical and logical structures? The answer to these questions is unknown at this time; what is more, it is unimaginable how we *can* answer it. But the fact that we are asking these questions underscores the computational view of mathematics—what mathematics ultimately is depends on the computational capability of the material structure that produces it.

Computers have had a significant impact on how mathematics is viewed. Digital computers perform discrete operations, they are finite machines (no illusion about the "infinite mind" here). Mathematicians use computers not because these machines are especially "smart," but because of their superior calculational power and speed. Mathematicians use them precisely because computers are basically dumb mechanical devices, in which they can have complete confidence—computers will do exactly what they are programmed to do. If a mathematician wants to check if the ten integers are evenly distributed in the first 143 million digits of the decimal expansion of π, a computer is the only practical way to do this (they *are* evenly distributed). Computers can be used to model mathematical equations, stochastic processes, and to aid in the construction of complex proofs, such as Haken and Appel's proof of the four-color-map theorem. Three decades ago Hao Wang, a logician and colleague of mine at Rockefeller University, used a computer program to prove many of the theorems, including all the theorems in elementary logic, in Russell and Whitehead's *Principia Mathematica*, a first demonstration that computers could prove theorems in logic. I was amused to learn that "equipment" is now an 8 percent item on the National Science Foundation's mathematics research support budget. A few decades ago no one could imagine what mathematicians needed "equipment" for. Computers are part of the repertoire of mathematics and are here to stay. They provide us with an image of reasoning, mechanical as it is, that lets us see precisely what is going on.

Because most computers are digital, finitistic devices, they correspondingly influence how we view mathematics. The computer cannot deal directly with the infinite number of points on a line or curve. Instead a curve is chopped up into discrete segments that approximate the curve for the purposes of numerical analysis. The mathematical world of a computer is a discretum, not a continuum. Yet a computer *can* deal with a continuum the same way that we do—by a series of discrete logical steps represented by symbol manipulation. For example, computer programs can be used to solve differential and integral equations exactly rather than numerically when the equations admit of a solution in terms of known simple functions. The computer is simply programmed to use the known properties of continuous functions in a logical fashion. In principle, it seems, computers can do what we can do. In practice, they still fall far short.

There is no programmable substitute for the activity of the mathematical imagination—at least for the foreseeable future. Computers can't make "intuitive" guesses (at least the way we do), and they are poor at global conceptual pattern recognition. Computers do not begin to touch human capabilities in this regard; they are simply intellectual tools. Someday true artificial minds may begin to explore the world of mathematics on their own. They might develop their "intuition" for integers up in the billions or for spaces of very high dimensionality in the same way we have intuition for the first few integers or three-dimensional space. Such aritificial minds could discover things that we might appreciate but could never imagine ourselves.

No matter how powerful computers become or how far they go in simulating the capacities of the human mind, they will always be material artifacts subject to the laws of nature. In this sense, then, the most powerful mind in mathematical and logical reasoning will be subject to the material limitations of the universe. In the early 1960s, Rolf Landauer, of the IBM Labs, following the lead of von Neumann, began to explore the ultimate physical limitations to computation. Since then a lot has been learned, but the field is still in its infancy. In 1982 a conference on the physics of computation was held at MIT that discussed the known fundamental physical limitations of computation (and there *are* such limitations). This is a curious situation because our comprehension of these material limitations is itself expressed and understood in terms of mathematical and logical reasoning, comprising self-referential feedback. Logical symbol manipulation must obey the laws of nature; the laws of nature are expressed by logical symbols. The relation between the transcendental world of mind and the natural world of matter is like the uroboros—the snake consuming itself.

I'd like to give at least one example of the interplay between the material world and the world of mathematical concepts. The notion of computability is specified in terms of Turing machines, devices I previously described. Usually Turing machines are "gedanken"—thought machines, not actual ones. But really, if we are talking about computers doing logic, we must consider actual Turing machines and imagine building them. A Turing machine works according to the laws of classical physics—we can imagine one built of gears and shafts with a paper tape running through it. One could get fancy and make it electronic, but that does not change the fact that it operates according to classical physics.

Many years ago I decided to design a quantum mechanical Turing machine. My purpose in doing this was that I wanted to design a non-Turing machine, a computer that could *not* be reduced to a simple Turing machine, for the reason that quantum mechanics cannot be reduced to classical mechanics. To accomplish this one must utilize an essential feature of quantum mechanics in the design of the computer. It is easily done by using the long-range correlations among quantum states. One imagines a source of photons (light quanta) that emits pairs of spin-correlated photons, each one of the pair going in opposite directions. These pairs of photons are then detected at two distinct stations after going through some polarizers. The pattern of detected photons— whether they get through a polarizer or not—can be represented as a random sequence of 0's and 1's (0 = no detection, 1 = detection). The two sequences of 0's and 1's at each station, where each is random, are correlated in a nonrandom way. Furthermore, that correlation cannot be accounted for by classical laws of physics; it is intrinsically quantum mechanical. These random sequences can be used as partial input for two ordinary Turing machines at each station, and these machines use the inputs for some computation. Now the whole apparatus consisting of both Turing machines can be viewed as a single computer. This computer is *not* reducible to a universal Turing machine for the simple reason that the correlations of quantum mechanics cannot be accounted for by classical mechanics.

While I had this notion of a non-Turing machine for many years (since then other people have proposed similar machines), I could not find a problem that this new machine could solve. At the Shelter Island II Conference in 1985, I saw Richard Feynman, a fellow physicist who, I knew, was interested in fundamental problems in computation, in part an interest generated by his discussions with Ed Fredkin, a computer scientist. I told Feynman my problem of not being able to find a suitable problem that the "quantum computer" could solve, a problem that couldn't be done on a standard Turing machine. He immediately said: "It can simulate the correlations of quantum mechanics. No ordinary computer can do that!" He was right, of course. Still, I was looking for a logical problem, not a simulation.

The difficulty is that a Turing machine *defines* what we mean by "computable," what we mean by "decidable." Standard mathematical problems are set up to be computable. So to find problems that the "quantum computer" can do that cannot be done on a Turing machine requires changing what we think of as the territory of mathematics. That is like the "tail wagging the dog." Nonetheless this example underscores that what we consider to be mathematically computable depends on the computer, and this, in turn, ultimately depends on the actual material laws of nature. There are probably lots of different kinds of non-Turing computers, and they serve to give new meanings to the idea of computation and mathematics.

Can the human brain be simulated by a Turing machine? If quantum correlations play a fundamental role in the neuronal network (and there is no evidence that they do), then the brain cannot be simulated by an ordinary Turing machine. Suppose, however, the brain's essential operation is correctly described in terms of classical physics. It is possible that deterministic chaos may play a role in brain function. Still, a Turing machine could, in principle, simulate the motion of every atom in the brain. But even if we used the largest supercomputer (equivalent to a Turing machine), the simulation of a millisecond of the brain's operation could take thousands of years. That's not a practical procedure.

Some people who suggest that the brain's intelligent behavior can be simulated by Turing computers, however, do not mean that the precise physical state of the brain is simulated. In fact, they don't care about the brain at all. Instead the simulation they suggest takes place at a much higher level, the level of concepts and symbols. This simulation problem, however, is not well defined because concepts and symbols are not well defined outside of their context, which is the entire world. It is not at all clear how or if one can program a computer to do such a simulation. So the answer to the question of whether the brain can be simulated on a Turing machine depends first on whether the brain's operation is essentially quantum mechanical or not, and if not, then in principle it can be simulated; in practice it is an all but impossible task.

The accomplishments of mathematics are awesome, stretching from its religious origins millennia ago to its abstract and universal formulation today. As a powerful component of human culture it will continue far into the future and, no doubt, surprise us still more. We may only be at the beginning of our explorations, and continents and universes of mathematics remain to be discovered. The end of this adventure of the human mind is not in sight.

It seems clear that the deep puzzles as to "where" and "how" mathematical objects exist and the nature of mathematical thinking are still locked in the secret of the mind and are not yet to be revealed. The puzzle is part of the general problem of the material representation of knowledge, being, and thought. If anything, we have gained confidence in this century that a transcendent order of reality (such as mathematical objects) can be productively thought about in terms of its material representation and actual physical process. And likewise, the material order of the universe cannot be rationally expressed other than by an appeal to transcendental concepts, many coming from mathematics and logic. The transcendental and the natural viewpoints are two complementary representations of a unitary reality, the full expression of which is still elusive because the very categories of our thought and language cannot yet accommodate it. Only through a transformation of the categorical structure of our experience, a transformation informed by the findings of empirical science and a deeper understanding of the mind, can such an accommodation be accomplished, if at all. Part of the answer, I believe, will turn out to be that we are asking the wrong questions, making a false distinction between the transcendent and the natural world. But to see that *that* is the answer will be quite the accomplishment. And when that day comes, it will transform our civilization.

Chapter 13

The Instruments
of Creation

Give me where to stand, and I will move the earth.
—ARCHIMEDES

As a twelve-year-old I used to build crystal sets, early versions of
the radio. All the parts, the wires, the resistors, and even the
crystals and cat's whiskers (a special wire used to probe the crystal
surface) could be bought at the local hardware store. I would
diligently wind the wire around discarded toilet paper roll cores to
make an induction coil, solder the wire, and carefully make the
connections on a breadboard. The antenna, a major component
of the system, stretched one hundred feet from the second-floor
window on my house to a neighbor's tree. A ground wire, part of
a lightning arrestor system, ran down the side of the house to a
steel rod buried deep in the ground. I pretty much understood
how the crystal set worked by imagining a fluid of electricity that
was set to vibrating in the antenna from the incoming radio wave
and then the crystal, the coil, and a condenser selected the right
vibrations because they filtered waves. But I was always amazed
when I finally put on the headphones and could hear the local
radio stations. Simply by assembling elementary parts, like putting
together a jigsaw puzzle, the world of radio was opened. I won-

dered what other incredible devices could be built out of simple parts if only we knew how. Selectivity on the crystal set was not great; but the satisfaction of having built it myself was immense.

With the help of a ham radio operator who lived down the street, I later built a short-wave receiver. I purchased the parts at electronic stores in Philadelphia with money I earned doing odd jobs, mostly mowing neighbor's lawns. Each subsystem of the receiver was tested independently, so when it was finally completed it worked the first time. I remember listening to European and African radio stations. That something I put together out of raw parts could draw in information from across an ocean never ceased to amaze me. It amazes me to this day that radio and television work.

I was reminded of my experience building crystal sets and radios when years later my wife and I were on safari with friends in the Issiolo Desert in northern Kenya. One of my friends, a game warden and hunter, had just shot a water buffalo that had been marauding local villages. I saw two teenage Samburu-Massai *morrans* (warriors) dissect the animal that had just been shot. The teenagers knew what every part of the buffalo could be used for and preserved with care what they needed. Their capacity to perceive interior detail was supreme. They knew the insides of animals the way I knew the insides of radios.

A few weeks after the trip to Issiolo I was wandering through the back streets of Nairobi (I love to check out the backyards of cities) and came across repair and maintenance shops. Here Kikuyu men, a generation or two removed from being bush hunters and herders, were hard at work fixing air conditioners, refrigerators, automobiles, radios—the equipment of a modern city. This local industry and the enthusiasm and the diligence displayed by the workers impressed me. The same skills of the hunters I had seen before, the capacity of the mind to spatially organize and categorize the world around it, was revealed by these workmen. Later that day I was with a group of people talking about education and new technology in Africa and how to accelerate development. An African expressed the view that they needed computers especially as educational tools. I asked if anyone knew what was *inside* a computer—how they worked, not in detail, but a few general ideas. No one did; and further, no one felt that it was important. I disagreed. I went on to say that I thought the future of developing nations like Africa lay more in the expansion of technological infrastructure—what I had seen in the back lots of Nairobi—than in trying to leapfrog the industrial nations by introducing inappropriate high technology. One has to know how things work from the "bottom up." Otherwise, the way things work is understood magically and is likely to encourage magical thinking about the world (as it does in industrial countries). By educating their people to master the technical world from the bottom up, the Japanese, who discovered that imitation and copycat technology can carry you only so far, came eventually to dominate many world markets. There are no substitutes to a "bottom-up" understanding in any field of human enterprise.

This "bottom-up" capability was vividly brought home to me when I was a graduate student at Stanford. Many of the physicists there were building the first giant linear accelerator—a two-mile-long monster that would cost $125 million. High-energy electrons were going to be accelerated down a long vacuum pipe and allowed to smash into nuclear targets. Nothing of this kind and magnitude had been attempted before, and it was a risky undertaking.

One day the scientists building the machine ran into a major problem. At a certain energy they found a new, unanticipated instability that disrupted the high-energy electron beam. Unless the instability could be gotten around, the whole project would fail. Wolfgang Panofsky, the physicist-director of the project, immediately stopped his administrative duties and jumped into action. He personally organized an expert team to study the problem and build new test equipment. He was not just the administrator giving orders, he was also a worker who knew how to get down to the details. Once, well after midnight, I remember seeing him in the machine shop working on a lathe, actually building the test equipment by hand. (How many officers of major technology-based industry could to that in a time of crisis? Many of the better ones, usually founders, can.) In two weeks or so Panofsky and his team overcame the instability. Only when he was confident that there were no further snags did he return to his administrative job. He knew that complex machine from the bottom up. This incident caused me to think of my own skills. I was a theoretical physicist, but still I knew how to operate a lathe.

The "hands-on" approach is the key to success in modern science; people who don't want to get their hands dirty have no business in science. Once I was carrying a viewgraph projector to a lecture room to be used by the afternoon seminar speaker. A colleague with a distinguished and noble Asian ancestry noticed me carrying the projector and asked why I was doing this. I said that since I was in charge of the seminars that year, I had to provide the visual aids for the speakers. My friend looked concerned. Then he said that since next year *he* was in charge of running the seminars he would have to get a secretary to carry the projector; he wasn't going to do it. I responded, "That, my friend, is one big reason that modern science began in the West instead of the East." He grasped my point immediately, and the next year I did see him conspicuously carrying the projector without complaint.

As my admiration for the "hands-on" approach to work and the "bottom-up" understanding of machines and equipment would indicate, I am disturbed by the tendency of some educators to promote a "top-down" approach, which can result in the loss of the sense of the material ground of existence. This can only help create a class of people who even as they operate and manage the complex technological equiment of our society hold magical beliefs about how it actually works.

The discoveries that transform the way we live are made by people who go back to the things themselves, get immersed in the material details of existence, and see them a new way. As Socrates observed, real knowledge comes from the streets or, in this instance, from the workbenches and shops. The rest of technical activity is a kind of intellectual confidence game, usually with economic and social consequences, that is played with human credulity.

God is in the details of existence. And anyone who refuses to look there is likely to be worshiping idols. But how do we get to the details of existence? How can we see what is going on? The answer to these questions lies in instrumentation—the tools we create and which, in turn, create our world. To an extent, greater than most people imagine, our instruments and experimental methods have revealed the world of modern science. Nature today is an instrumentally perceived reality in which crucial points of observation are connected by the web of theory. Long ago Archimedes said, "Give me where to stand, and I will move the earth," referring to the instrument of the lever. If a lever is long enough and one has a fulcrum and a place to stand, one can indeed move the earth.

It is our instruments, the artifical extensions of our several senses and our mind, that move us into a new world. Theoretical ideas follow after the instruments and experiments; and these theoretical ideas, in turn, lead to the construction of new instruments. A few examples will suffice to get my point across—the history of science is as much a history of instrumentation as it is a history of theoretical ideas.

Galileo may not have built the first telescope, but he was among the first to use it for seriously exploring the heavens. (He also used it as an instrument to enhance his patronage, especially with the Medici.) Galileo saw things no other human being had ever seen before—the moons of Jupiter, the phases of Venus, mountains on the moon—and concluded that the universe was quite different from the prevailing Ptolomic cosmology supported by the Church and more in line with Copernicus's view. His difficulty with the religious authorities in Rome helped the nascent scientific revolution to migrate north, where it took firm root. Subsequently other men began to build improved telescopes for the express purpose of viewing the heavens. Optically assisted astronomy was born. Issac Newton developed the reflecting telescope—a device that used a curved mirror instead of a lens as its focusing element and anticipated the first large reflecting telescopes built centuries later on Mount Wilson and Mount Palomar in the United States.

The history of astronomy can be traced by studying astronomical instruments and their improvements. William Herschel's fifteen-inch reflecting telescope, built in the early 1780s—a superior instrument of its day—guided his eye to first see the complex, dynamic universe we know today. During the nineteenth century, accurate timing devices were added to the telescope mount to compensate for the rotation of the earth, photography was introduced, and the line spectra of stars was revealed, opening the door to astrophysics and the study of the chemistry of stars. It was also clear by the end of the century that the refracting telescopes that used large lenses had reached the limit of practical size. By building the first large reflectors, American astronomy passed European astronomy, and the center of gravity of science shifted West.

Both the First and Second World Wars were a stimulus to the development of new instruments—fallout from military applications. The use of photographic films with quality emulsions, optical technology, the development of radiotelescopes from radar, and rockets to carry astronomical equipment aloft were all examples of this fallout. No major discovery in astronomy has not been preceded by a new instrument or technique. Today the universe is explored across the entire electromagnetic spectrum—visible light, infrared light, and X rays, gamma rays, radio and microwave radiation. Earth-orbiting satellites will soon include the Space-Telescope, a device that, unhampered by the effects of the earth's atmosphere, can see about ten times deeper into the universe. Who can imagine what we will see? It is not even imaginable what we would think of the universe today if we did not have these instruments and were always restricted to using the unaided eye. And probably compared with the instruments of the future, our modern instruments are comparatively "blind."

While the telescope and its progeny explored the macrocosmos, another development occurred—the exploration of the microcosmos. Utilizing similar techniques of lens grinding already developed for telescopes, microscopes were made. Anton van Leeuwenhoek, the superintendent of the Guelf town hall in Holland, built the best microscopes with high resolving power. He looked at everything, particularly organic substances—blood, the deposits around peasants' teeth, excrement—and first saw the "little animals," bacteria. When he communicated his results to the Royal Society in London, his letters were first received with incredulity, but soon it was clear that a new window on the organic microcosmos was opened. His methods were imitated. A powerful instrument had fallen into the hands of scientists that began to reveal the material basis of the processes of life.

The next several centuries saw vast improvements in microscopes and their resolving power and contrast. The introduction of photographic methods created a permanent, accurate record of observations. The phase-contrast microscope, which enormously improved the ability to see distinctions between almost transparent tissues, was a major breakthrough. But the biggest change came from an entirely new development in the 1930s—the electron microscope. Using the much shorter wavelike properties of electrons and bending magnets as lenses, a new microscopic world—the detailed interiors of cells—could be seen using the electron microscope. Biologists availed themselves of the new instrument to explore the living microcosmos, and other instruments and techniques—X-ray diffraction, radioactive tracers, mass, infrared and microwave spectroscopes for detailed chemical and molecular analysis, chromatography to reveal the presence of large organic molecules. Physicists, meanwhile, were building "matter micro-scopes"—high-energy accelerators. These huge machines came into existence following World War II and in the subsequent decades explored the world beyond the atomic nucleus. They eventually probed down to the level of the quark—the very constituents of the proton and neutron.

Usually new instruments are first built by scientists who design them for their own work. If the instrument proves to be especially useful and has commercial applications, some company will pick up on it. The route from the laboratory to the marketplace can be as short as a few years or in some instances as long as decades. The key to this development depends on whether the instrument can be designed so that nonexperts can use it and if there is a market for it. The mass-commercial availability of precision scientific instruments is one of the cornerstones of modern science and technology.

Today a new instrument, the electron tunneling microscope, can actually detect and "see" individual atoms. An electron tunneling microscope consists of a very fine pointed needle delicately suspended over the sample to be observed with the point of the needle almost touching the sample surface. An electric voltage is applied between the needle and the sample. According to classical physics, no current will flow between the needle and the sample because the needle does not actually touch the surface. But according to quantum physics, electrons can actually "tunnel" across the gap, producing a measurable current. The amount of this current is extremely sensitive to the gap distance, so sensitive, in fact, that as the point of the needle is moved over the sample surface, the bumps and valleys produced by individual atoms can be detected. That is a long way from the time eighty years ago when many physicists and chemists did not believe atoms existed.

In some instances the material or logical instrument that advances science is not so evident. An example is Charles Darwin's creation of the theory of natural selection—surely a major shift in the way scientists, and eventually most people, thought about the origin of life. Darwin stands as the greatest synthesizer of our thinking about living organisms since Aristotle. What was his instrument? He certainly used the microscope, was familiar with the instruments available to naturalists of his time. Yet these were not essential to making his great discovery.

Darwin's instrument was the *Beagle*, the ship he used to sail around the world for five years gathering specimens. Ships had existed before, yet this match between the man and his instrument provided a vista of life on our planet never before available. What Darwin saw on the voyage of the *Beagle* informed his thinking and helped him develop his view about the evolution of life.

To support this contention—that the ship was Darwin's instrument—I refer to an article by Stephen Jay Gould about the voyage of Louis Agassiz, the influential nineteenth-century American naturalist and scientist. Agassiz was a creationist and thought that Darwin was simply wrong. So he decided, late in his life, to follow in Darwin's footsteps, retracing Darwin's voyage in South America and to the Galápagos Islands in the hope of showing Darwin was wrong. Although he never gave a detailed report of his trip, what he saw must have been deeply unsettling for a man of Agassiz's knowledge and faith; he certainly did not contest Darwin after that. Unlike the cardinal who reputedly refused to look through Galileo's telescope, Agassiz did "look through" Darwin's instrument. And what he saw must have shaken him.

Today we have spacecraft voyaging to other planets, radio telescopes, high-energy accelerators, electron microscopes, machines that do biochemical assays of complex molecules, computers, a cornucopia of new, powerful instruments. These are the instruments creating the modern world of science, transforming it beyond recognition. We make our instruments, and then they make us, changing our perceptions, our image of ourselves.

Although I believe that many dramatic scientific changes can be traced to the introduction of a new technique or to an old technique used in a new way, it is clearly not all so determined, and it would be foolish to insist on this viewpoint. Technology does not exist in a cultural vacuum; it is culture-supported. Chance discovery, it is said, favors the prepared mind—a mind surely prepared by a culture. But to provide no instruments for such a mind is a guarantor of scientific failure—instruments are necessary, though not a sufficient, condition for discovery.

This view that material instruments are crucial to the creation of science is not new, although scientists and philosophers emphasize it insufficiently in my opinion. What they do emphasize is the *thinking* that goes into a discovery. Instruments, and to a lesser extent the instrument makers, are mute, and the thinking types get all the coverage by the intellectuals. This attitude ought to change; it is a leftover attitude from the classical culture that emphasizes thinking and writing rather than doing and making.

I also think that the notion of instrumentation is conceived of too narrowly. When we think of instruments we think of microscopes, telescopes, electronic measuring devices—material artifacts. However, people also fashion "cognitive instruments," especially mathematical techniques that can be tools used by the human mind to promote discovery. An example would be the nineteenth-century invention of the Riemannian geometry of curved space, which became a cognitive instrument in the hands of Einstein when he created his general theory of relativity. Newton had to fashion the calculus as the proper mathematical language to express his mechanical laws. Likewise the mathematics of probability was appropriated by physicists from the mathematicians when it came time to develop statistical mechanics.

Another, more contemporary example of a cognitive instrument is innovative software. New, powerful mathematical algorithms that enable scientists to utilize computers more effectively and solve previously intractable problems are one example of cognitive instruments that are used in software. Possession of a program with unique analytic capabilities puts a scientist in as much of a privileged position to make new discoveries as the possession of a powerful telescope. These cognitive instruments are in the realm of concepts and information; nonetheless they are used by scientists as tools, extensions of our ordinary human analytic capability.

Today there is a vast array of material and cognitive instruments exploring the macrocosmos and the microcosmos, two major frontiers representing the limiting extensions of the human sensorium. We now have a good sense of the territory of material reality, the "lay of the land." No doubt there are big surprises in store for us as our instruments improve, and new major discoveries will be made. We will surely see the territory differently in the future. I believe that from the perspective of several centuries hence the evolution of science for the last several centuries, supported by the instruments of its creation, will be seen as only a beginning— simply an exploration of the territory of reality, a staking out of claims. We have yet to learn to live in that territory, to comprehend it, and significantly, to bring it to serve human purposes.

Our instruments have shown us the visible and the invisible world of matter—atoms, molecules, protons, and cells; we know what is there. What we do not know is how, in detail, it is organized—a problem in complexity. If the first three centuries of modern science have extended the human sensorium, learned the properties of matter and life, the next three centuries will see the rise of the sciences of complexity. The arrival of these sciences will mark the completion of the scientific enterprise as we now know it, for complexity is the last frontier of science as far as we can see.

To get a glimpse of this new frontier we only have to remind ourselves that all matter is made of atoms—the basic building blocks of the world we see around us. It is amazing, but true, that the complexity of the world is a consequence of the arrangement of only some six dozen different atoms. From atomic combinations we build up molecules, cells, and living organisms. Yet the existence of life is only one out of many complex and interesting arrangements of molecules—one that suits the environment of earth. There could be other equally complex and interesting combinations of molecules which could be constructed artificially. No one knows the limits of what can be made from atoms. If we did not know of the existence of life (assuming we were something else), no one would have guessed that it was possible. There is no reason that atoms and molecules could not be arranged very differently. Physicist Richard Feynman gave a talk in 1959 entitled "There's Plenty of Room at the Bottom." He described molecular cities, factories, and repairmen that could be sent to a damaged site in the human body to repair it. Molecular computers would control this tiny world and turn it to human benefit. New entities —molecular robots—distinct from life, but possessing some of its properties, could be created. Once one grasps the potential of this vast microscopic realm and its possible arrangements, the direction of the future of science is apparent.

This molecular world and its implications for our world are described in Eric Drexler's book *The Engines of Creation*. Drexler foresees the future "assembler revolution" when the first true assemblers are built—self-replicating and organizing molecular machines, controlled by molecular computers and operating on a nanosecond time scale. These assemblers released into the environment could mine minerals, grow plants, clean cities—in short, become the miniature molecular slaves of the human species. Biochemists have been heading in this direction for a long time using organic molecules. But there are lots of ways of arranging atoms into molecular systems other than using clues from biochemistry. Perhaps we can build mechanical computers out of molecules thousands of times smaller than a living cell. This nanotechnolgy can completely repair damaged bodies and build new life forms. Whether such a technological fantasy is indeed possible remains to be determined, but there is nothing in the laws of chemistry and physics that says it is impossible. Perhaps the only thing that stands in the way of such a revolution is human ignorance of how to accomplish it and the will to bring it about.

Not only will the mastery of complexity enable us to create new worlds and new beings, it will enable us to understand the complex components of our ordinary world. The body and brain are the most complex entities we know, and because of this fact and the new instrumentation that is available, the neurosciences, medicine, and biology are at the frontier of modern research and are likely to remain there for a long time. The work in cognitive sciences such as on the mind and vision or the quantitative study of the social world, economics, language, and the evolution of culture are also examples of the sciences of complexity. What is the instrument that will bring this world to comprehension?

The computer, the instrument of the sciences of complexity, will reveal a new cosmos never before perceived. Because of its ability to manage and process enormous quantities of information in a reliable, mechanical way, the computer, as a scientific research tool, has already revealed a new universe. This universe was previously inaccessible, not because it was so small or so far away, but because it was so complex that no human mind could disentangle it.

Often we think of computers as aids in work, in terms of their commercial applications or as potential artificial intelligences. What I would like to emphasize here, however, is the computer in its role as a research instrument—the first of a new generation of instruments that will open up the realm of complexity. This opening is going to be one of the great adventures of science, part two of the scientific revolution. The new science of complexity, like the computer, cuts across disciplinary boundaries. Certain problems in biology, physics, electrical engineering, economics, and anthropology can be dealt with using similar methods, not because of any overlap in the nature of these fields, but because the specific abstract techniques required to solve the problems are similar. The future organization of the sciences, as exemplified by the way departments of science are categorized in universities, will change reflecting this new interdisciplinary problem structure. Either that will happen, or new institutions will emerge that themselves embody this new architectonic of the sciences.

Once we grasp that the complexity of the world is a challenge and not an obstacle—an opportunity, not a barrier—the vision of the future of science expands. The instruments to explore this world are being built today, complex computers—instruments whose own improvement depends on the progress in the sciences of complexity.

Many of the problems that I have described in this part of the book—problems coming from cognitive sciences, the mind-body problem, the problems of thinking about the scientific enterprise —will be solved, changed, or modified as the sciences of complexity mature. Scientific discovery profoundly informs philosophy. With the emergent sciences of complexity, natural scientists will begin to think about the mind—the traditional intellectual territory of the philosophers. This could mean the end of "armchair philosophy" and a return to the spirit of the old natural philosophers who did not hesitate to roll up their sleeves "to do philosophy" in the laboratory or at the workbench. Philosophers are already writing software. Of course there will still be the metaphysical purists who insist that science must be epistemologically grounded in philosophy. But if I am correct and the model for the development of science is the evolution of life, then this philosophical way of thinking about scientific practice and scientific truth is simply inappropriate. Science is not grounded or justified by philosophy any more than the evolution of life is grounded or justified by philosophy.

I believe that the most dramatic impact of the new sciences will be to narrow the gap between the natural and the human world. For as we come to grasp the management of complexity, the rich structures of symbols, and perhaps consciousness itself, it is clear that the traditional barriers—barriers erected on both sides—between natural science and the humanities cannot forever be maintained. The narrative order of culturally constructed worlds, the order of human feelings and beliefs, will become subject to scientific description in a new way. Just as it did during the Italian Renaissance, a new image of humanity will emerge in the future as science and art interact in their complementary spheres.

It is my conviction that the history of the contemporary world will be seen in the future as a history of *science* and *technology* dominantly shaping the course of international events. The future of the world lies with the nations and people that master this new realm of complexity, a mastery that will be a source of their wealth, security, and well-being.

Francis Bacon said that knowledge is power. How right he was. But his remark leaves open the question of whether we possess the wisdom to exercise that power, and whether we who possess it are ready to extend it to the billions who are powerless. Sometimes I wonder if it will be the poverty of the poor or greed of the rich that will be our undoing. Yet I remain an optimist and believe that the liberating capacity of our knowledge, along with a little wisdom, will affirm the power of life over death. I continue to believe that the distant day will come when the order of human affairs is not entirely established by domination. And even if that day should never come, it seems worthy of our hope.

CONCLUDING
REFLECTIONS

Chapter 14

The Dreams
of Reason

The dreams of reason bring forth monsters.

—FRANCISCO GOYA

In this book I have been exploring the frontiers of science and the boundaries of human reason. Science provides a vision of reality seen from the perspective of reason, a perspective that sees the vast order of the universe, living and nonliving matter, as a material system governed by rules that can be known by the human mind. It is a powerful vision, formal and austere but strangely silent about many of the questions that deeply concern us. Science shows us what exists but not what to do about it.

Other visions of a different reality are provided by politics, law, art, and religion. These visions of reality are informed by the first-person perspective and the principles of practical or aesthetic reason that orders the immediacy of our lived experience and our values reflected in our ethical and aesthetic judgments. As Vico pointed out centuries ago, it is this reality—the world of civil society and culture—that we can truly grasp because it was made by us and not by God.

There are still other visions of reality that seem to lie outside of reason altogether, visions that have little to do with rules or judgments, but instead tear back the facade of ordinary existence and for brief, intense moments show us the reality that emotionally supports that facade. Reason is like the fragile, encompassing shell of an egg that holds the vital substance of our being together. When that shell cracks in a moment of intellectual or emotional crisis, we see what cannot normally be seen. We can see that the entirety of human life—our lives—are but so many complex motions within a vast game played with rules of which we are usually unaware. These crises can be moments of true creativity or absolute despair—transcategorical experiences that shift the order of our personal universe and subsequently transform our ideas and values.

Wolfgang Pauli, the physicist who did so much to discover the laws of quantum theory and an individual who embodied the principles of rational criticism to an extreme, faced such a crisis during his terminal illness. I have the following story told to me by Gilles Quispel, a Dutch historian of religion. Quispel had been sent to Egypt by Carl Gustav Jung, the depth psychologist, to purchase a manuscript, an ancient gnostic text, which interested Jung (later called the Jung Codex). Some years later Quispel was delivering a series of lectures on gnosticism at Jung's request. Pauli, who at the time had collaborated with Jung on their paper on synchronicity (the phenomenon of coincidental but symbolically correlated events), came to the lectures and a dinner preceding them. Quispel sat next to Pauli, and they were engaged in an intellectually stimulating conversation. All at once Pauli abruptly changed the subject and asked Quispel with great emotional intensity, "Do you believe in a personal God?" Quispel, taken aback, deflected the question. Pauli, he later learned, was confronting his death and was engaged in a search for a deeper meaning to his life, a search that led him to reassert his Jewish ancestry and heritage.

After the lectures on gnosticism, Pauli came up to Quispel and said, "This God, the God of the gnostics, I can accept. I could never accept the existence of a personal God. No such Being," Pauli went on darkly, "could possibly endure the suffering of humanity." A few months later Pauli died. But he had seen a vision of the God of faith, the God of Jerusalem, and not the rational God of Athens.

In the late 1960s I was traveling in Asia and visited the Indian city of Calcutta, where I gave a lecture at the Statistical Institute.

I spent several days in the city alone wandering around the neighborhoods teeming with people. Calcutta is an extremely poor city with hundreds of thousands of homeless individuals who live on the streets. While I saw poverty I also saw a coherent and often joyful life, lived amidst almost incomprehensible suffering, a social world in which religion was undifferentiated from the ordinary transactions of life. But this scene also made me angry because I felt that by changing the social arrangements and through the acquisition of education and administrative and vocational skills, much of the misery I saw could be alleviated.

One day I was walking down a deserted alley in a very poor neighborhood. There was a large trash heap along the narrow path, and as I was about to pass it I saw something stirring in the trash, something about the size of a large dog, but I knew that there could be no dogs about in such a poor neighborhood. Whatever it was sprang forth all at once right into my path. It moved like an immense spider, with the head of a man but no limbs save stumps where the legs and arms should have been, grinning strangely at me. I was striken with fright at this horrible sight and turned immediately around to flee. But as I retreated I heard a human voice behind me, an indescribably beautiful voice, singing a hymn of praise to the Lord Shiva, celebrating the beauty of existence. Awestruck in the presence of this hierophany, I turned and saw the spider-man singing, a divine voice emerging from the midst of utter wretchedness. I knew then that in my heart I had just denied the humanity of a living person, and that this was my lesson. Ashamed of my fear and repulsion, I pledged never again to allow them to overcome me or to deny the humanity of a person again. I was connected to the spider-man.

Learning is most intense and effective when it has an emotional, not just an intellectual, component, when there are no explicit rules and the organism is thrown upon its basic resources for survival. These need not be negative emotions; Plato saw the erotic as an essential component of any real education. Our emotional life lies outside the framework of reason (although it can be examined by reason), and at its most intense we realize that there are no rules or regularities to guide us into new territory. This is an opportunity for creativity, and we often emerge from an emotional crisis with newly learned rules and values.

The crisis may be provoked by confusion and uncertainty, and there is the danger of slipping into one or another form of intellectual, political, scientific, or religious fundamentalism. The characteristic of all fundamentalism is that it has found absolute certainty—the certainty of class warfare, the certainty of science, or the literal certainty of the Bible—a certainty of the person who has finally found a solid rock to stand upon which, unlike other rocks, is "solid all the way down." Fundamentalism, however, is a terminal form of human consciousness in which development is stopped, eliminating the uncertainty and risk that real growth entails.

It is important to distinguish between such fundamentalistic certainty and our real convictions, which as morally responsible individuals we need to live by. The nature of fundamentalism is that it projects the internal convictions of the individual into the objective external world as a form of certainty about the world. The certainty thus becomes a property of the world and not the person. The nature of conviction, by contrast, sees one's belief as purely an internal matter, a part of one's subjectivity and not necessarily a part of the objective world. Our convictions, consequently, while they may be strongly held, are subject to evolution and growth because they are not seen as part of a bedrock external reality, but rather as part of our creative individual being.

Given the enormous power of human emotions, their potential for creativity and fulfillment as well as destruction, one wonders about the role of fragile reason in regulating our lives, especially given its insufficiency in the face of deeply conflicting human values, values informed by our nationality, culture, race, age, and sex. Further, what insights can the new sciences of complexity, struggling to come to terms with the intricacies of mind and nature, offer us as we try to interpret our lives? Martin Luther, that fortress of faith, decried "that whore reason" even while he rationally pressed his case. Thomas Aquinas saw reason as a manifestation of the divine within us but knew that faith was the "bottom line." Goya saw the dreams of the Enlightenment and reason transformed into the monstrosity of the Napoleonic Wars. Is the vast empire of reason, in the last analysis, but an instrument in the service of unconscious, primitive feelings, or is it in the driver's seat? How, in short, can the third-person perspective enlighten the existential passions of the first person?

First and foremost, the findings of science provide a view of material reality that represents the evolving edge of our knowledge about the universe. Minimally, our beliefs and philosophical outlook must be consistent with that view without necessarily being founded upon it. One takes a considerable risk if one maintains beliefs that fly in the fact of the discoveries of science—the risk that one's beliefs are false and contradict the order of nature. Holding such beliefs cannot, in the long run, promote survival of either the individual or the group.

While deeply held beliefs should not contradict science, they also cannot be founded on science. This is especially true of religious beliefs. The Catholic church for centuries saw its faith supported by Ptolemy's cosmology, which placed the earth at the center of the cosmos. When that cosmology was overturned by Copernicus, the Church saw the faith threatened. A conflict arose because the findings of science are always temporal, while faith is intended to be eternal. If belief is founded on science, then when science changes its mind about the nature of reality, it can upset the faith.

Today some people in the West, attracted by Eastern religions, suggest that the findings of modern quantum theory are somehow more congenial to Eastern rather than Western religions. Such a connection between the concepts of physics and religious notions is totally superficial and does no credit to the depth of either the scientific ideas or the religious insights. The claim made by some proponents of Eastern philosophies that states of meditation are related to quantum fields is at best simply wrong and at worst fraudulent. Trying to relate the findings of natural sciences directly to our subjective state of mind is, if one reflects about it only slightly, completely silly. No moral good can come from what is false.

The new sciences of complexity show us how complex consequences can arise from simple elements and rules. Many of the computer models we described are predicated on this idea. Some aspects of our moral behavior—behavior that either reflects or constitutes our moral values—seem extremely complex, but conceivably they arise from simple elements that can be understood. While science cannot judge, it can help us understand.

I am unaware of any computer models of moral behavior, but there are lots of models of economic behavior, and it is instructive to examine them. One feature of those models that I find intriguing is how counterintuitive they often are. I remember economist friends posing problems for me. They would ask if I did this or that, would the interest rates go up or down. In spite of my reasoning through the problem, my answer would as often be wrong as right. The correct answer was often counterintuitive because I often overlooked some factor.

I suspect that many of our moral values are also like that. We hold certain values because we want to effect some desired goal, one that is at least good for us. But if we could model the complex consequence of those simple values, we might find out, as often as not, that there are counterintuitive consequences of our moral actions. There are things we leave out in our thinking. The direct good that we want to realize is not realized, or there are disastrous side effects of our pursuit of a specific moral action. The new sciences of complexity and the perspective on the world offered by computer modeling may teach us things that we did not realize about the values we hold. Science cannot resolve moral conflicts, but it can help to more accurately frame the debates about those conflicts.

Take, for example, the act of lying. We hold the telling of truth as a value; we are not supposed to lie. Yet if everyone told the truth all the time so that one could have complete trust in what one is told, then the advantage that would accrue to a single liar in society would be immense. This is not a stable social situation. On the other hand, in a society of individuals in which everyone lied all the time, society would be unworkable. The equilibrium state seems to be one in which people tell the truth most of the time but occasionally lie, which is how the world really seems to be. In a sense, then, it is the liars among (and within) us that keep us both honest and on our guard. This kind of scientific analysis of lying can help us understand why we do it.

The new sciences of complexity are also going to challenge our values directly. This is already evident in the biomedical ethics debates involving the modification of human, animal, and plant genomes, the artificial prolongation of life, and transplant priorities. There will be more such problems in the future. The day will come when people will have moral concerns regarding artificial life—what are our obligations to the beings we create? Can we permit such beings to hurt and kill one another? We may have a moral problem in determining what actions we allow our artificial creatures to undertake. Perhaps we ultimately have to let our creations be free to come to terms with themselves.

The sciences of complexity, because they will alter the architectonic of the sciences, will create a new image of reality. They cannot but influence how we think of ourselves and the nature of our humanity.

William Butler Yeats, the Irish poet, remarked at the end of his life that he had tried to find and to represent deep truth in his writing. He came to realize that this was impossible, but he did realize that it was possible for a human being to embody that truth. In other words, the real receptacle of the truth of our being is our actual flesh and blood, a truth that is reflected in all our life and actions.

Yeats's insight expressed in terms of complexity theory asserts uniqueness of unsimulatable systems. That's one way of thinking about who and what you and I are—unsimulatable biological systems. No one can possibly simulate you or me with a system that is less complex than you or me. The products that we produce may be viewed as a simulation, and while products can endure in ways that our bodies cannot, they can never capture the richness, complexity, or depth of purpose of their creator. Beethoven once remarked that the music he had written was nothing compared with the music that he had heard.

Seen in this light not only are individual human beings unsimulatable systems, but so is the entirety of culture and life—a vast "computational system," perhaps working out the solution to the Demiurge's master problem, a problem currently beyond our comprehension. We are like a complex three-dimensional cellular automata enacting our own game of life by working out the complex consequences of the elementary rules reflected in the laws of nature—a bizarre image of our existence. And like all unsimulatable systems, our future existence is unpredictable and blind as to where it is headed. Some individuals may have faith in the "wisdom" of our evolving existence to come to its own best realization; others plan, control, and try to predict it; all, in acting as they do, compete and cooperate within the system. Like the Chinese tale of the arrogant monkey king who wanted to challenge the Buddha to a jumping contest only to discover that even if he jumped to the ends of the universe he was still in the hand of the Buddha, we cannot exit the game of life.

The reasoning process, although it takes into account the nature of the world, logically begins with certain axioms—basic propositions—and then arrives at conclusions. One cannot deduce values or the correct course of moral action from reason alone because people with different values will simply choose different axioms. But what can regulate the formation of our values—where do we turn for guidance?

Over the centuries people concerned about how they should act have given answers to this question. Some think that a transcendental foundation outside of humanity can be the only basis for our values—essentially God. Others find the basis for value in authority—the Church, the Party, the Constitution, a revered teacher, or they simply accept the cultural "hand-me-downs." Still others with a secular philosophical bent argue for universal principles like Kant's "categorical imperative," John Rawls' "veil of ignorance," Feyerabend's "relative democracy." It should be clear, however, by this time that no such universally agreed upon standard of values is in fact possible in the sense that it is accepted by all rational men and women. The diversity of human culture, the plurality of human needs imply a spectrum of human values that range from the justification of cruel inhumanity to saintly altruism. Others argue that we must trust our innermost feelings of what is good and right. Yet that trust is easily misplaced, and individuals and whole nations have been monstrously deceived by following their feelings. Where then do we turn when confronted with a moral decision?

The problem of searching for an absolute standard of moral truth has certain similarities to the search for absolute truth in science. Some philosophers of science have wanted to secure scientific knowledge for all time. Now we know that this is impossible; science is a selective system and is subject to what we discover in the real world. Likewise the moral order is actually embodied in the real plurality of changing human culture and the immediate conflicts of our existence and not in transcendent, abstract, or emotional principles. And that is the source of its resolution as well. Our actual decisions must take place within existing power relations, a specific cultural and social environment, not some imagined world. Abstract moral principles without being realized in an immediate personal choice, in a world of unanticipated complexity, are of no more guidance than a science divorced from experiment. Asking to what do we turn for guidance in making a moral choice is like asking to what does an animal species turn as it takes the next step in evolution. Is it possible that our moral actions represent a selective system embodied in our culture, laws, and behavior? If so, we see that what is selected through such actions is the moral order itself, just as the pattern of species is selected through natural selection.

Even though values can be viewed as competing and cooperating in an environment of choices, of what use is this notion if you or I are confronted with a decision? Such a selective systems view does not help decide the actual choice we make but does help inform us of the consequences of that choice. Our actions become self-constituting; they inform our character and define it in relation to the culture in which we live. And by constituting our character through exemplary actions, we help constitute the culture. Our freedom lies in the recognition of necessity.

How we act as individuals ultimately depends on how we are connected to deep primitive feelings, a connection that is mediated by the fragile and fallible faculty of reason. The process of the legislation of our moral actions is, like evolution, an unsimulatable process, a process that defines the edge of our present cultural development. There is no answer to how we must act to achieve an explicit goal any more than there is an answer to determining the future development of an unsimulatable automata.

Reason dreams of an empire of knowledge, a mansion of the mind. Yet sometimes we end up living in a hovel by its side. Reason has shown us our capacity for power, both to create and to destroy. Yet how we use that power rests on our deeper capacities which lie beyond the reach of reason, beyond our traditions and culture, stretching far back into the depths of the evolutionary process that created our species, a process that ultimately asserts the power of life over death. And, ironically, even death, as part of the process of life, asserts that power. That is how we have come into being and now find ourselves committed to the unrelenting moral struggle of ordinary human existence.

We surely stand at the threshold of a great adventure of the human spirit—a new synthesis of knowledge, a potential integration of art and science, a deeper grasp of human psychology, a deepening of the symbolic representations of our existence and feelings as given in religion and culture, the formation of an international order based on cooperation and nonviolent competition. It seems not too much to hope for these things.

The future, as always, belongs to the dreamers.

Bibliography

This is a list of books and articles that I have found useful in preparing this book. It is not complete but will serve as an introduction to the formidable and rapidly growing literature on the topics covered in the text. The exploratory and curious reader will find that this bibliography is but "the tip of the iceberg."

Anderson, Walter Truet. *The Upstart Spring, Esalen and the American Awakening*. Menlo Park, Calif.: Addison-Wesley Publishing Co., 1983.

Ashby, W. Ross. *Design for a Brain*. New York: John Wiley, 1952.

Attewell, Paul, and James Rule. "Computing and Organizations: What We Know and What We Don't Know." *Communications of the ACM*, vol. 27, no. 2 (December 1984): 1184.

Ayer, A. J. *Logical Positivism*. New York: Free Press, 1959.

Bennett, Charles H., and Rolf Landauer. "The Fundamental Physical Limitations of Computation." *Scientific American*, vol. 253 (1985): 48.

Bernstein, J. "Profiles: Marvin Minsky and Artificial Intelligence." *New Yorker* 57 (1981): 50–126.

Bower, Bruce. "Who's the Boss." *Science News*, vol. 129, no. 17 (April 1986): 266 (article on Ben Libet's experiments).

Boyd, Robert, and Peter J. Richardson. *Culture and the Evolutionary Process*. Chicago: University of Chicago Press, 1985.

Brain, The. New York: Scientific American Books, W. H. Freeman and Co., 1979.

Bruner, J. S. *In Search of Mind*. New York: Harper and Row, 1983.

Campbell, David, James Crutchfield, Doyne Farmer, and Erica Jen. "Experimental Mathematics: The Role of Computations in Non-Linear Science." *Communications of the ACM*, vol. 28, no. 4 (1985): 374.

Carnap, Rudolf. *The Logical Structure of the World; Pseudoproblems in Philosophy*. Berkeley, Calif.: University of California Press, 1967.

Carruthers, Peter. "Emerging Synthesis in Modern Science." Los Alamos preprint LA-UR-85-2366 (1985).

Chaitin, Gregory J. "Randomness and Mathematical Proof." *Scientific American*, vol. 232 (1975): 47.

Charlesworth, Max. *Science, Non-Science and Pseudo-Science*. Melbourne, Australia: Dankin University Press, 1982.

Chomsky, Noam. *Rules and Representations*. New York: Columbia University Press, 1980.

————. *Aspects of the Theory of Syntax*. Cambridge, Mass.: MIT Press, 1965.

Churchland, Patricia Smith. *Neurophilosophy*. Cambridge, Mass.: MIT Press, 1986.

Computer Culture. The Scientific, Intellectual and Social Impact of the Computer, ed. Heinz R. Pagels. Published NYAS *Annals*, vol. 426, 1984.

Computer Software Issue, Scientific American (September 1984).

Crick, F.H.C. "Thinking About the Brain." *Scientific American* 241 (1979): 219–323.

Crick, F.H.C., and Graeme Mitchison. "The Function of Dream Sleep." *Nature* 304, 5922, (1983): 111–14.

Critchley, MacDonald. *The Divine Banquet of the Brain*. New York: Raven Press, 1979.

Crutchfield, James, J. Doyne Farmer, Norman H. Packard, and Robert S. Shaw. "Chaos." *Scientific American*, vol. 255, no. 6, December 1986, 46.

Dawkins, Richard. *The Blind Watchmaker*. New York: W. W. Norton & Co., 1986.

————. *The Selfish Gene*. New York: Oxford University Press, 1976.

Dennett, D. C. *Brainstorms: Philosophical Essays on Mind and Psychology*. Cambridge, Mass.: MIT/Bradford Books, 1978.

Descartes, René. *The Philosophical Works of Descartes*. Cambridge, Mass.: Cambridge University Press, 1968.

Dreyfus, H. *What Computers Can't Do: A Critique of Artificial Reason*. New York: Harper and Row, 1972.

Dreyfus, Hubert L., and E. Dreyfus. *Mind over Machine*. New York: Free Press, 1986.

Duhem, Pierre. *The Aim and Structure of Physical Theory*, trans. by Philip Weiner. Princeton, N.J.: Princeton University Press, 1962.

Dyson, Esther. *Release 1.0* (July 9, 1987). Published by Edventure Holdings, Inc.

Edelman, Gerald. *Neural Darwinism*. New York: Basic Books, 1987.

Fang, J. *Bourbaki, Towards a Philosophy of Mathematics I* and *Hilbert, Towards a Philosophy of Mathematics II*. Hauppauge, N.Y.: Paideia, 1970.

Feyerabend, Paul K. *Philosophical Papers*, vols. 1 and 2. Cambridge, Mass.: Cambridge University Press, 1981.

Feynman, Richard. *Surely You're Joking, Mr. Feynman*. New York: W. W. Norton, 1985.

Fodor, J. A. "The Mind-Body Problem." *Scientific American* 244: 114–23.

———. *Representations: Philosophical Essays on the Foundations of Cognitive Science*. Cambridge, Mass.: MIT Press, 1981.

———. *The Language of Thought*. New York: Thomas Y. Crowell Co., 1975.

Ford, Joseph. "Chaos: Solving the Unsolvable, Predicting the Unpredictable." In *Chaotic Dynamics and Fractals*. New York: Academic Press, 1986.

———. "How Random Is a Coin Toss?" *Physics Today*, vol. 36, no. 4 (April 1983): 40.

———. "What Is Chaos That We Should be Mindful of It?" *The New Physics*, ed. S. Capelin and P.C.W. Davies. Cambridge, Mass.: Cambridge University Press, 1986.

Frege, Gottlob. *Translations from the Philosophical Writings of Gottlob Frege*, trans. and ed. P. Geach and M. Black. Oxford: Basil Blackwell, 1952.

Gardner, Howard. *The Mind's New Science: A History of the Cognitive Revolution*. New York: Basic Books, 1985.

———. *Frames of Mind*. New York: Basic Books, 1983.

Gazzaniga, Michael S. *The Bisected Brain*. New York: Appleton-Century-Crofts, 1970.

———. *The Social Brain*. New York: Basic Books, 1985.

Gleick, James. *Chaos*. New York: Viking Press, 1987.

Goodman, Nelson. *Fact, Fiction and Forecast*. Cambridge, Mass.: Harvard University Press, 1985.

———. *Ways of World Making*. Indianapolis, Indiana: Hackett Publishing Co., 1978.

———. *Of Mind and Other Matters*. Cambridge, Mass.: Harvard University Press, 1984.

Gould, Stephen Jay. *Ever Since Darwin*. New York: W. W. Norton, 1977.

———. *Hen's Teeth and Horse's Toes*. New York: W. W. Norton, 1983.

———. *The Mismeasure of Man*. New York: W. W. Norton, 1981.

———. *The Panda's Thumb.* New York: W. W. Norton, 1980.

Griffin, Donald R. *Animal Thinking.* Cambridge, Mass.: Harvard University Press, 1984.

Harrington, L. A., M. D. Morley, A. Scednov, and S. G. Simpson, eds. *Harvey Freidman's Research on the Foundations of Mathematics. Studies in Logic,* vol. 117. Amsterdam: North-Holland, 1985.

Hempel, Carl. *Aspects of Science Explanation.* New York: Free Press, 1965.

Heppenheimer, T. A. "Mathematics at the Receiving End." *Mosaic,* vol. 16, no. 4 (1985). Published by the N.S.F. Advanced Scientific Computing II.

Hillis, W. Daniel. "The Connection Machine." *Scientific American* (June 1987): 108.

Hinton, Geoffrey E., and James A. Anderson, eds. *Parallel Models of Associative Memory.* Hillsdale, N.J.: Erlbaum, 1981.

Hofstadter, Douglas R. *Gödel, Escher, Bach: An Eternal Golden Braid.* New York: Basic Books, 1970.

———. *Metamagical Themas.* New York: Basic Books, 1983.

Holton, G. "Do Scientists Need a Philosophy?" *The Times Literary Supplement* 2 (November 1984): 231–34.

———. "Constructing a Theory: Einstein's Model." *The American Scholar,* vol. 48, no. 3 (1979).

———. *Thematic Origins of Scientific Thought: Kepler to Einstein.* Cambridge: Harvard University Press, 1973.

Holyoak, Keith J. Review of *Parallel Distributive Processing,* by David E. Rumelhart, James L. McClelland, and the PDP Research Group. *Science,* vol. 236 (1987): 992.

Kandel, Eric R. "Small Systems of Neurons." *Scientific American* 241, 3 (1979): 66–77.

———. *Cellular Basis of Behavior: An Introduction to Behavioral Neurobiology.* San Francisco: W. H. Freeman, 1976.

Kant, I. *Critique of Pure Reason,* trans. N. Kemp Smith. New York: Random House, 1958.

Kirkpatrick, S., C. D. Gelatt, Jr., and M. P. Vecchi. "Optimization by Simulated Annealing." *Science,* vol. 220 (1983): 671.

Klein, Morris. *Mathematical Thought from Ancient to Modern Times.* New York: Oxford University Press, 1972.

Kolata, Gina. "What Does It Mean to Be Random?" *Science,* vol. 231 (1986): 1068.

Kosslyn, S. M. *Ghosts in the Mind's Machine: Creating and Using Images in the Brain.* New York: W. W. Norton, 1983.

———. *Image and Mind.* Cambridge, Mass.: Harvard University Press, 1980.

Kuhn, Thomas S. *The Structure of Scientific Revolution*, 2nd ed. Chicago: University of Chicago Press, 1970.

Lax, Peter D. "Large Scale Computing in Science, Engineering and Mathematics." Talk delivered at the Joint Academia Nazional dei Lincei and IBM Sci. Ctr./Rome, May 1985.

———. "Mathematics and Computing." *Journal of Statistical Physics*, November 1985.

Libet, Benjamin, E. W. Wright, B. Feinstein, and D. K. Pearl. "Subjective Referral of the Timing for a Conscious Sensory Experience: A Functional Role for the Somatosensory Specific Projection System in Man." *Brain* 102 (1979): 191–222.

Maor, Eli. *To Infinity and Beyond*. Boston: Birkhäuser, 1987.

Marr, D. *Vision: A Computational Investigation into the Human Representation and Processing of Visual Information*. San Francisco: W. H. Freeman, 1982.

Medawar, Peter. *Pluto's Republic*. New York: Oxford University Press, 1984.

Mind's Eye, The. Readings from *Scientific American*. New York: W. H. Freeman, 1986.

Minsky, Marvin. *The Society of Mind*. New York: Simon and Schuster, 1986.

Minsky, Marvin, and S. Papert. *Perceptions*. Cambridge, Mass.: MIT Press, 1969.

Nagel, Thomas. "What Is It Like to Be a Bat?" *Philosophical Review* 83 (1974): 435–450.

Newell, A., and H. A. Simon. *Human Problem Solving*. Englewood Cliffs, N.J.: Prentice-Hall, 1972.

Non-Linear Phenomena, Physica D. "Evolution, Games and Learning," vol. 22D (1986). Amsterdam, North-Holland: Proceedings of the Fifth Annual International Conference of the Center for Non-Linear Studies, Los Alamos, N.M. Eds: Doyne Farmer, Alan Lapidis, Norman Packard, Burton Mendroff.

Norman, D. A. *Memory and Attention*. New York: John Wiley, 1969.

Pagels, Heinz. *Perfect Symmetry*. New York: Bantam Books, 1986.

———. *The Cosmic Code*. New York: Bantam Books, 1983.

Patrusky, Ben. "Biology's Computational Future." *Mosaic*, vol. 16, no. 4 (1985). Published by the N.S.F. Advanced Scientific Computing II.

Peirce, Charles Sanders. *The Collected Papers of Charles Sanders Peirce*, vols. 1–6, eds. C. Hartshorne and P. Weiss. Cambridge, Mass.: Harvard University Press, 1931–35.

Physics Today, May 1984. "Advances in Computers for Physics." Published by American Institute of Physics.

———. October 1987. "Computational Physics." Published by American Institute of Physics.

Pines, David, ed. "Emerging Synthesis in Science." Proceedings of the Founding Workshops of the Santa Fe Institute. Santa Fe, N.M.: The Santa Fe Institute. Articles by M. Gell-Mann, Manfred Eigen, Irven DeVore, John Tooby, S. Wolfram, Felix Browder, Harvey Freidman, and Charles Bennet.

Pitts, W. H., and W. S. McCulloch. "How We Know Universals: The Perception of Auditory and Visual Forms." *Bulletin of Mathematical Biophysics* 9: 127–47, 1952.

Plato. *Plato: The Collected Dialogues*, ed. Edith Hamilton and Huntington Cairns. New York: Bollinger Foundation, 1961.

Popper, Karl R. *The Logic of Scientific Discovery*. London: Hutchinson, 1959.

———. *The Open Universe, An Argument for Indeterminism*. Totowa, N.J.: Rowan and Littlefield, 1982.

———. *Quantum Theory and the Schism in Physics*. Totowa, N.J.: Rowan and Littlefield, 1982.

Popper, Karl R., and John C. Eccles. *The Self and Its Brain*, parts I and II. Berlin: Springer-International, 1977.

Pribram, K. H. *Language of the Brain: Experimental Paradoxes and Principles in Neuropsychology*. Englewood Cliffs, N.J.: Prentice-Hall, 1971.

Putnam, Hilary. *Realism and Reason*, vol. 31. Cambridge, Mass.: Cambridge University Press, 1983.

Pylyshyn, Z. W. *Computation and Cognition: Toward a Foundation for Cognitive Science*. Cambridge, Mass.: MIT Press, 1984.

Quine, W.V.O. *From a Logical Point of View*. Cambridge, Mass.: Harvard University Press, 1953.

Reichenbach, Hans. *Philosophy of Space and Time*. New York: Dover Publications, 1958.

———. *The Rise of Scientific Philosophy*. Berkeley, Calif.: University of California Press, 1951.

Resnik, Michael D. *Frege and Philosophy of Mathematics*. Ithaca: Cornell University Press, 1980.

Rorty, R. *Philosophy and the Mirror of Nature*. Princeton, N.J.: Princeton University Press, 1979.

Rumelhart, David D., James L. McClelland, and the PDP Research Group. *Parallel Distributed Processing, Explorations in the Microstructure of Cognition*, vols. 1 and 2. Cambridge, Mass.: MIT Press, 1986.

Ryle, G. *The Concept of Mind*. London: Hutchinson, 1949.

Schank, R. C., and R. Abelson. *Scripts, Plans, Goals and Understanding*. Hillsdale, N.J.: Lawrence Erlbaum, 1977.

Searle, John. *Minds, Brain and Science*. Cambridge, Mass.: Harvard University Press, 1984.

Shepard, R. N., and J. Metzler. "Mental Rotation of Three-Dimensional Objects." *Science* 171 (1977): 701–3.

Simon, H. "Cohabiting the Planet with Computers." Preprint, Department of Psychology, Carnegie-Mellon University, 1986.

———. *Sciences of the Artificial*. Cambridge, Mass.: MIT Press, 1981.

Sloman, A. *The Computer Revolution in Philosophy: Philosophy, Science and Models of Mind*. Hassocks, Sussex: Harvester Press, 1978.

Solomonoff, R. J. "A Formal Theory of Inductive Inference, Part I." *Information and Control*, vol. 7 (1974): 1.

Soros, George. *The Alchemy of Finance*. New York: Simon and Schuster, 1987.

Stent, Gunter S. Review of *Neurophilosophy* by P. S. Churchland. *Science*, vol. 236 (1987): 990.

Swinney, Harry L., and Jerry P. Gollub. "The Transition to Turbulence." *Physics Today*, vol. 31, no. 8 (1978): 41.

Thomas, Lewis. *The Medusa and the Snail*. New York: Viking Press, 1979.

———. *The Youngest Science*. New York: Viking Press, 1985.

Traub, J. F. "Information Complexity and the Sciences." University Lecture, Low Library, February 6, 1985, Columbia University.

———. "The Influence of Algorithms and Heuristics." Preprint Department of Computer Science, Carnegie-Mellon University, 1979.

Traub, Joseph F., and Edward W. Packel. "Information-Based Complexity." *Nature*, 1987.

Von Neumann, J. *The Computer and the Brain*. New Haven, Conn.: Yale University Press, 1958.

Waldrop, M. Mitchell. "The Connection Machine Goes Commercial." *Science*, vol. 232 (1986): 1090.

Wang, Hao. "Computer Theorem Proving and Artificial Intelligence." *Contemporary Mathematics*, vol. 29 (1984): 49.

———. *Reflections on Kurt Gödel*. Cambridge: M.I.T. Press, 1987.

Winson, Jonathan. *Brain and Psyche, The Biology of the Unconscious*. New York: Vintage Books, 1986.

Winston, P. H. *Artificial Intelligence*. Reading, Mass.: Addison-Wesley, 1977.

———. *Psychology of Computation Vision*. New York: McGraw-Hill, 1975.

Wittgenstein, L. *Tractatus logico philosophicus*. Trans. by D. F. Pears and B. F. McGuinness. London: Routledge and Kegan Paul, 1961.

Wright, Robert. *The Grand Design, Three Scientists and Their Gods*. New York: Times Books, 1988.

Index